. . . and then what happened?

... and then what happened?

Harold Harris and the
Early Development of Aviation

Alta Mae Stevens

authorHOUSE®

AuthorHouse™ LLC
1663 Liberty Drive
Bloomington, IN 47403
www.authorhouse.com
Phone: 1-800-839-8640

Published by AuthorHouse   01/22/2014

ISBN: 978-1-4918-1405-5 (sc)
ISBN: 978-1-4918-1404-8 (e)

Library of Congress Control Number: 2013916994

To my mother and my brother.

Contents

"Airplanes took off, they flew around. They landed— it was an accomplishment."

—Harold R. Harris

Preface

A few years before he died in 1988, Harold Ross Harris decided to write a book detailing some of the incidents of his rich and eventful life. He couldn't decide between writing his autobiography or the history of his part in the creation and development of Pan American Grace Airways (Panagra), the first American scheduled airline in South America and indeed anywhere in the world south of the Equator.

Since we were living together, he consulted me as to which avenue to follow. Knowing his love for Panagra, I urged him to the latter. Now I regret his choice. After leaving Panagra at the start of WW II, Harold Harris embarked on what turned out to be in many ways the most fulfilling part of his career in which he made perhaps his greatest contribution to worldwide aviation. I have no way of uncovering the scope of his role in the Air Transport Command during WW II. However, I have documented—using his own words wherever possible—many of his subsequent experiences leading American Overseas Airlines, or as head of the Atlantic Division of Pan American Airways, as CEO of Northwest Airlines, as founder of Aviation Financial Services, a company dedicated to locating funding for new airlines, and finally as a U.S Government consultant participating in the creation of U.S. aviation policy abroad.

Harris gave his collected papers to the Air Force Museum at Wright Patterson Field. From there they traveled to Wright State University Archives, where they were sorted and made available to the general public that for a boiling hot week one June included me.

There are several edited versions of the book he did write but not publish: the history of Panagra, which provided much of the material used by William Krusen in his history of Panagra, *Flying the Andes*. Using this and a few other sources I was able to eke out for my own satisfaction the important steps that led to the development of American commercial aviation and Harold Harris' role in helping implement those steps.

In the following narrative wherever possible I cite Harold Harris's own words, his own descriptions. Against these I attempt to provide a generalized background of events both within and outside the world of aviation.

Harold R. Harris was a large genial man, 5'10", as Richard Hallion noted, "in appearance more closely resembling an account executive than the public image of a test pilot."[1] He had a hearty laugh and his humor, his love of puns and jokes—inherited surprisingly from his staunchly religious father—carried him through many personal and business crises. (From his mother he inherited his business acumen and enormous courage.) Anyone close to him came to take for granted both his physical strength and ingenuity. The Harris family was famous for its large-sized appetites and Harold Harris was no exception. He had an outsized appetite for work, for play, for food, as well as for competition. I won't forget the triumphant laughter that accompanied his winning every card game I ever played with him.

Through the years our Dad shared many anecdotes about his experiences with my brother and me. Many, involving hairbreadth escapes from sure death, always led us to ask, "And then what happened?" This question seemed perfectly to sum up Harold Harris' crowded and fabulous life.

This book, then, in my words and from my perspective, is by way of an homage to him and to the aviation industry that he helped foster and in which he was immersed for over seventy years. It was a glorious story well worth the telling and retelling many times over.

---

[1]   Richard Hallion, *Test Pilots, The Frontiersmen of Flight.* Doubleday & Company, Garden City. New York, 1981,78.

Introduction

This book is devoted to detailing the exploits of Harold R. Harris, our father, perhaps the least celebrated and certainly among the most deserving of celebration of all the truly great early pilots and aviation visionaries.

Born in Chicago Dec. 20, 1895, Harold R. Harris played hookey from school to attend the first national aviation meeting at Dominguez Field, Los Angeles, January 10-20, 1910. By the time of his death in 1988 at the age of 92 he was perhaps the only man who, devoting his entire career to both military and civilian aviation over a span of almost 80 years, had personally witnessed and participated in the changes occurring in the field of aviation.

The items on the following short list of his most notable exploits are dealt with in more detail chapter by chapter.

During WW I between March and July, 1918, at Foggia, Italy, Harris was chief instructor of day and night flying in Farmans and Capronis. He helped establish an aerial ferry route from Ilan to Paris for the United States Navy.

On July 25, 1918, Harris along with his co-pilot, George Lewis, made the first flight by American pilots over the Alps from Italy to France.

Put in charge of the flight test section at Dayton's McCook Field Harris competed in many aviation meets, by 1926 holding 13 world flying records. He flight-tested the first Martin Bomber equipped with Liberty engines to be supercharged. And June 8, 1921, he was the first pilot to test a pressurized cabin, nearly losing his life in the process.

Harris, Don Bruner, and other military pilots played an active role in setting up and operating the first lighted airway, an

80-mile stretch of land between Columbus and Dayton, Ohio, thus allowing the introduction of regular night service vital for carrying the mail on a 24-hour basis.

August 11, 1921, he flew the first plane designed to pick up airmail sacks from the ground. He became famous as the first pilot willing and able to fly that enormous triplane, the Barling Bomber, the Army's answer to the ZR-1 (the Navy's first American-built rigid Dirigible), and on Feb. 23, 1924, was one of the first pilots to fly an Emile Berliner helicopter, one of the earliest prototypes. In 1924 he made the first cross-country flight of the Stout plane, an all-metal single winged or monoplane.

By the end of his test pilot career, he held 16 American and 10 world flight records.

On October 20, 1922, at McCook field, in what until this point proved to be perhaps his sole lasting legacy, celebrated even in the comics, Harris was the first pilot in the U.S. to save his life using a parachute in an emergency when, his monoplane's wing disintegrating, he bailed out, landing safely in a grape arbor! Because the parachute canopy was made of silk he became the first member of what ever since has been known as the Caterpillar Club and was awarded the Leo A. Stevens parachute medal.

"For having made the first emergency parachute jump from a U.S. Army airplane which resulted . . . in the U.S. Army Air Force issuing an order requiring all airmen to wear parachutes on all flights."

Harris became vice president and operations manager of Huff Daland Dusting Company. Although he himself did not fly the dusting planes for actual dusting, he was one of the pilots who developed the specialized flying techniques that are still in use for crop dusting today, He probably also performed demonstration flights in the duster plane.

In 1924 C.E. Woolman and Harold Harris joined together to help underwrite what actually became Delta Airlines. James Hoogerwerf, chronicler of the founding and early days of Delta Airlines, noted that at a time when aviation was almost the exclusive prerogative of the military, Harris, in his landmark testimony in 1925 before the Morrow Board assigned by President Coolidge to investigate the future of non-military aviation, laid out commercial aviation's huge possibilities while also pointing out the safeguards that would be required to assure passenger safety and future airlines' economic stability.

In 1928, before his inauguration as President, Herbert Hoover [1929-1933] made a trip down the west coast of South America on a U.S. Navy cruiser in order to determine for himself the viability of an airline located there. Thanks to Harris' help, Hoover was not just convinced; he was enthusiastic. "He assured me," Harris wrote, "he would give us full support in our efforts to grow and expand internationally."

Harris presented a proposal for an airline connecting the west coast of South America with the U.S. that led in 1929 to the establishment of Pan American Grace Airways, a joint venture between Pan American World Airways and Grace Shipping. In order to get the mail concession, Peruvian Airways Corporation was created with Juan Trippe, president of Pan American Airways, listed as president and Harold Harris as vice president.

At Harris's insistence, the four passenger Fairchild plane ordered for the new airline, the first U.S. flag airplane to make schedule anywhere in the world south of the equator, contained a toilet, the first in any U.S. airplane. This historic plane is now in the Smithsonian Air Space Museum.

In the decade between 1929 and 1939, Harris, in Peru, held the position of Vice-President and Chief Operations Officer of Panagra with New York-based John MacGregor, acting as Vice President and General Manager. Juan Trippe, president of Pan American, had insisted that there be no president. (This situation lasted until 1941 when Harold Roig of Grace was elected president of Panagra.) Through careful negotiation with warring governments, the recruitment of skilled air crews, and helped by both Pan American and Grace in the acquisition of aircraft and landing sites, Harris and MacGregor were able to oversee the rapid development of the infant airline under some of the most difficult circumstances and over some of the most forbidding terrain in the world.

In 1942 Harris accepted a commission as Colonel in the Air Transport Command, resigning his position with Pan American Grace Airways to do so. During World War II Harris served as Assistant Chief of Staff, Plans; Assistant Chief of Staff, Operations; Commanding Officer of Domestic Transportation Division; and was Acting Chief of Staff of the Air Transport Command with the rank of Brigadier General when he left the service in 1945 to join American Overseas Airlines.

Harris was Vice-President and General Manager of American Overseas Airlines until 1950 when the airline was incorporated into Pan American Airways. Working for Pan American Airways, Harris became Vice-President in charge of the Atlantic Division.

Between 1954 and 1955 he was President and Chief Executive Officer of Northwest Airlines, resigning because of ill health and irreconcilable differences between himself and the Northwest Airlines Board of Directors.

For the next decade he was President of Aviation Financial Services, Inc., a company dedicated to helping infant airlines acquire adequate capitalization. He retired in 1965 at age 70. Aged 92, he died in his home at Falmouth, MA. in 1988.

Decorations that Harris received are the Distinguished Service Medal, the Legion of Merit, and the Air Medal (U.S.), Commander of the British Empire (Great Britain), Corona di Italia, Fatiche de Guerra (Italy), Abdon Caldern (Ecuador), and Orden del Sol (Peru).

"I have been researching early Delta Air Lines history," wrote James Hoogerwerf, author of a study of C.E. Woolman and the rise of Delta Airlines," and it turns out Harold R. Harris was a significant figure in the company's early days as a crop dusting outfit. Harris was a test pilot for the military and took a leave of absence to join Huff Daland Dusters, the world's first crop dusting company. Harris was an advocate for the commercial uses of aircraft and so testified before the Morrow Committee . . . These points briefly highlight Harris' importance to my study. Outside the purview of my present work, his role as a WWI aviator, test pilot after the war, manager of Panagra, service in WWII, and activities after the war are also significant. Harris, in my mind, is a figure deserving of more recognition for the part he played in the development of aviation."

Justin H. Libby, known for publishing a series of articles covering the exploits of early aviators, observed, ". . . how many people [besides Harold Harris] have ever had 26 flying records . . . [as well as being] inducted into probably the two most prestigious air societies: the American Institute of Astronautics and Aeronautics and the Society of Experimental Test Pilots?

"Your dad," he continued, in an email, "for many reasons I find impossible to fathom, is truly invisible; if you check my bibliography of your father's life and times, he is omitted from many biographies, dictionaries, almanacs, bibliographies as if he did not exist and indeed for those editors he did not exist—truly strange when others like Eaker, Spaatz, Doolittle, Rickenbacker, Lindbergh, and other notables all with better PR representations throughout the years—captured the imagination not of all Americans who have no interest in such matters, but at least of those interested in aviation—not even Muir Fairchild gets much ado as well and Macready gets a mention here and there."

Libby continued, ". . . he [Harris] was man of action and masterful technical-engineering skills, not of self promotion without a corps of reporters and photographers following him around to record his achievements. Perhaps his personality and character were more confident or introspective or even passive (although that is a strange term given all that he accomplished) than those who need constant adulation and admiration. Thus, he becomes easier to ignore and forget. Historical amnesia is I believe become a hallmark of the American character."[2]

As Harold Harris's daughter, I hope the following will help to rectify that situation.

---

[2] Justin H. Libby, personal correspondence.

Chapter 1: Early Flight

The universal desire to fly, to emulate the free-soaring birds is embodied in the legend of the Greek architect Daedalus and his overly ambitious son Icarus. Because he gave King Minos' daughter, Ariadne, a ball of string in order to help Theseus, the enemy of Minos, survive the Labyrinth and defeat the Minotaur, Daedalus and his son Icarus were to be exiled from Crete. To avoid this fate Daedalus fashioned two pairs of wings out of wax and feathers for himself and his son. Before they took off from the island, Daedalus warned his son not to fly too close to the sun, nor too close to the sea. Overcome by the giddiness that flying lent him, Icarus soared through the sky curiously, but in the process he came too close to the sun, which melted the wax. Icarus kept flapping his wings but soon realized that he had no feathers left and that he was only flapping his bare arms. And so, Icarus fell into the sea in the area that bears his name, the Icarian Sea near Icaria, an island southwest of Samos.

A Montgolfier balloon ascent in 1783

Humanity's attempts to reach into the sky really began with balloons. "The balloon," observes Richard Hallion, "gave the world its first astronauts, and these courageous individuals, many of whom were motivated by scientific and technological curiosity and not merely a desire for acclamation or adventure, can rightly be considered forerunners of modern test pilots and flight researchers."[3]

A Brazilian cleric at the beginning of the eighteenth century is said to have initiated

---

[3] Richard Hallion, *Test Pilots: The Frontiersmen of Flight*. New York: Doubleday, 1981, 7.

ballooning. But it was the Montgolfier brothers, papermakers, experimenting with steam-filled paper balloons, who actually introduced the craft and science of ballooning.

In 1782 they experimented with a free flying taffeta balloon that rose to 983 feet. In 1783 they lost one beautiful balloon 74 feet high to a storm, but quickly built another to fly before the royal court.[4]

> The balloon, named the Martial, lifted off from the courtyard of Versailles, swathed in noxious smoke and carrying three passengers: a sheep, a duck, and a rooster! As Louis and his queen, Marie Antoinette, watched, the colorful balloon, radiant in blue and gold, drifted along for over two and a half miles before landing in Vaucresson Forest eight minutes after lift-off, its barnyard animals dazed but safe.[5]

November 21, 1783, a Montgolfier handcrafted hot air balloon—the hot air generated by a bonfire—was flown by two French noblemen, the Marquis d'Arlandes and Pilatre de Rozier who, flying from the Chateau de la Muette in the Place d'Italie became the first humans to make a free balloon flight.[6]

Preparations for the flight had been extensive. "Early in the morning Pilatre, the Montgolfier brothers, and d'Arlandes inspected the balloon. A strong wind gust damaged the balloon slightly and delayed the flight, to the annoyance of the large and growing crowd. Finally, seamstresses repaired the damage, and at 1:54 P.M. the aeronauts cast off. A subsequent report prepared the same day for the Journal de Paris by the Duc de Polignac and other distinguished luminaries including the

---

[4] Hallion, A hydrogen-filled balloon was launched that same year by a rival.
[5] Ibid.
[6] Hallion, 7. Unfortunately, Pilatre de Rozier died in 1785 when his hydrogen-filled balloon exploded.

American minister to France, Benjamin Franklin, stated that it left in a most majestic fashion.

"And when it reached about 250 feet above the ground, the intrepid travelers, taking off their hats, bowed to the spectators. At that moment one experienced a feeling of fear mingled with admiration.

"Soon the aerial navigators were lost from view, but the machine, floating on the horizon and displaying a most beautiful shape, climbed to at least 3,000 feet at which height it was still visible; it crossed the Seine below the gate of La Conference, and, passing between the Military Academy and the Hotel des Invalides, it was borne to a position to where it could be seen by all Paris . . .

"They made a gentle descent into the a field beyond the new boulevard, opposite the Croulemarge Mill, without suffering the slightest discomfort, with two-thirds of their supplies still intact, so they could, if they had wanted to, have journeyed three times as far. Their voyage had taken them 20 to 25 minutes over a distance of 45,000 fathoms."[7] Human ascension into and passage "through once unreachable heavens became a reality."[8]

In 1784, Jean-Pierre Blanchard fitted a hand-powered propeller to a balloon, the first recorded means of propulsion carried aloft. In 1785, he crossed the English Channel with a balloon equipped with flapping wings for propulsion, and a bird-like tail for steerage.

Jerome Lederer, Harris's close friend and in the 1920s the Aeronautical Engineer for the U.S. Post Air Mail Services, reported that the first Air Mail in the U.S. was a letter of introduction by George Washington carried by the French

---

[7]   Hallion, 8, quoting from the *Journal de Paris*, Nov. 22, 1783.

[8]   Aero.com

balloonist, Jean Pierre Blanchard, in a free balloon flight in 1793 from Philadelphia to Woodbury, New Jersey.

In 1870, noted Harold Harris, during the siege of Paris in the Franco-Prussian War, "the only communications with the outside world by the people inside Paris was by free balloon. In 127 days of the siege, sixty-four balloons were launched. Five were captured by the Prussians, six were lost at sea, 53 arrived safely with 4,000,000 letters, several hundred homing pigeons to bring messages back to Paris, and 88 passengers. As much as 1500 pounds of mail was carried in a single balloon."[9] It is a remarkable coincidence that Otto Lilienthal, the father of modern flight research, took part in this war that marked the emergence of modern Germany.[10]

Harris observed that Eduardo Bradley crossed the Andes in a free balloon June 16, 1916.

Balloons have been used for spying purposes; tethered, as defenses against enemy bombers—as in the Battle of Britain—and, more recently, as forms of sport competition and tourist attractions, perhaps the most famous being the Albuquerque International Balloon Fiesta, the world's largest hot air balloon festival, that takes place each October.

Dirigibles, navigable powered balloons, were developed at almost the same time as balloons. In France wealthy Alberto Santos-Dumont, whose passion was flight, created 18 different examples of dirigibles before turning his attention to fixed winged aircraft in 1907.

Many inventors were inspired by Santos-Dumont's small airships and a veritable airship craze began worldwide. "The "Golden Age of Airships" began in July 1900 with the launch of the Luftschiff Zeppelin LZ1. This led to the most successful

---

[9]   Harris memoir.
[10]   Hallion, 15.

airships of all time: the Zeppelins. These were named after Count von Zeppelin who began experimenting with rigid airship designs in the 1890s.

In 1910 at the first international air show at Dominguez Field, outside Los Angeles, Harold Harris noted that "the best flying was done by Roy Knabenshue in a lighter than air dirigible."[11]

The prospect of airships as bombers had long been recognized in Europe. During World War I the German dirigibles known as Zeppelins were terrifying but inaccurate weapons. Navigation, target selection and bomb aiming proved to be difficult under the best of conditions. Further their hydrogen gas was flammable. The Graf Zeppelin burned blau gas, similar to propane, stored in large gasbags below the hydrogen cells, as fuel. Since the density of hydrogen was similar to that of air, it avoided the weight change when fuel was used, and thus the need to valve hydrogen. In peacetime the "Graf" was a great success and compiled an impressive safety record, flying over 1,600,000 km (990,000 mi) (including the first circumnavigation of the globe by air) without a single passenger injury.

By the mid-1930s only Germany still pursued the airship. The Zeppelin company continued to operate the Graf Zeppelin on passenger service between Frankfurt and Recife in Brazil, taking 68 hours. The Hindenburg (LZ 129) completed a very successful 1936 season carrying passengers between Lakehurst, New Jersey and Germany. But in 1937 the Hindenburg burst into flames and crashed. Of the 97 people aboard, 36 died: 13 passengers, 22 air crew, and one American ground-crewman died. The disaster happened before a large crowd, and was filmed so theatergoers could see and hear it the next day. On that same next day, the Graf Zeppelin landed at the end of its flight from Brazil, ending intercontinental passenger airship travel.

---

[11]   Harris memoir.

Hindenburg's sister ship, the Graf Zeppelin II (LZ 130), could not perform commercial passenger flights without helium, which the United States refused to sell. The Graf Zeppelin flew some test flights and conducted electronic espionage until 1939 when it was grounded due to the start of the war. The last two Zeppelins were scrapped in 1940. Development of airships continued only in the United States, and in a small way, the Soviet Union.

Winged flight could be said to have begun with George Cayley, born 1773, who was the first to apply scientific methods to the development of flight technology.[12] As a child initially interested in balloons, through studying the flight of birds, particularly their wing structures, he quickly developed an interest in aeronautics.

"By 1799", notes Hallion, "he postulated the shape of the modern airplane, a configuration having a fixed main wing, a control car for the pilot, and cruciform tail surfaces."

Most important, Cayley recognized that the problem of control "was just as important as the problems of lift and propulsion."[13]

Today hailed as the father of the modern airplane and the science of aerodynamics, Cayley is less well known for flight testing and flight research. In 1809 he constructed a full-sized glider "having a wing span of 200 square feet and flew it successfully, both unmanned and piloted by a small boy (whose name is regrettably lost to history.)

"That same year he published his monumental treatise *On Aerial Navigation*, one of the most important works ever written on aviation."

He created two more gliders. The last was piloted by his very reluctant coachman, who is alleged to have said after his flight,

---

[12]   Hallion, 33.
[13]   This and following quotations are from Hallion,12-18.

"Please, Sir George, I wish to give notice. I was hired to drive, and not to fly!"

Between Cayley and Otto Lilienthal in the late 19th century, the latter considered the father of modern flight testing, came many others along with the development of what became an essential testing tool: the wind tunnel that led in turn to the general public's acceptance of the scientific validity of the concept of flight.

Born in 1848 in Anklam, Pomerania, Lilienthal and his younger brother worked to create an ornithopter (winged glider) that was not successful. Technically educated, Lilienthal worked for several engineering firms. His studies on the flight of birds culminated in *The Flight of Birds* as the Basis of *The Art of Flying (1899)*. This research and subsequent success in glider design led to his fame throughout Europe. By the time of his fatal crash in 1896 people had become convinced that human flight was possible.

Hallion writes, "After Lilienthal, aviation would never be quite the same, for he had given the world a vision of the future: the repeated sight of a man confidently gliding through the air with swiftness and skill, in a vehicle of his own making."[14]

---

[14] Hallion, 18.

Chapter 2: Mae Plumb Harris and Ross Allen Harris

Harold Harris's mother, Mae, was the daughter of Samuel Plumb (b.1812) and Levancia Holcomb Plumb (b.1841). Once the mayor of Oberlin, OH., Samuel and his brother together founded the town of Streator, Illinois, where Samuel became president of Streator's Union National Bank. After he died in 1882, Levancia took charge of his estate, was elected President in his stead and remained in that position for 24 years. This despite the fact that she spent most of those years in a wheelchair, a result, noted her granddaughter Jessica, of a serious injury incurred when a disgruntled former employee pushed her down the stairs.

Levancia's obituary noted that she was one of only two women bank presidents in the United States, "an honor not often accorded to a woman, and although unable for some years to work actively in this capacity, she retained a keen interest in the affairs of the Union National Bank, talking over matters of finance almost daily with her son, S. W. Plumb, vice-president, upon whom the duties of president developed."

Nothing if not determined, when her children entered Wheaton College, Levancia had moved there in order to be able to continue to supervise their activities. Levancia and her grandson Harold Ross Harris were very close. Much to her delight, on her eighty-eighth birthday in April 1923, from McCook Field where he was chief test pilot at the time, he buzzed her house. (Her daughter Mae was still alive and participating in the festivities.)

"Who's Who of American Women, 1890" described Levancia as "a woman of liberal education, sound business judgment, great tact and wide experience in practical affairs." It continues, "She is interested in temperance work. Her work in that reform began in 1877. She was one of the charter members of the Women's Temperance Publishing Association. She was one of the charter members and originators of the temperance hospital in Chicago, IL. Since1890, while retaining her business interests in Streator, she has made her home in Wheaton, IL in order to superintend the education of her four children."

I was born too late (1928) to know Levancia's daughter, my much-loved grandmother Mae (June 14, 1869-March 18, 1926). The photographs, taken in her early middle age make it clear that—unlike her husband—she was no beauty. That she was a woman of administrative talent is evident from the fact that, as her daughter our Aunt Jessica pointed out, at Wheaton College where Mae met her husband, who was her harp teacher, she "was student body president when her two sisters and brother were students there." Mae had flaming red hair, a beaky nose,— in middle age the face of an Irish washerwoman—and an undeniably corpulent body.

She wore spectacles. (This latter may have been at her husband's behest. He eventually got the entire household— wife and three children as well as himself—in spectacles.)

It is also apparent that for our grandfather, brilliant, occasionally irascible, domineering, stubborn, yet devoted to his family, she was the perfect mate. Indeed, Mae ran her household as effectively as her mother ran the bank.

The household fulcrum and yet running to fulfill Ross's every whim, even determining, when he sought to become a medical missionary in China, that she would take nurse's training, Mae was in every way as much a true Victorian as her husband. She died in her mid 50's, by today's standards much too young.

Why did Ross pick Mae to be his wife? He was, after all, handsome and accomplished in his own right. Was it because he had always been poor and she, on the other hand, came from a well known and financially sound family? Did Ross truly love his wife or did he consider her simply a good household manager? The answer lies in his self-description in 1908 for the Oberlin alumni records. Fifteen years after his wedding he noted that he was married Aug. 16, 1893, "to Mae Irvine Plumb, of Streator, Illinois, the best girl in the United States." It was a startling burst of enthusiasm.

Mae with Ross and her daughters June and Jessica

Daughter of the first woman president of an American bank, Mae, gentle and kind to a fault, had a steely interior and cool nerves, characteristics she appears to have passed on to her son Harold. Without appearing to, she provided the essential strength of the family. My cousin Dorothy recounted a story concerning Mae's "cool" that her mother Jessica had told her. The year was 1886. Mae, aged 18 or 19, was quietly studying one evening in her Wheaton College dormitory room. It was either spring or fall and so the windows were all open. The window next to Mae's desk opened on a fire escape. As she studied, intent on her book, a man slid from the fire escape into the room. Startled, she turned, saw his dark figure and, most especially, the knife he carried in his hand. She gasped.

The man spoke. "God told me to come kill you tonight," he said in the flattest of tones. She got up out of her seat to face him. Quietly and with great determination she said, "Oh no, you're wrong. God didn't tell you to kill me tonight. He told you to kill me <u>tomorrow</u> night!"

The intruder looked puzzled and paused for a moment as if trying to figure things out. Then, having decided that this clearly determined woman must be right, he turned and fled out the window and down the fire escape from where he had come.

Literally quaking, Mae pulled herself together and went for help. Later she found that the man, an escapee from the local insane asylum, had been apprehended. She would not have to dread what might occur the following night!

Besides raising her own children, Mae took in and raised several neighborhood children from families that had encountered unfortunate circumstances. I was able to meet one of these, already in late middle age by the time I met him. This was Holland Kinkaid who never forgot Mae's kindness and never renounced his wholesale admiration for the teenage buddy of his youth, Harold Ross Harris.

Ross Allen Harris

Many stories have grown up around the dominating figure of Ross Allen Harris (b.1864), our father's father, a remarkable and difficult man. He and his wife Mae came from very different backgrounds. According to our Aunt Jessica, our father's younger sister, Ross Allen's background was somewhat problematic.

His mother married a Mr. Allen. They had a daughter, Louisa, later known as Aunt Lou Langdon, and a son, who, according to Aunt Jessica, "married Aunt Josie; their one child was named Perlina." I believe Mr. Allen abandoned his wife, returning to her to be nursed only when terminally ill.

Upon her husband's death, Ross's mother married his best friend, a Squire Harris. The family lived in Oberlin, Ohio. One of the couple's two sons, Ross Allen, was born May 11, 1864. Squire Harris, a local judge whose constituents called him "Square" Harris, was not renowned for his humanity. He sold William, the other of his two sons, to a local farmer because he had taken a dislike to the child, an act then permissible. (A letter from Aunt Jessica to her brother Harold Ross Harris dated June 26, 1982, notes that she remembered that Harold had gone to Vermillion, Ohio, to see Ross Allen's brother, his uncle William, and found him "a poor farmer.")

The Squire also abandoned his family—for what reason or what was his subsequent fate, I have no idea. To maintain herself, his wife set up a boarding house for Oberlin students and thus made a scanty living. Ross Allen, the remaining son, whom the Squire had "adored", was raised there primarily by his half-sister Louisa Allen. She considered him "difficult, full of tantrums and furious tempers but at the same time loving and bright." Aunt Jessica notes there may have been some "shameful" mystery surrounding Ross Allen's mother, since hers was the only family portrait that was not allowed in the living room of their house, reposing instead in Ross Allen's bedroom.

The description of Ross Allen's education is somewhat confusing. The Oberlin College Archives file states that Ross Allen "was enrolled in the college between 1882-1886, [that is between the ages of 18 and 22]. In 1882 he was enrolled in the College, and in 1884-5 in the preparatory and it appears he was enrolled in the Conservatory in 1885-6 [when he was 21-22]. He did not graduate from the college or the Conservatory, though."

Ross Allen himself wrote that he attended Oberlin High School and spent 3 years at Oberlin Academy (cited in Oberlin Academy records as "both a private secondary school and as the first of four departments of Oberlin College to admit students", this allowing his obituary to claim him as an Oberlin College student.)

Oberlin Conservatory of Music, one of the few American conservatories to be completely attached to a liberal arts college (Oberlin College) is where, thanks to a scholarship, Ross, a "musical prodigy", as Aunt Jessica described him, said he spent four years, not the single year assigned to him by the Oberlin Archives.

Ross followed this with enrollment at Chicago Musical College, where he took instruction in the pipe organ with Clarence Eddy, known as the dean of American organists. He became a teacher of piano and pipe organ, a choirmaster and organist with membership in the Organists' Guild of America. Let's give him two years to do all this—although that's very unlikely.

He subsequently attended Wheaton College and at the age of 21 became Director of the Wheaton Conservatory of Music between 1885-93. There he met his future wife Mae, who was student body president when her two sisters and brother were students there. Their relationship was established when he taught her the harp.

Married and with two of his three children already born, in response to a questionnaire from Oberlin Alumni Association, Ross Allen provided a summary of himself and his manifold achievements. (Additional information comes from a brief biography published in The Youth's Companion for Sept. 14, 1898.) He said he was 5'8" tall, and that he had had lobar pneumonia at age 18 but made a "perfect recovery. "His father had died at age 72 of "catarrh [inflammation] of the bladder" and his mother, at 64, of "phthisis"[pulmonary tuberculosis].

Ross determined to become a physician—graduating from medical school in 1899 at the age of 35—as a path to becoming a medical missionary to China. His ambition was thwarted however by his wife's pregnancy with their first child,

Harold Ross Harris. Children were not allowed to accompany missionaries to China.

Two daughters were to follow: June, six years younger than Harold and Jessica, 10 years younger.

That same year he moved his family to California and went into private practice as an eye, ear, nose, and throat specialist at Redlands, California. The family moved once more, to Los Angeles where he was the first eye, ear, nose, and throat doctor in the LA area. His last letterhead read:

Ross Allen Harris M.D.,

Eye, Ear, Nose and Throat

Hay Fever—Asthma, Sun and Diet Therapy

623 So. Bonnie Brae, Los Angeles, California.

(Previous addresses include: 207 West Broadway; 301 Broadway, Central Building, Suite 300; 424 South Broadway. One wonders why he moved his office so frequently. Was it due to diminishing funds, and if so, why did they diminish? Did the diminution of his funds have anything to do with his property investments?)

Ross Allen became a clinical instructor in Ophthalmology, College of Medicine, University of California, and Associate Professor of Ophthalmology at the Los Angeles Post-Graduate School. He was a member of the Los Angeles Medical Association, the Southern California Medical Society, the American Medical Association, and the American Academy of Medical Sciences.

Somewhere along the way he gained a working knowledge of Latin, Greek (both probably requisite for the medical degree), German, as well as "some French and Spanish."

Seeing his son Harold go overseas as a military pilot in 1917, Ross Allen, then 54, determined to enlist. In 1918 he applied to and was rejected by the U.S. Army. Instead, undoubtedly aware that the demands of the military caused an acute shortage of physicians domestically, he became a substitute intern that summer at the Chicago Eye and Ear Infirmary.

A genuine Victorian patriarch, Ross Allen Harris was an eccentric legend in his own time. A stern Congregationalist, a poet and essay writer, Ross had a quirky sense of humor that emerged in his travel essays. His religious principles were strict. Deeply devout and committed to the literal truth of the Bible, when the new minister at the church the family had attended for many years declared himself unable to believe in the divinity of Christ, despite the longtime friendships his wife and children had developed among fellow parishioners, Ross Allen marched them out of the church never to return.

Although married to Mae Plumb, whose mother was America's first female bank president, and a formidable advocate for women's rights, he was no early feminist. He saw to it that his wife, gentle daughter of a powerful mother, was not either.

Ross Allen's eccentricities, all too familiar to his family, became evident to Grace, his future daughter-in-law, the year she lived with the Harris family while Harold was in Italy. She noted, for example, that Ross loved motorcars that he always purchased second-hand. The longer and the flashier they were, the better. On a running board Ross installed his beloved—and ugly—Cop, a red-haired Chow dog. To commemorate Cop's death, Ross wrote a sad elegy.

Perhaps as a result of a financially pinched childhood, Ross loved buying land. The problem was that, once having acquired a piece of property, he never bothered to pay the taxes on it and consequently ultimately lost back to the City whatever he had acquired.

Ross' younger daughter Jessica, found this characteristic unforgivable. "All the most valuable property in Los Angeles, including the land on which the Hollywood Bowl now sits, at one time or another belonged to Father," she moaned. "We could have been millionaires many times over!"

Living with her in-laws the year (1917) Harold Harris was stationed in Foggia, Italy, Grace observed and sympathized with the extraordinary difficulties encountered by Mae and her daughters in Ross Allen's household. As was true of most middle class housewives, Mae had a "hired girl" to help with the housework. Considering her girth and the weight of the feminine attire of the time—corsets, several petticoats and a full-skirted gown—as well as her manifold duties, particularly during the family's "camping" summers (without the hired girl) in a cliffside Catalina Island cottage where it was Mae's (and her daughters', as they grew older) job to carry buckets of water from a spring forty feet down, it is not surprising that Mae's blood pressure became dangerously high. Her husband, the doctor, ordered her to bed, the recommended remedy. There, Mae spent the last part of her life. When her daughters, aware of their father's religious strictures against most forms of entertainment, smuggled in a pack of cards so Mae could entertain herself by playing solitaire, Ross was furious and appropriated the cards as easily as he had his wife's small inheritance, with which she had hoped at one time to finance her trip to Europe.[15]

---

[15] Family histories soon become mythical and—where the proponents or their closest relatives are still alive—far easier to modify so as—hopefully—to correspond more to the circumstances of the original incident. First and foremost one needs to take into account the personality and motivation of the person recounting the story. Take, for example, the story that our paternal grandfather, Ross Allen Harris, appropriated his wife's inheritance that she had hoped to use for a trip to Europe. I heard this story in two versions: one from our mother, who disliked R.A., and one from our Aunt Jessica, R.A.'s younger daughter. The

Using the inheritance, instead, in 1921 Ross took his family to Europe (without Harold, married and living in Dayton). The only other trip outside the U.S. that he took was in 1929 when, upon her graduation from college, Ross took his daughter Jessica, the only child still living with him, on a trip to South America to visit his son Harold Ross and family.

Despite the genuine affection both felt for each other, Ross Allen's relationship with his only son, the light of his life, was strained. Growing up, Harold Ross had demonstrated the high intelligence, sheer stubbornness, and will power—as well as the sense of humor—that characterized the father.

Harold Ross was tenderly attached to both his mother and grandmother. Yet Ross Allen's anxiety about his children's health that led him to imagine that none of the three would ever live to adulthood, drove a wedge between father and son.

Only a few months before he died, at the age of 92, Harold Ross still bitterly recalled the fact that his father, claiming that his son was in delicate health, would not allow him to participate in his team's out-of-town football games. There were other problems, as well. Unlike his father, given to brooding and introspection, Harold Ross was outgoing and serenely confident. The father seemed always to compare himself with other men; his son never bothered. Yet both men had a deep well of affection for family and friends.

Harold Ross at seventeen

---

latter noted that her mother would have gladly given the money for that purpose.

Chapter 3: Harold Ross Harris—The Early Years

Harold was Ross and Mae's first child and a son. The two facts conspired together to produce a birth announcement noting the arrival of HRH—"His Royal Highness" December 20, 1895. In time he had two sisters: June and Jessica. To Harold they were always "the girls", whose friendship in later years he cherished and who, from earliest childhood, adored him. It might have been the infrequency of their encounters that kept the relationship between the girls and their brother free of the normal childhood hassles. As an older brother, he was somewhat remote, involved with his own adventures shared with his own group of friends.

Harris, seated upper row center, with the other children of his extended clan

Harold was fortunate in several ways. His immediate family— that included a physician father noted in the tiny Los Angeles community for his eccentricities as well as for his profession as an ear, nose, and throat specialist—doted on Harold, indeed, from his infancy put him on a pedestal. As surviving photos demonstrate, Harold also had a large extended family whose members he was close to from childhood on. There is a charming photo of Harold, his two sisters, June and Jessica, along with other children of his clan: Fraziers, Plumbs, a Scryver, seated on the front steps of a house belonging to their wealthy cousins, the Bishops. Another surviving photo shows extended family members standing in front of a 1909 Pierce Arrow, one of Ross Allen's numerous large secondhand cars, parked in front of the Bishops' house.

Further, as a teenager Harold was fortunate in that the Manual Arts High School provided the right combination of nurturing and challenge, as it did also for Harold Morton, Harold's friend, future corporation lawyer and future husband of Dorothy Haines, the only other true love interest claimed by Harold Ross; Jimmy Doolittle and Josephine Daniels, his future wife; as well as Holland Kinkaid.

Finally, Harold Harris was fortunate in choosing a career that was still in its infancy.

This meant that initially anyway, there were few rules; pilots were encouraged to pioneer, to use their own initiative in all ways with no or few questions asked. We see this in a letter he sent home to California after being installed as a Dayton test pilot. He observed, "This ship is in poor condition and I don't care if it is struck by lightning before I leave. It has not enough gasoline capacity either. I am having an extra tank installed." Much later when, as Manager of Panagra and himself an engineer, he saw a need for improving the ability of his aircraft to fly bulky machinery up to remote Andean mining operations, he thought nothing of ignoring flight engineers' advice and simply having a section of the roof made removable so that the machinery could be installed.

As I noted in my memoir of Harold's father, Ross Allen was an overprotective parent. Convinced that none of his children would survive into adulthood, he had everyone in the family in glasses and, much to his teenage son's fury, forbade him to travel with his football team to play outside games because he considered it too much of a risk to Harold's health.

Yet Harold Harris was not to be caged. Unlike his father, Harold Harris was physically strong, mentally tough, a natural-born leader, someone whose leadership, even when young, inspired his peers. As a teenager Harold quickly developed a gang of admirers. To Holland Kinkaid, an early playmate who finally joined the Harris household in 1918, Harold was a shining star. Together the gang found ways to elude Ross Allen, ways that Mae didn't approve of, but which she kept secret from her husband. Thus when he was old enough to drive, in an evening Harold was accustomed to climb out the window, over the geraniums in the window box, and down the drainpipe to where his friends were waiting for a ride in Ross Allen's car. One day his younger sister Jessica, then a small child, accompanying her mother into Harold's room, pointed out a pile of dirt from the window box displaced by Harold's window-climbing expeditions. Jessica started to say something only to have Mae hush her by putting her finger to her lips. They cleaned it up and no one subsequently mentioned the discovery.

The Throop Polytechnic football team, with Harris gripping the football

Growing up, Harold Ross was tenderly attached to both his mother and grandmother. Yet Ross Allen's strict religious principles and anxiety about his children's health created a divide between the father, on the one side, and the son and older daughter on the other. As June pointed out, "When Harold went to college, Father said, 'I don't want you to join a fraternity.' So he did. And when I came along, he said, 'I don't want you to join a sorority.' So I did. And when I was in high school, 'I don't want you to learn to dance,' so I did. It's a wonder we weren't all drunkards!"

Jessica noted that Mae's fears for her son's safety during WW I, when she "had all sorts of horrible visions about it, maimed or killed in an accident, or something like that" had some basis in Harold's teenage antics. "Of course she knew what went on even in high school, so she had some justification. She was well aware and always kept it a secret. She didn't even tell father. Father did know that he had to pay through the nose for all the times he [HRH] was arrested for speeding, all the speeding tickets. But outside of that, he didn't know about all the other shenanigans [which] she took in her stride . . . I don't know exactly what they were; nothing was ever told to me; I was kept in the dark . . . There were usually a lot of boys around the house who were helping Harold and up in his room talking about things, and little sisters were not invited."

Harold Harris and Jimmy Doolittle, about the same age, were both speed freaks when young, but Doolittle was the real daredevil. Noted Harold in 1987, chatting with a Mr. Towner of Brewster, "He [Doolittle] was really a terrible roughneck when he was in high school, the head of the gymnastics team, extremely agile and completely fearless. Years ago, the streetcars in Los Angeles were on rails which were quite far apart and Jimmy got himself on a motorcycle and rode between the street cars going in the opposite direction. . . . He broke both ankles must have been in 1925 when he hung onto the balcony of the club in Santiago until he finally couldn't hang on anymore and let go and fell down 18 feet there, nearly broke his neck."

According to *The Spirit of the Toilers,* its 1977 memoir, Los Angeles's Manual Arts High School, up-to-date and very modern, was built in 1910 to replace the Olive St. High School, an outcast of the LA educational system.[16] Olive St. was a dirty, dingy grey building with no play yard whose interior initially lacked a science lab. Lacking an auditorium, the Olive St. staffers were forced to use an extra-large classroom for school affairs. Fortunately, young and eager, they made up for the school's physical deficiencies. By way of compensation, they could lunch at the elegant Fremont Hotel next door, or on Wednesday afternoons enjoy a performance of the nearby Los Angeles Symphony.

In 1910 Olive St. faculty and students, the latter including Jimmy Doolittle, Harold Morton, Dorothy Haines, Holland Kinkaid and Harold Harris, moved on to the shiny-new Manual Arts High School with its science labs and spacious shop facilities. To enhance the students' sense of involvement, the principal enlisted their aid in finishing off the surrounding grounds, an ocean of mud during the rainy season.

A new century was bringing many changes in education. The late 19th and early 20th centuries—with wholesale immigration and the beginnings of an enormous population shift from farms to urban areas—saw a new emphasis in classrooms on multiculturalism, cooperation and social awareness. Religion, a foundation stone of American education, promoted the rise of the YM and YWCAs to keep young people new to the city on the straight and narrow. In addition to the classical curriculum, educators determined to teach what it seemed students needed to become responsible adults in this ever-changing world. Hence, the emphasis on manual arts. As the head of the new

---

16   Florence Sprenger, *Spirit of the Toilers,* V. 1, Taylor Publishing
     Company, 1977.

Mechanic Arts Department noted: "By manual training we mean a thorough instruction and practice in tool and machine work designed to improve the powers of the worker."

The school principal elaborated: "Vocational education has for its object efficiency, ability to do one's share of the work of the world . . . The evolution of civilization may be studied in clay, wood, and textiles of the metals. To come in contact with basic elements is a distinct and unique experience."

Despite this, the principal did not neglect the liberal arts. He boasted that his shop teachers could pinch hit in Latin, math, modern languages, or science classes. His teachers learned a new concept: they were not "potters shaping clay" but only facilitators for the opening of youthful minds. His teaching staff joked that they were merely "a bunch of adults hired to help the seniors run the school". Indeed, the students felt that "the school was theirs; they could make of it what they would".

Chasing a Dream

Among the first Boys' Self-Government leaders were Harold Morton and Harold Harris, the latter cited in *Spirit of the Toilers* as one of those brave soldiers who during WW I were to make "the World safe for Democracy."

Thus, during WW I, "Carleton Henley, in the Aviation section, wrote home that 'With me in camp are several well-known Manualites of the early days . . . [including James Doolittle . . . and Holland Kinkaid, who followed his idol, Harold Harris, into the military.] We have all promised to take the name of Manual Arts into Berlin with us."

The memoir continues: "At least twenty-two of Manual's own were fliers. In addition to those in camp with Carlton Henley there were other known leaders from the school—Cliff Henderson, George Comeny, who earned a croix de guerre; Harold Harris, who was the first American to fly over the Alps."

It was an exciting time to be alive; huge technological changes were occurring on an almost daily basis. The Wrights flew at Kitty Hawk in 1903 when Harris was an 8-year old schoolboy. In 1904 the St. Louis World's Fair demonstrated in its Palace of Electricity "dynamos and motors of many kinds and new electrical machinery for a multiple of uses". Progress in the use of electricity in the treatment of diseases was illustrated with X-ray apparatus and "the famous Finsen light, " not to mention the progress in electric lighting and the use of electric power" as well as the use of "small but powerful electric locomotives for mining purposes" as well as "the wonders of electrochemistry." (Quoted from advertising literature about the Fair.) And then there was the promise of a brilliant future for manned flight.

The aged Harold Harris recalled his youthful passion for all things mechanical "from the two-cylinder Maxwell Runabout of my rich Aunt, whose chauffeur taught me to drive in 1909, to the first aviation meet in California" on January 10-20, 1910. Harold was 14 when, along with his schoolmates Jimmy Doolittle and Josephine Daniels, Jimmy's future wife, he played hookey from school to attend the first American air meet held at Dominguez Field in Los Angeles. Billed as "the world's first International Aviation Meet", it featured "ten aeroplanes, seven balloons, three dirigibles, and 200,000 awed spectators."[17]

---

[17] For the complete meet schedule, see *Dominguez Air Meet 1910*, published by Hatfield History of Aeronautics, Northrop University, 1976.

Since the Wright brothers were embroiled in a fierce patent dispute with other aircraft builders, no Wright planes were involved. D.D. Hatfield notes that at an earlier air meet in Rheims, France, although Orville Wright operated a flying school not far from Rheims, "The Wrights did not favor competitive flying and, feeling secure in the validity of their patents, went to great lengths to prevent anyone else from flying. The effects of this attitude were to be felt in aviation for many years to come."[18]

The basis for this and successive meets was a sequence of tests requiring pilots to fly around a series of pylons, thus demonstrating their speed and skill. Monetary prizes—the highest, $10,000—were awarded even including one prize of $500 for "any aeroplane which makes the slowest lap at any time during the meet."

Guaranteed a significant sum of money, world famous Louis Paulhan came with his Farman biplane from France. Some of the other stars included Glenn Curtiss, Charles Willard, and Charles K. Hamilton.

Glenn Curtis and Louis Paulhan

Writes historian Don Dwiggins, "Thus, were heroes born, in a day when the smell of castor oil and the sound of singing wires brought flying down to the grassroots level."[19]

It is difficult today, when air travel is mundane, to appreciate the aura surrounding the early pilots. Even the media glorification of

---

[18] Ibid.
[19] Op cit.

the first astronauts did not equal the early pilots' fame. For the first time in history humans, gazing up at the sky, could see and wonder at a machine that carried another or several other humans. And thanks to the photography of early pilots such as John A. Macready, for the first time people could see what their world looked like from hundreds even thousands of feet up.

Looking back many years later at events at the early aviation meets, Harold Harris recalled a grisly product of all this fame. At another meet also held at Dominguez Field a year later, "when Arch Hoxie in a 'Wright Flyer' descended from an altitude attempt, went into a vertical dive, and was killed, I was horrified when the crowd rushed out to the crashed plane and tore the clothing off his body for souvenirs!"

Convinced, despite his father's apprehensions, that aviation was his chosen career, Harold Harris graduated from Manual Arts High School in Los Angeles and subsequently from Throop Polytechnic Institute, or Throop College of Technology, later known as the California Institute of Technology. He had developed into a tough, resourceful man. At Throop, despite his father's concerns, he played three years of varsity football. An engineering major, he joined an engineering fraternity. A resounding baritone, he joined the college's all-male chorus, noting wryly that the difference between him and Lawrence Tibbett, another chorus member, subsequently a world-famous baritone, was that "Tibbett had a voice."

Almost 21, in 1916 at Monterey, California, the site of the only one of the "Citizens Military Training Camps" set up by the Federal Government throughout the U.S. that had an aviation section, Harris was taken on his first plane ride by one of the site's two Navy instructors. All of the military planes were being used to attempt to locate Mexico's Pancho Villa, so his first ride was in a plane loaned by a civilian to the camp.

Harold Harris and Grace Clark met at a Los Angeles church social. They eloped and were married July 14, 1917, the same day Harold graduated from the first ground school class at the University of California, Berkeley. Their witnesses were Holland and Marjorie Kinkaid—who had also eloped and married.

Grace always insisted that if Harold hadn't married her, he would have ended up with any one of a dozen other girls, perhaps pretty Dorothy Haines. I disagree. Rather it seems as though Harold felt when he met Grace that it was the right time to wed and she was the right girl. In later life his sisters twitted him for his youthful adoration of the opposite sex. When young, they joked, the "R" of his middle initial stood for Romeo! Yet they also noted that of all the beautiful girls Harold admired, Grace was the most beautiful and also the liveliest. Harold replied quite seriously that he and Grace had contemplated marriage for a long time before eloping—at least a year.

Grace

The biographies of great men seldom have more than a passing reference to their wives, certainly in one way or another their most important relationship. In the case of Harold R. Harris, there is no doubt that as a complement to his need to explore and create, in Grace Clark he had found a beautiful woman whose intelligence, creativity, and inner steel matched his own and who, despite continuing ill health, ultimately became an unrelenting watch dog over his career.

The third and undoubtedly the liveliest of four children, Grace, born August 16,1894, in Colfax, Illinois, to Daniel A. Clark, a prosperous Colfax shop owner, and Nellie (Sutton) Clark, was her father's favorite, a romantic figure, as a young adult always the centerpiece or ringleader of a cluster of warm friends both male and female.

At some point, Daniel was diagnosed with TB and recommended to a warmer climate in which, to recover, he could spend most of the year outdoors. It can be assumed that the family's move to California took place somewhere around

1912, following Grace's graduation from Colfax high school. She attended Illinois Wesleyan University, graduated from California State Normal School June 22, 1916, and briefly became a teacher in rural Nevada. Home again in Los Angeles, she soon developed a devoted coterie. She was pretty, a good dancer, loved a good time, and played the piano: all popular attributes. One evening she attended a church social where she met Harold Harris, at that time an ambitious young Lieutenant in what was to be the Army Air Corps. And the rest, as they say, is history.

World War I was dwindling down in early 1917 when our parents married, very much against Grace's parents' wishes. From my perspective, their opposition was baseless. It is well to remember, however, that in 1917 the lives of many aviators were tragically short. Daniel Clark, former owner in Colfax, Illinois, of a largely prosperous dry goods establishment, was nothing if not practical and was not eager to hand his beloved "Grayla" over to be pointlessly rendered a widow.

Why Grace and Harold felt it necessary to run away from both families is a puzzle.

That the Clark family reluctance to accept the marriage was not shared with the Harris family is demonstrated by the fact that shortly after Harold was shipped overseas, and despite her father-in-law's domineering ways, Grace went to live with his family and stayed there until Harold returned and they moved to Dayton. At the Harrises she quickly learned about life with a Victorian patriarch.

Chapter 4: Foggia and World War I

Caproni bomber pilots, from left: Lt. Harris, naval Ensign Robert Hudson, Lt. Spencer Kerr, Lt. Ed Lewis, and Lt. Will Agar

In the summer of 1916 it became evident that the U.S. would have to join the war in Europe. In Monterey, California, Harris attended one of the Citizens Military Training Camps. There, since the six Army planes had been conscripted to fight Mexico's Pancho Villa, he learned to fly in a plane loaned to the Army by a private owner.

Having learned to fly, Harris became Engineering Officer of an Army unit called the "First Provisional Aero Squadron." When the United States declared war on Germany in April, 1917, he enlisted in the Aviation Section of the Signal Corps. Shipped out with 75 other American pilots to Foggia, Italy, where, learning from a Swiss who spoke little English, after three hours of flight training in a Maurice Farman Pusher, Harold soloed. Here is what he noted about this initial experience:

"The instructor in the rear and the student in front. The plane was a Pusher with a ten-cylinder radial, air-cooled Anzani engine developing about 80 horsepower. The only instruments were a tachometer and an oil pressure gauge. When it was part of the instruction course to climb to a particular altitude, the student was issued an altimeter which he strapped on his leg to carry on the flight, and then turned back to the office when he landed!"

He quickly graduated to flying instructor and then to test pilot of some Caproni bombers being constructed at Milan for the U.S. Navy.

Fiorello LaGuardia, a former Congressman and future Mayor of New York, Captain of the American cadets at Foggia, was fortunately bilingual.

A Caproni Ca. 5 with Italian air force markings

Sometime in 1917, LaGuardia and his instructor, an Italian, took off for a routine training session in a Farman biplane. Returning to the field proved a real adventure. Harris notes: "We watched the plane come in for a landing, very slow and flat, and about to spin. It hit the ground flat, bounced several times, and finally stopped. The two men jumped out, screaming at each other in Italian. It turned out that each thought the other was making the landing!"

Harris became identified with the Caproni, a plane other pilots were reluctant to attempt to fly. In a memoir, he recounts how a certain Lieutenant Zelch voiced his concern:

Lieutenant Zelch had been turned over to me as a doubtful pilot of the Caproni Bomber. I was amazed in making the circuit with him that his landing judgment had been questioned. After we landed a couple of times, this being daylight and not night flying, it looked as though Zelch was an able guy and I didn't anticipate any problem, but he seemed to have some worry.

[I said,] 'Tell me, do you really think you can fly one of these things?'

'Oh yes, sure.' [Shakily, I suspect.]

'Well, I'll tell you what I'm going to do. I'll let you fly solo and you make two or three landings and we'll see how it goes.'

As soon as I got out of the plane, he passed the test very nicely . . ."

Between March and July, 1918, Harris was chief instructor of day and night flying in Farmans and Capronis. July 16 he left Foggia and reported for duty as a test pilot at the Caproni factory in Milan. On July 25, 1918, Harris, along with his co-pilot, George Lewis, and R. S. Hudson, USN, were the first American pilots to fly a Caproni bomber on a reconnaissance mission over the Alps from Italy to France.

Lewis' World War I letters to his wife were preserved and many years later published by his son. Reproduced were not only the letter he wrote her before departure on the Alps mission but also the mission's official report in which at times he became almost lyrical.[20]

Dearest, . . . a letter to you before I start over the Alps tomorrow. We're passing thru the same country now I flew over Sunday morning. The weather has been warm and clear this side and the sky is cloudless. Let's go. My

---

[20] This and the following official report are from *Dear Bert: An American Pilot Flying in World War I Italy*, by Edward Davis Lewis, George's son. Logisma Editore, 2002.

pilot partner is Harry Harris, an old high school buddy of Bill Creighton in Calif. He is the best pilot we have in Italy. We're taking a Naval officer along to help with the compass readings... Two machines are making the trip and we hope to keep together between the glaciers by means of smoke bomb signals... Well, here's a salute until I get another chance to write.

Lots of love, George.

Edward Lewis also included his father's official report:

From: George M.D. Lewis, 1st Lieut., Air Service, U.S.A.

To: Chief of Air Service (Information Section) A.P.O. 717, France

The first American owned and American flown, machine to cross the Alps was of the 600 H.P. Caproni biplane type, CA5. The power plant consists of three Fiat A-12 Bis motors, each with a block test of 312 H.P. The wingspan of the plane is 23.4 meters, the gap 2.75 meters and the chord of the wings 2.75 meters. The plane was designed and tested to carry a load of 900 kilograms, including seventeen bombs, four men, two machine guns, and a ton of gasoline and oil for 5½ hours flight. One of the machine guns is designed to be operated by the observer, sitting just in front of the two pilots, the rear (central) motor, is operated by the mechanic. The fuel is carried in three tanks, one large tank directly behind the pilots and two smaller ones in each fuselage. The machine was equipped with a Universal compass, altimeter and speed-meters of the Pensuti type on each side of the carlinga. There were also the usual gages [sic!] indicating the pressure of gas and oil... Besides the crew, the machine carried a load of 400 pounds, which consisted of personal luggage and spare parts.

After all the necessary preparation had been made, the initial lap of the flight was covered from Taliedo to Milan, to Turin. This flight was made July 21, 1918. The trip was made in one hour forty minutes without incident . . .

The trip from Turin, Italy, to Lyon, France, was delayed for three days. Telegraphic reports from Modane and Lyon indicated contrary winds and low clouds. During this time the motors were gone over and tested on the ground by the Italian mechanics. Finally, conditions being favorable, the trip was made on the 25th of July. Entering the mountains in the valley of the Dora Riparia and passing over Susa to Mount Cenis, an average altitude of 3,500 meters was maintained. The highest altitude reached was 4,290 meters over Mount Cenis and Mount Thabor, which range about 3,200 meters above sea level. The atmospheric conditions were ideal except for the unusual agitation of the air over snow capped peaks and glaciers where the variations in temperature made the flying very uneven. Here the temperature was very low, causing ice to form on the face coverings of the pilots.

Worthy of mention is the remarkable beauty of this phase of the trip. The light of the morning sun reflected from dazzling snowcaps with an impression of utter isolation from the rest of the world. The first half of this trip was made over the rugged snow-covered peaks and steep ravine passes. During the entire passage over these mountains there did not appear to be a single possible landing place, except one built by the Italian government on the frontier alongside Iago di Monte Cenis about 2,500 meters above sea level.

After a flight of two hours and forty minutes over a distance of 2790 kilometers, the landing was made at Lyon, where the pilots were met by a party of French and Italian aviators, including the inventor of the machine, Signor Gianni Caproni.

(signed) George M.D. Lewis, 1st Lieut. Air Service, U.S.A.

Notes Justin Libby, "Averaging 60 miles per hour and using a
hand-held barograph to measure their altitude and a railway
tourist map for navigation ... they left Turin and two and a half
hours later, with their faces covered with ice, landed at Lyon,
France."[21]

When both men were in their 80s, they met again at our
Falmouth house. Lewis, a remarkably successful architect, in
the interim had been responsible for most of the important
buildings in Scranton, PA.

This early experience was a suitable preparation for a man
who dreamed up an airline crossing the high Andes and who
subsequently in the Air Transport Command had to deal during
World War II with problems arising from the need for regular
transport across the Hump, the name given by Allied pilots to
the eastern end of the Himalayan mountains.

Harris subsequently helped establish an aerial ferry route from
Ilan to Paris for the United States Navy.

Despite his father's admonitions, Harold Harris had embarked
on a career that seemed destined to cut his life short. Yet,
fortune's child, he possessed the skill and nerve to emerge alive
from even the riskiest flights. Following is an example of his
"cool"—and hubris!—while based at Foggia in his own words.

> I had heard that a pilot could not safely fly [a Farman]
> in a cloud. An overcast day tempted me to try and I flew
> through the solid cloud cover to the sunlight, collecting
> ice in a "Vee" on the front of all the brace wires. After half
> an hour above the clouds, I looked for a hole just where I
> knew where the airfield should be. No cloud hole. So I flew
> toward a mountaintop I had never seen before. This was
> fine; I could follow a river to the sea and orient myself.
> However, I had not noted that the strong wind had blown

---

[21] from Justin H. Libby's biographical sketch of HRH.

me across Italy—and the river was flowing to the western sea! As I got into the lee of the mountain, the mountain wave turbulence took charge, turning the plane upside down.

I knew it was the end for me! In those days no airplane parachutes existed.[22] Fortunately, I had my half-inch seat belt fastened, and there was plenty of time for my descent from 12,000 feet to consider my situation—hands gripping the scissors control, stomach straining against the seat belt, heels locked against the rudder pedals—and my lower lip trembling with fright! Close to the ground I regained control and landed in a cultivated field.

Once down, the airman was met by pitchfork-wielding farmers who, since he didn't speak Italian, initially mistook him for an Austrian (enemy). "I must have said something in English, and one of the old men answered in English! He had been an elevator operator years before in Chicago and remembered enough English to recognize it! . . . I had landed where they had never seen a plane before, at least not closely."

Harris continued by noting his foolishness in attempting to move the plane to a neighboring less muddy field, in the course of which he inadvertently caused an engine fire that nearly destroyed the plane and alerted the local population, many of whom probably had never seen an airplane before. Because of the damage to the plane, Harris was forced to stay overnight in a nearby village. The village Mayor welcomed him handsomely and provided him with overnight food and shelter. Italian officials, with no English and only broken German, attempted

---

[22] This is not quite correct. In 1917 although the American military didn't adopt parachutes as routine gear until 1918, when the plane of a German pilot was destroyed by machine gun fire from an Allied plane, the pilot leaped overboard using a Heinecke-type parachute equipped with an eight-foot static line and landed safely. See "Parachutes" on Aero.com.

to interrogate him. Fortunately, a local Italian count, who spoke excellent English, rescued him and made provisions for shipping what was left of the plane back to the Americans at Foggia.[23]

The Hero Returns

From right to left: Jessica, Harold, Grace, Mae and Ross and others.

World War I not quite over, Harold Harris returned to the bosom of his loving family where he had been sorely missed. Following is an excerpt from the series of interviews I conducted with Harold Sr. and his sisters June and Jessica in 1981 that deals with that moment.

> Je: Well, time went by and Harold stayed in that war, it seemed like forever. We sent him Hershey bars. And then his letters would come to our house and there would be very little letter. It was mostly cut out [by the censors.] We all had these songs like "It's a long way to Tipperary" and "Bring back my Daddy to me." And all these songs about the war, and the tears would run down mother's cheeks

---

23   Harris's unpublished memoir.

when father would play those. June and I would sing them, especially "Bring back my Daddy to me."

HRH: I never could understand how mother could let her only son go off to war. And yet, as far as I could tell, there wasn't any reluctance, no hovering over . . .

Je: No pleading. She certainly loved that son of hers.

AMS: You said that she would pore over the censored letters trying to figure out what had been cut out.

Je: She'd read them over and over again. They were very precious to her. He finally came back from the war.

Ju: We were waiting for you [HRH] to come back. We knew you were coming that day. And I would go out in front to see if you would come on the Sixth Street streetcar. And one time I went out and there he was . . .

Je: In his uniform?

HRH: This was Christmas time, 1918, when I came back . . . to Los Angeles. I had borrowed a hundred dollars from Grace because there was a special round-trip Christmas fare on the railroads. (She went for Christmas to her sister's in Chicago, and I went out to Los Angeles.) I was coming from Dayton, the fare was for the boy who had gone to fight the great big war, the last war ever to be fought . . .

Ju: That's when I went out to see if you were coming. I was seventeen.

HRH: Well, at that time I had not given anyone any advance notice that I was coming.

Ju: I remember that you were waited for. You must have phoned from the railroad station.

HRH: I called the house and the line was busy. So I called again later. Mother came on the telephone. I didn't say who I was. I said, "You shouldn't talk so much on the telephone." And she got a little bit uppity.

Ju: She didn't recognize your voice. Did she weep?

Je: Of course. She wept about everything."

Chapter 5: Dayton and Flight Testing

Harris's memoir recalls that although previously the Capronis and the Handley Page aircraft had been built in Europe, by the waning days of the war the Air Service "had contracted with the Fisher Body Co. in Detroit to build Capronis and the Standard Aircraft Co. in New Jersey to manufacture the Handley Page, multi-motored bomber planes, both with modified engines."

However, since the manufacture in the U.S of Caproni bombers, a specialty of test pilot Harold Harris and others, was going so slowly, in August, 1918, Lieutenant Harris, along with two other lieutenants, was told to return to the U.S. to report to Wilbur Wright Field, the predecessor of Dayton's Wright-Patterson Air Force Base, for flight test work.

Almost from the outset of flight testing there have been three groups or categories of test pilots who are trained to observe different aspects of the experimental craft. These are: the research pilot who flies to acquire knowledge useful to the whole field of aeronautics; the corporate test pilot who tests specific plane designs; and the service test pilot who tests in relation to the specific needs of his branch of the military.[24] Some test pilots, noted Richard Hallion, "were excellent in demonstrations... Others were true engineering test pilots, capable of analyzing aircraft behavior from a stability and control standpoint". Harold Harris, "one of the most distinguished of the

---

[24]   Hallion, 52-3.

early band of Army test pilots" exemplified the early test pilot who despite his profound engineering knowledge was nevertheless a jack-of-all trades not overly concerned with precisely evaluating aircraft handling qualities.

Rather, as Harris recalled, early test pilots "viewed flying in nearly philosophical terms: 'Airplanes took off, they flew around, they landed—it was an accomplishment.'"[25]

In Dayton the military pilots operated from two bases: Wilbur Wright and McCook. McCook Field, an airfield and aviation experimentation station operated by the Aviation Section, U.S. Signal Corps and its successor the United States Army Air Service from 1917-1927, was named for Alexander McDowell McCook, a Civil War general and his brothers and cousins, who were collectively known as "The Fighting McCooks".

It was located approximately one mile (1.6 km) north from downtown Dayton, Ohio. Its very short landing field was in the area between the Greater Miami and Stillwater rivers, almost in the heart of the city, with a dangerous fence at one end that proved to be the bane of pilots who landed too close. In fact, the warning—"This Field is Small, Use It All!"-was painted atop the airfield's hangars. Urban growth encroached on the space and larger aircraft being developed overtaxed the field's surface. Ultimately, the field became too small for its purpose.

"To add to the problem, there was a steel truss bridge over the river, directly in the takeoff path which could be disastrous if you couldn't climb fast enough."[26]

Wilbur Wright Field was built six miles out of the city on the Huffman Prairie where the Wright brothers conducted their early glider flights.

During WW I, Wilbur Wright Field, writes Harris,

---

[25]   Hallion, 53.
[26]   *Newsletter of the Florida Aviation Historical Society*, May, 2009.

was the experimental testing ground for the U.S. Army Air Service. McCook Field, also in Dayton, was, during the war, the testing ground for production aircraft rather than experimental. Shortly after the war was ended in November 1918, Wilbur Wright Field was de-activated and the few remaining flight test officers transferred, together with their activities to McCook Field under the command of Major Rudolf Schroeder, Chief Flying Section, Engineering Division, Air Service.

Schroeder was described by Harris as "one of the greatest natural pilots I have ever known." Test piloting was very dangerous; there were so many crashes that Schroeder finally had a trophy made. It read, "We Crashed Not Because We Ran out of Gas, but Ran Out of Knowledge." At McCook between May and September 1919 Captain C.H. Walsh was Schroeder's successor. Harris became Chief in September 1920 and served until October 1925.[27]

Harris and General Patrick

[27] General Harold R. Harris, "The First 80 Years", *Twenty-First General Harold R. Harris 'Sight' Lecture.* New York City, 1984.

In January 1919, after serving in aeronautical-related duties in Washington, D.C., Col. Thurman Bane was placed in charge of McCook Field. He was successful in brokering a division of labor between industry and the Army's in-house aeronautical development efforts. The two Dayton military aviation facilities: Wilbur Wright Field and McCook Field—switched functions so that production work, initially at McCook was relegated to Wilbur Wright, and flight testing given to McCook.

At McCook Col. Bane organized the Air Service's Engineering Division. At the same time, he founded an Air Service School of Application, the forerunner of the Air Force Institute of Technology. He also introduced modern industrial methods of research, design, and manufacture.

Harold Harris noted in his speech at the dedication of Thurman Bane Hall (at Wright Patterson Air Force Base in 1982), that the atmosphere at McCook was "informal, to say the least." Bane told his officers, "'Gentlemen, when you pass through that gate under the sign reading <u>Engineering Division—Army Air Service</u>, you leave your rank outside. Here we are all students of aeronautical science.' No one at McCook worked *for* Col. Bane. They worked *with* Col. Bane." When General Pershing came to inspect, although many pilots were WW I returnees, "the military people had a difficult time finding all the necessary military clothes and insignia for this important visit."

Despite being generally ignored by other branches of the Army, under Col. Bane the Engineering Division became the Air Service Engineering School. Harris commented on what he considered the three classes of military officers who were assigned there.

> One class were the men who really wanted to advance themselves in the science and art of military aviation. One class was made up of officers whose immediate commander didn't know what to do with them, so he sent them to school. And the third class were the dumb bunnies

who were unable to properly carry out any military orders. Harris did observe, however, that members of the second class frequently found their air legs and went on to make real contributions to aviation.[28]

McCook Field was the center of military flight testing. In addition to various types of planes captured during WWI, it was open to current domestic inventions. The test pilots were responsible for testing all new designs with the purpose of weeding out those of no real use.

McCook's test pilots were a brave and dauntless crew. Knowing their deep attachment to him and the peril in which he found himself as a test pilot on an almost daily basis, I doubt whether Harold ever discussed details of his test pilot experiences with either his wife or his family. I suppose in those early days wing walking was even more dangerous—but not by much! Yet the contribution to flight safety made by Dayton's test pilots all too often at the expense of their lives as described by Richard Hallion is completely unknown outside the aviation industry.

Hallion writes:

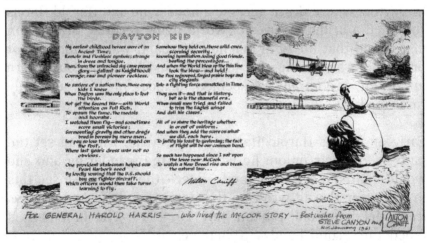

"Dayton Kid" drawing by Milton Caniff

---

[28]   Harris's personal memoir.

Every time a weekend pilot goes aloft in a light plane, every time a military pilot slams into afterburner, every time a businessman or a tourist relaxes in an airline seat, every time an oil rigger flies out to a drilling platform—in short, every time any of us fly as flight crew or passengers, we follow in the wake of the test pilots and flight engineers who have gone that way before.

They have acquired the detailed scientific knowledge that designers have put to use in building the aircraft upon which we rely. They had spent thousands of hours proving out the vehicles we fly, so that we may fly with confidence. They have chosen to verify the expectations of the engineers and to furnish the manual writers with the information pilots and flight crews need to know about the aircraft. Above all, they have demonstrated the products of the drawing board aloft, in actual flight, away from the static conditions of the laboratory. And they follow in the trappings of a long and noble tradition, for flight testing of new aircraft, systems, and concepts is as old as flight itself[29]

In Dayton, where Grace became a housewife and Harold Harris compiled a brilliant series of world flying records, Grace soon discovered that life with her new husband was nothing if not predictable and even—for him—downright dangerous. More important, events always seemed to focus on him, and only rarely on her.

Early on, it was Harold Harris, not his wife, who had set the pattern for their union: he would do the wandering and she would maintain the home and—later—the family. We see this in the letter Harold wrote to the Harris family in Los Angeles from McCook Field, Dayton, July 10, 1919. The first part is typed; the second, hand written in pencil.

---

[29]   Hallion, x-xi.

Dear Folks: At last another letter, and about time, too. Grace and I are here in Dayton for a few days till I start South again with the other plane. I reached here last Sunday and hope to get away again about Monday or Tuesday . . . Grace and I went to Chicago together and saw her grandmother for a few hours between trains. Grace came on to Dayton and I went up to Detroit.

[Handwritten.] This typewriter is on the bum so will end with a pencil. I left Detroit on the 9th but had to return on account of motor trouble. We are living in a furnished room here in Dayton as we haven't yet found an apartment. Grace is going to stay here while I am on my trip and will hunt for a place. It is terribly sultry and rotten here and we surely wish we were in L.A. with good weather. If this Army reorganization bill goes through, it looks as though we might be out there sooner than we think.[30] Love to all from both of us, Harold and Grace.

Other than the birth of my brother, Harold Jr., Oct. 18, 1924, the only other thing I know about their Dayton sojourn is that they adopted a stray female dog of indeterminate parentage that they called Jane. When friends asked what breed she was, our father, who exemplified the Harris family sense of humor, was quick to reply, "Curbstone setter."

---

[30] Probably this refers to the Army Reorganization Act of 1920 whose increased appropriations were later undermined by "A penny-pinching Congress and an economy-minded Executive" that "allowed equipment to become obsolescent and personnel to drop far below the strength" authorized by the Act. (see Nick A. Komons, *Bonfires to Beacons*: Federal Civilo Aviation Policy Under the Air Commerce Act, 1926-193, Smithsonian Institution Press, 1989, 42.

Harris, Grace and Harold Jr.

In 1920, Harris was made Chief of the Flight Test division at McCook. He remained Chief until 1925 when he quit the Army for commercial crop dusting. At McCook he tested different types of aircraft including his specialty, heavy bombers.

The title of this account, *"...and then what happened?"* is epitomized by Harris's experience with General Billy Mitchell in a Martin bomber.

Harris wrote,

In early December 1920 the Martin Company in Cleveland said their first MB-2, which was the Martin Bomber equipped with Liberty engines to be supercharged, was ready for flight testing which I did on the 12th. It was the first flight of this type of airplane. The plane was satisfactory... On the 15th, General Mitchell was having an inspection at McCook and I flew this new type for him, including the first loop that had been made by the Martin Bomber.

I did a bad job of looping it. The negative G built on the top of the loop, and both engines stopped. They resumed operation as soon as the plane had leveled out after the loop. General Mitchell was very annoyed at the inability of the Liberties to operate properly at negative G and he had the entire program delayed while the engine carburetion was reworked to give full operation at any angle of flight.[31]

---

[31] Harris's personal memoir.

Chapter 6: Heavy Bombers and Other Experimental Craft

The Barling Bomber. Muir Fairchild stands at far right of photo, with Harris to his right. At far left is Walter Barling. The man in uniform in the center is General Patrick.

Harris became famous as the only pilot willing and able to fly that enormous triplane, the Barling Bomber, the Army's answer to the ZR-1 (the Navy's first American built rigid Dirigible). Powered by four tractor and two pusher engines, the gigantic triplane was 65 feet long, 28 feet high, and had a wingspan of 120 feet (the exact distance of the first sustained heavier-than-air flight.)[32]

---

[32] William A. Krusen, in *Flying the Andes: The Story of Pan American Grace Airways*, Tampa, University of Tampa Press, 1997, 8, notes that "the Barling was a ridiculous example of too much of a good thing, with engines, wings, and wheels in profusion, all laced

Harris's commentary on his test flight noted that "... at the top of a Barling test climb to absolute ceiling with a full load ... a stream of liquid was observed coming out the trailing edge of the top wing. All fuel was in the fuselage, so that wasn't it. Investigation on the ground showed that the wing had become full of rainwater and the test was valueless since the actual total aircraft weight at takeoff was unknown.

All testing had to be stopped until a hanger large enough to house the plane could be built."

Following is a description of the Barling as flown by Harris at the International Air Meet of 1923.

INTERNATIONAL AIR MEET, 1923

PROGRAM OF EVENTS (From the St. Louis Post-Dispatch

Rotogravure Picture Section, September 30, 1923)

The Leviathan of airplanes. This is the Barling bomber, the largest heavier-than-air flyer ever built. Flown by Lieut. Harold R. Harris ...

The arrival of the Barling Bomber at the St. Louis airport was in a way the most remarkable event of a week's crowded aerial demonstrations. To say that this six-engined triplane is huge, does not in the least convey the impression it creates on the ground or in flight. 'Monumental' would perhaps best express it.

The Barling Bomber remained at the St. Louis airfield throughout the week, stupefying the thousands who inspected it. The pride of the Army weighed 27,132

together with guy wires, almost as though someone decided that to make a big bomber, all you had to do was to wire together a dozen Spads."

pounds empty, and with its gross weight of 42,569 pounds, it could reach 95.5 miles per hour. The ship cost $500,000 to construct and . . . required a special hangar at a cost of $700,000.

In actuality, the Barling flew very little, mainly because when officials requested it be flown from Dayton to Washington, D. C. for display purposes, it was discovered that the vehicle was too heavy to make it across the Appalachian Mountains! At the order of General H.H. ("Hap") Arnold, to avoid taxpayer outrage it was destroyed quietly in 1928.

The GAX

Soon after the end of WW I, the US Army sought to explore highly armored and armed specialist ground attack aircraft. This was a pet project of General William Mitchell. The Army Air Service Engineering Division issued requests for proposals to U.S. aircraft producers on October 15, 1919. There were no designs offered, so the Engineering Division ordered one of its engineers, Isaac M. Laddon, to attempt what the aviation industry clearly considered impossible. His design, designated GAX, first flew at McCook Field on May 26, 1920. The GAX was McCook Field Project P129 and wore AAS serial number 63272.

Harris became the first (and only?) pilot to fly the beast. He recalls, "This was a triplane with twin Liberty engines, 420 horsepower each. Complete armor around each engine and the portion of the fuselage occupied by the crew—pilot and gunner, one 37mm. cannon swiveled forward and four Lewis guns in the floor of the armored section firing vertically down. To protect the engine water-cooling, ribbon radiators were constructed above each engine, protected by the armor around the engine . . . I had a battle with [the designer] since I felt the engine would not cool. He was sure it would as soon as we got flying and air flowed above the engines."

The Boeing GA-I experimental ground effect airplane

On April 3rd, I was assured the plane was ready for its first flight. The Chief Engineer, Lt. Col V. E. Clark, told me privately that because of the big box fuselage behind the armor, and the small fuselage area forward of the plane's center of gravity, the plane might be spirally unstable, so don't attempt the first turn below 5000 feet altitude. This altitude would give me room to attempt to regain control if trouble arose.

The Chief of the Equipment Section, a Lt. Colonel, quietly informed me that they had fudged a little on the size and strength of the tires and wheels to save weight, so be sure to land easily.

I taxied down to the south end of the field, peeking out the six inch deep section of armor plate on the right side of the fuselage, which could be folded down to give the pilot some vision (otherwise had none.)

The flight test observer, Lt. George Elsey, and Lt. Charles Monteith, the Army officer who had done much of the engineering of the plane went aboard for the first flight.

After the engines cooled off, since they boiled in taxiing, I took off the long way of the field. Just as I got to the north fence, about 20 feet high, both radiators burst—directly above the carburetors. Liberty engines don't run well on water. No structures were between the fence and the deep narrow riverbank, so I urged the engines to help, which they did, and I turned around and headed back to the field—came low to the fence but still got some power, jumped the fence and landed without more trouble—not even a blown tire! (I forgot both warnings I received before I took off)![33]

As I recall from what I heard from our Dad, one other problem with the original version of the GAX was that the machine gun, mounted over the hood in front of the pilot, was not synchronized with the spinning of the propeller, so that, if fired in flight, it would surely have splintered the wooden prop to pieces! So much for good design!

I will cite only three more of the experimental models Harold Harris tested during his days as head of the flight testing section at Dayton.

The Helicopter

Although an early prototype in a child's toy appeared as early as the fourteenth century, it was several hundred years before a full-sized man-carrying helicopter was developed. In the early 1920's a Spanish designer, Juan de la Cierva, developed the Autogiro, "an aircraft having a large, free-wheeling rotor mounted above the fuselage and a conventional piston engine and propeller to drive it through the air." The rotor and the engine were not connected, making it incapable of true vertical takeoff or a hover. This was cured when the inventor "hinged the rotor blades at their roots to compensate for the differences in lift generated by an 'advancing' and 'retreating'

---

[33] Harris Sight Lecture, *The First 80 Years*, 1984.

blade."[34] This and various other models of Autogiros were tested for military use but all required considerable modifications. Soon it was recognized that the Autogiro was only a step toward a true helicopter.

Despite the fact that there were no training manuals, helicopter schools, or tips from experienced pilots, helicopters were developed, built, and tested during the first half-century of flight. One of the earliest designers of a helicopter was Emile Berliner who, as early as 1907, had designed an unmanned helicopter. Igor Sikorsky, the originator of what would prove in the late 1930's to be the first successful helicopter design, began experimenting in Kiev shortly before WW I. In 1922 De Bothezat, a Russian émigré to the U.S., created "a large, ungainly craft having four six-bladed 'paddles' for rotors" that was first tested by Thurman Bane, McCook's commandant.[35]

Shortly after returning from Wright State University at Dayton, Ohio, where the Harris memorabilia are archived, I received a letter from William Ringle, who publishes a little newsletter for his retirement community. Mr. Ringle had interviewed Richard Sanders, a 96-year old member of his community, who said that because he was Emile Berliner's grandson—and Henry's nephew—when he was 11, on Feb. 23, 1924, he was allowed to witness Harold Harris flying an Emile Berliner helicopter, one of the earliest prototypes, on what Sanders thought was the maiden flight of this vehicle.[36] He said that Navy personnel were on hand to witness the flight.[37] As for choice of a test pilot,

---

[34] Hallion, 144-5.

[35] Ibid, 147.

[36] William Ringle, personal correspondence. Writes Ringle, "Two years earlier, on June 16, 1922, a manned Berliner helicopter had made a flight, according to a chronology by the National Aeronautics and Space Administration (NASA). Sanders says he has no personal knowledge of that date, which he concedes may be correct."

[37] Henry, his father Emile's collaborator, was the inventor of the Ercoupe, a small plane that was created so as not to stall or spin.

"for the Berliners—father and son Henry—it was Harold R. Harris, a daring 27-year-old Army test pilot and record setter who went on to become a true legend in American aviation, and a major general [sic!]"[38]

The Berliner helicopter prototype was a fixed-wing triplane with two wing-mounted rotors to give vertical lift

Ringle continues, "I found this in a document from the War Department Air Service dated April 4, 1924. It is a 'Report on 1924 Model of Berliner Helicopter Tested During February and March, 1924' by Harold R. Harris, Chief, Flying Section." On page 3 he [Harris] writes, 'A large number of controlled flights were made by me with this helicopter in January, February and March of 1924. These experiments showed that the helicopter has insufficient lift to clear the ground reaction but that the control system is satisfactory and, except in case of lateral control, adequate. The maximum duration of flight was 1 min. 35 sec. on February 23 at a maximum altitude of 15 feet.'"

I met Henry Berliner, since WW I Harold Harris's friend, when I accompanied our father to dinner at Henry's home.

[38] William Ringle, personal correspondence.

In actuality the Berliner-Harris experiments at College Park Airport occurred between 1920 and 1924 using what Hallion calls "a primitive convertiplane having twin rotors mounted on the end of the wings," which never climbed higher than 15 feet.[39] It was not until 1942 that a helicopter designed by Igor Sikorsky reached full-scale production, with 131 aircraft built. Though most earlier designs used more than one main rotor, it was the single main rotor with anti-torque tail rotor configuration of this design that would come to be recognized worldwide as the helicopter.

The Stout Plane

Henry Ford had made his initial entry into aviation in 1923, when he came to the financial rescue of William Bushnell Stout, who was experimenting with an all-metal trimotor monoplane known as the "Tin Goose', "a nearly indestructible aircraft."[40] The Ford Motor Company began building this plane itself in 1924.[41]

The Dayton Daily News published the following:

> Harris Flies the Stout Plane, 1924

> Lieut. Harold R. Harris, Chief of the McCook field flight test section, made a trial hop in the plane Wednesday.

---

[39] Hallion, 147.

[40] Marylin Bender and Selig Altschul, *The Chosen Instrument*. New York: Simon and Schuster, 1982, 66.

[41] Komons, 67.

At 2:30 o'clock, the plane took off for Detroit on the return trip. It is to be brought back to McCook field and subjected to army tests at a later date.

The flight to Dayton Wednesday was the first cross country trip ever made by the Stout plane. Most of the distance was covered at an altitude of approximately 3000 feet and the passengers aboard declared they could see the rain below, although they were not in it themselves.

All members of the aerial cruising party said the trip was delightful, being devoid of the rocky, jumpy sensation usually accompanying an airplane trip loaded so heavily. The Stout plane is powered with one Liberty motor and has a normal speed of more than 110 miles an hour with a full load.

Chapter 7: The Pressurized Cabin

Reinforced entrance hatch of the modified DeHavilland D-9A

Harris competed in many aviation meets, by 1926 holding 13 world flying records. On June 8, 1921, he was the first pilot to test a pressurized cabin, nearly losing his life in the process.

By the 1920's based on the experiences of high-flying pilots like John Macready and "Shorty" Schroeder, the latter Harris's predecessor as chief of the Dayton flight test section, it had become clear that heights of over 30 thousand feet were untenable for ordinary aircraft. Planes, noted Macready, had absolute ceilings above which they could not go. Pilots, too, have ceilings, above which their minds grow mushy and their judgment is severely affected. Further, there was the question of crew comfort. "Under the best of circumstances, "Richard Hallion noted, "flight crews toiled in uncomfortable conditions, chilled to the bone, operating in a low pressure environment, absolutely miserable. The ideal solution, of course, would be an enclosed, pressurized cabin . . ."[42] This situation is what Harris for the first time attempted to endure.

In fact Harris was the first pilot to test a pressurized cabin, nearly losing his life in the process. Hallion called this attempt "pure comedy". Yet, without Harris's quick thinking, the attempt could have resulted in pure tragedy.

Artists' rendering of the DA-9 in flight

Here is the report that Harris submitted as part of his speech titled "The First Eighty Years" to the Wings Club in New York City May 16, 1984.

Pressurization Invented.

June 8, 1921, I made what I believe to have been the first pressurized cabin flight in the world. We learned a great deal about the possibility in one short flight—and I lived to tell the tale!

---

[42]   Hallion, 78.

The plane was the US D-9A, a single Liberty-engined observation plane built from the designs of the British DeHaviland DH-9. It was a two-seater, but for the purpose of this experiment, the seats were removed and the area filled with an oval pressurized compartment made of steel. As I recall it, it was riveted and the joints were brazed. The minimum of controls were brought into this tank—the spark advance, throttle, mixture controls, ignition switch, the control for elevator and ailerons, and the rudder cables. Packing glands surrounded all controls where they went through the sides of the tank.

The only instrument inside the tank was an altimeter. All other instruments were on a special board just forward of the 6-inch porthole in the front of the tank so that they would be readily visible to the pilot. No controls were furnished for the pressurizing unit.

There were five six-inch portholes in the tank, on the bottom, the top, one on the left side, one forward, and the fifth in the removable door on the right: the door was about three feet in diameter. In unpressurized flight the door was hung on hooks on the right interior wall of the tank. This door was steel of considerable weight, and had to be lifted off the suspending hooks and placed on the retaining tracks on the inside of the opening, and then rotated about one-eighth of a turn to make a tight seal against a rubber gasket. A normal pilot seat was installed in the tank. In the ceiling was a three-quarter-inch globe valve, with a manual control easily reached from the pilot's position, presumably to make pressure control easily available to the pilot through adjustment of the rate of exhaust of the pressurized air. A propeller-driven blower, I believe of the Rootes type, was installed in the leading edge of the lower left wing with a 1 to 1 1/2 to 2 inch pressure line running from the blower to the lower forward part of the tank. Other than the above, no special changes were made to the standard US D-9-A airplane.

There was no supercharger installed on the Liberty engine, since this was strictly an experimental installation to try out a pressurized cabin. If the tests had been successful, the super-charged engine could have been installed at any time.

I do not know who invented the idea of the pressurized cabin, but I suspect that it was Major L.L. Hoffman, who was head of the Equipment Section, and very much interested and working intently on problems of high-altitude photography, for which an aircraft of this type would be very useful.

The pilot assigned to the first flight was Art Smith, a very well-known World War I exhibition pilot, who was employed as a civilian test pilot by the Air Corps. He was about 5 feet 3 inches, quite husky, but not as tall as the average pilot. He took the experimental plane up with the door mounted in the rack aft through which the pilot entered the tank. Smith climbed to 3000 feet and tried to lift the door to pressurize. Because of his poor leverage, he was unable to maneuver the heavy steel door into its closed position, so he brought the plane back.

Since I am taller than Smith and would have better leverage, I took the plane up myself. At 3000 feet I lifted the door into place and rotated it into its locked position.

Immediately things began to happen. The cabin supercharger had been designed on the assumption that there would be a large leakage through all the packing glands carrying the cables for the control mechanisms, and that the regulation of pressurization would be easily taken care of by the manually-operated globe valve in the roof. For an effective test, the designers had increased the compressor capacity by 100 percent. Almost immediately after the door was closed, pressure built up in the tank, until the altimeter inside the tank registered 3000 feet below sea level, although the altimeter outside the tank showed that the plane was flying at 3000 feet above.

My first action was to make sure that the manually-operated exhaust valve in the roof was wide open. It was as I could feel the rush of airflow through the opening in the valve. Then I searched for something with which to break a window. But I had nothing, not even a pocketknife, and since I did most of my flight testing wearing tennis shoes (because of a better feel on the controls), I didn't even have the heel of a shoe. Opening the inward-opening door was impossible because of the tons of air pressure inside the steel tank. There was no way to stop the wind-driven compressor from operating as long as the plane was flying because it was driven by its own propeller, separate and distinct from the engine propeller.

The only thing left was to assume as slow speed a glide as I dared and land as quickly as possible. At no time from shortly after closing the door until the plane came to a stop was the cabin pressure less than 3000 feet below sea level.

There was no possible escape from this ever-increasing pressure. I do not recall any particular area of discomfort, although it has been reported that I complained of pain in my ears. The air in the tank was uncomfortably warm from the action of the compressor, and I was wringing wet from perspiration on landing. However, this was doubtless due in part to my anxiety about the outcome of this test, and irritation at myself for having gotten into such a situation without having intelligently considered the possible difficulties and taken the necessary precautions.

Although many years passed before pressurized aircraft were perfected, that strange failure contributed to ultimate success..."

Chapter 8: The First Emergency Parachute Jump

THE FIRST BAIL-OUT

Lt. Harris bails out of his disintegrating Loening monoplane. Ink and wash drawing by M. Corning

The beginnings of powered flight—neither as slow or as low as balloons or dirigibles—saw some terrible fatalities that led to safety concerns. These concerns regarding not only the fragility of the aircraft but also the need to ensure pilot safety in case of an accident arose as a result of an aircraft crash that involved two of aviation's then leading figures. In 1908 a plane piloted by Orville Wright, on a demonstration flight at Fort Myer, 125 feet above the ground, shattered a wing and crashed. Wright's passenger, Lt. Thomas Selfridge, was fatally injured. He was the first person in the U.S. to die in a crash of a powered airplane. Selfridge was not wearing any headgear. If he had been wearing a helmet of some sort, he most likely would have survived the crash. As a result of Selfridge's death, the US Army's pilots were required to wear large heavy headgear reminiscent of early football helmets.

Yet the military was very slow to address the need for parachutes. Actually Germany was the first military organization to do so, installing in its war planes static—line parachutes. (These are used in order to make sure that a parachute is deployed immediately after leaving the plane, regardless of actions taken or not taken by the parachutist.) Finally during World War I the U.S. military authorized the use of parachutes, but before they could reach American pilots in Europe, the war was over.

The war ended, American pilots, whether at home or overseas regarded the parachutes as more of a nuisance than a safeguard and frequently didn't bother to wear one. In 1922 parachutes had yet to be made mandatory. Harris, a big man, had been reluctant to don one over the bulky flight suit of the type all pilots wore to maintain body temperature inside unheated cockpits. His narrow escape changed that. Fortunately, as a consequence, instead of becoming yet another sad statistic, Harris became the first pilot in the U.S. to save his life using a parachute in an emergency. It happened during a test flight of a monoplane when, the wing disintegrating, he bailed out, finally managing to open the chute, and landed safely in a Dayton grape arbor, thus becoming the first member of what became known as the Caterpillar Club—because the parachute canopy was made of silk which originated from a caterpillar cocoon.

Notes Justin H. Libby, "The parachute eventually opened at 500 feet (he jumped at 2500 feet) and the only injury Harris suffered were leg bruises, some bruising on the right hand and after landing safely stated that he never felt any fear but decided relief when the parachute billowed."[43]

Many years later Jimmy Doolittle recalled to Harold Harris his reaction at the test site on seeing the wing collapse: "I was standing at the trap range with Lt. Colonel Thurman L. Bane and Lt. Bob Worthington when your Loening monoplane experienced aileron flutter and disintegrated. I can still see Bane wringing his hands reiterating, "Oh, my god, Oh my god," until your blessed parachute finally 'blossomed out'."[44] In the Introduction to William Krusen's *Flying the Andes*, I note that ". . . when I went to comment poetically on the experience of typing for him the text of a speech to the Dayton Stamp Club in which my father described the circumstances surrounding his making the first emergency parachute jump over McCook Field, I simply filled in what I considered the essential details he had omitted."

Unfortunately, and to my later great embarrassment, I confused the situation of the two airfields. Harris did indeed, along with Muir Fairchild, a fellow test pilot and close personal friend flying the other plane, take off from McCook Field in the heart of the city. Wilbur Wright Field, the other airfield, was situated on a prairie—exactly as I had described but at the time was quite the wrong field for pilots intent on testing new equipment.

---

[43] Justin H. Libby, unpublished article on Harold R. Harris.
[44] Doolittle letter to Harold R. Harris.

Here is what I wrote:

Starting and Stopping at the Wrong Places

He should have begun with the Wrights'
kites or the first international airshow
for dirigibles, balloons, and airplanes
in a Los Angeles field.

He played hookey to watch, and there was only
one fatality that day.

But he began with two planes: his
one-winged (an experimental model)
and Fairchild's, two.

We have to assume the prairie,
golden fan flipped wide
to accommodate a speckless October sky,

the farmer, his head later severed by some lowflying pilot's
wheelbrace,

busy among the dead cornstalks
clattering in a light breeze.

Since he spoke of pheasants,
ground squirrels, rabbits, eyes

squeezed shut against
the exploding prop wash,
we must imagine them, too;
the coffee cup, half empty
left on the hangar sill;
the bulky flying suit crammed grudgingly and
at the last minute
in an undersized parachute harness,

the jaunty thumbs-up
to Fairchild next to him.

The Dayton Stamp Club knows
two Army pilots went up to test ailerons.

They executed mock combat. His plane crumpled.
He jumped. After four frantic tries,
his parachute opened.

He floated into history, and never thought
to mention Muir Fairchild's

joyous smile at finding him alive,
though bruised, in a military infirmary.

In later years Harris did, indeed, speak of Fairchild's probable reaction when he saw Harris' wing begin to collapse. "He supposed," wrote Harris, "until he landed at the airdrome that I was in the wreck and that I was dead. This was a tremendous shock to him as we had known each other since May, 1917, when we entered the University of California Ground School together. He arrived at the Field Hospital about ten minutes after I was brought there and I'm sure he was whiter and more frightened than I was myself."

While he was still alive, for many years Harris's exploit was noted by the media. It even made its way into the comics as well as providing an historical landmark for USA Today. What I remember best, however, is the trip our father and I took in the early1980's to Dayton where he was slated to recall the event in a speech to the Dayton Stamp Club.

During that visit he was invited to tour the latest site on the new Aviation Trail: the very spot at 337 Troy Street, property of Mr. Dan Baree, where the grape arbor had stood in which in 1922 he had landed.[45] Escorted by a covey of reporters and photographers, we arrived and were greeted by the home's current owners. The grape arbor was of course long gone. However, as we stood amidst the clicking of camera shutters, an elderly man approached Harold and held out his hand. "General", he said, "You may not remember me, but I'm the little boy who lived across the street and, seeing you crash into the arbor, asked my mother what to do to help. 'Go take him a glass of water,' she said. So I did, and as I recall, sitting there in the ruins, you even drank it!"

Snap, snap went the cameras, as our Dad and the elderly man shook hands. I thought to myself, How wonderful that these warm memories should persist among so many whose lives became entangled in one way or other with Harold Harris's adventures.

Harris' Account (from "The First Eighty Years")

Several flying officers were gathered at McCook Field on October 20, 1922, when a visiting officer asked about the parachute. We explained the way the parachute worked and the visitor seemed impressed. Several others expressed doubts of a pilot's ability to release himself from an airplane and operate the parachute in an emergency. Little thinking my words would soon be put to the test, I remarked that it was surprising what a man could do when put to it. Although freefall parachutes were tested and being worn, no pilot had yet used one to save his life.

Subsequently I suggested to Muir Fairchild that he fly the Thomas Morse fighter for further test of new tail surfaces while I took the Loening monoplane up to test some new and experimental types of ailerons.

---

[45] Specifics of house and owner thanks to Justin H. Libby, unpublished article on Harold R. Harris

I had just had a new seat cushion installed on my parachute and found that the harness was a trifle tight; I sent the time keeper to get another parachute. The one he brought had an even smaller harness. I almost yielded to the temptation to conduct my test flight without a parachute, but eventually decided to wear my own chute.

Fairchild meanwhile took off and I followed. At an altitude of about 2,500 feet the other machine was waiting for me. We had maneuverability tests to carry out on both airplanes; therefore, it was logical for us to practice a little combat.

Fairchild began a slight left turn. He told me afterward that his indicator then showed slightly more than 150 miles an hour; I was therefore going about that seed when he began his turn. I also began to turn to the left. As soon as the turn started, all hell broke loose!

The whole airplane shook violently, laterally and the control stick began to oscillate rapidly from side to side. I knew immediately what the trouble was—the experimental ailerons. As soon as the motion of the ailerons started they began to operate themselves, due to their overbalance, making it impossible for the pilot to control their action. As the aileron on one wing goes up, the aileron on the other wing goes down; and that was exactly what was automatically happening at a high rate of reversal speed.

The only way I could control this oscillation was to slow the speed of the airplane, so I closed the throttle and tried to climb. By this time however, the aileron whip had become so great that the wing structure had been torn apart internally. The control stick oscillations became extremely violent and were being stopped on each side by my legs. (Three days after the accident I could hardly walk, suffering from severe bruises.) My right hand, with which I was trying to control the airplane, was also badly bruised by the lateral oscillations of the stick.

I knew it was impossible to regain control of the airplane. There was only one thing to do. In a collapse of the sort I was experiencing, if I stayed in the airplane I would undoubtedly be killed. The next thing for me to do was to leave my airplane and trust my parachute.

This was not hard to do because the airplane was descending at an angle of about 25 to 30 degrees with the horizon, and portions of the wing structure were beginning to blow off. I had only to release my safety belt and climb on top of the fuselage. The tremendous wind pressure, probably 250 miles an hour, blew me clear of the airplane. Now to pull the ripcord of my parachute.

I had piloted airplanes for about fifty live parachute jumps, and as I watched the expression on the man's face as he was about to jump, I decided it was too much of a mental strain to suit me. A surprising thing about the jump that I made is that during the whole experience I did not become fearful or feel any faintness or failure of my faculties.

After leaving the airplane, I looked down at my feet and realized that my feet were pointing to the sky! I located what I thought was the rip ring and pulled. Nothing happened. I was spinning like a top, head down and feet up. Three times I located what I thought was the release ring, but each time I was pulling on a leg strap. Finally I pulled the right ring.

I felt something snap and found that I was looking down at the ground. I then looked up at my parachute—not with any sense of relief because I had none. It all seemed part of the program that the parachute should open without argument, and I can remember admiring the beautiful silk. I could not understand how silk could be kept so white and clean around an airplane hangar!

I looked down again to see just where I was going to land. I saw a grape arbor and knew the frail laths could easily give way and break my fall to the ground. This is exactly what happened. The only damage was a tear on the best pair of pants I owned and some cuts on my shoes as I went through the arbor. The brick sidewalk below the arbor was not particularly resilient, but I was not rendered unconscious by the fall although my physical condition was low on account of the terrific beating I had received on my legs from the control stick.

My first thought on finding that I was all right was the possibility of injury or death to anyone from the falling airplane.

A couple of hours later I learned that the airplane was completely demolished without injury to anyone and with little damage to surrounding property.

Since flying officers had to purchase their own uniforms, Harold's most bitter memory of the event concerned the fact that landing, he tore his best pair of trousers Since officers in those days paid for their own uniforms, this was a real blow!

The parachute that saved Harris' life draped over the broken grape arbor

Harris was awarded the Leo A. Stevens parachute medal "For having made the first emergency parachute jump from a U.S. Army airplane which resulted ... in the U.S. Army Air Force issuing an order requiring all airmen to wear parachutes on all flights."[46] Although parachutes remained optional until 1924, at McCook Field, a sign in large letters proclaimed:

DON'T FORGET YOUR PARACHUTE.

IF YOU NEED IT AND HAVEN'T GOT IT,

YOU'LL NEVER NEED IT AGAIN!

Guy Bell—whom Harris called "the father of the American Parachute"—who had been experimenting with parachutes as early as 1918, on his wife's advice used Chantilly silk, which became the standard material for all future parachutes." Once, preparing to jump, Bell's cord caught accidentally and the chute opened inside the cockpit. The release design improved, this cord became the "rip cord," and Bell's "McCook Field Lifesavers Club" soon became known as the Caterpillar Club."

---

[46] "Parachutes" under aero.com.

Chapter 9: Landing Fields and Night Flying

While in Foggia, Harris had remarked on the lamentable condition of the Italian landing fields. "The airfields in those days," he noted, "were nothing but raw land. Whenever it rained, it became almost impossible to operate in the mud that developed. Several hundred square feet in front of the hangars at the [Caproni] factory were paved which made it very easy to maneuver the planes on the pavement. When I asked one of the Italian Caproni pilots why they didn't give consideration to paving the landing areas, he said it wouldn't work at all because the only way you could see to land was to see the blades of grass and know just what your altitude is above the landing field. If you just had cement or macadam to land on it would be impossible to know when you were actually very close to the ground!"

Once back in the U.S., although he was probably not provided with the same explanation, Harris discovered very much the same conditions. On April 30, 1919, his apparent cloak of invulnerability was slightly torn when after departing Detroit he seriously damaged his hand crash landing a Caproni bomber in the deep mud at Cleveland's improvised airport.

"Cleveland didn't have a landing field at that time," he later recalled, "but the Martin Company had just built a factory there and in connection with the factory had put in a landing field."

The bomber was loaded with leaflets endorsing the Government's bond drive. A certain Major Norman J. Boots, a passenger on that flight, apparently eager to gain personally from the publicity ensuing from this stunt, had insisted before reaching Cleveland on changing seats with the co-pilot Wilcox, presumably in order to make it appear that he had flown the plane from Detroit.

Unfortunately the landing area at the Martin plant was very soft and the plane finally nosed over as it was coming to a stop. Writes Harris, obviously with some satisfaction, "Major Boots and I were pinned under the top wing in the mud until enough manpower was on the job to lift the wing off. Wilcox had been standing between fuel tanks in the rear section of the fuselage and was not hurt but Boots broke his collarbone. The first finger of my right hand was caught between the entering edge of the top wing and the mud, breaking the lower half of the finger.

> The military ambulance finally made it to the Martin Plant and Major Boots and I were carried into town in this ambulance over extremely poor roads. A most unsatisfactory ambulance ride as you can imagine into the hospital at Cleveland. We were later transferred by rail from Cleveland to the Ford Hospital in Detroit.

> An amusing incident occurred in connection with my forefinger having been broken with the lower part of the bone sticking out of the flesh and the top of the finger being at almost right angle to its normal position. The net result being that it looked as if the finger had always been that way because there was practically no blood showing. The medical orderly who was manning the rear of the ambulance took a look at my hand and said, 'Did your hand always look like that?'[47]

It is important to remember the circumstances under which the Dayton test pilots operated in 1919. The first airfields were any flat ground with predictable winds where the surface was relatively smooth. The earliest glider and fixed-wing flights required steady but gentle breezes to fly. Kill Devil Hills, North Carolina, where the first powered, controlled flight took place, had sand dunes bordered by a grassy slope that was swept by Atlantic Ocean winds. Other early flights took place on prairies

---

[47] Harris memoir

or near water because the series of warming then cooling air masses created predictable wind patterns.

The 1905 flights of the Wright brothers' Flyer 3 occurred on Huffman Prairie outside of Dayton, Ohio, with its short grass and thermal-driven air currents. "We have to assume the prairie", I wrote in my (inaccurate) description of the area from which Harris took off for the soon-to-be famous parachute jump:

> golden fan flipped wide/ to accommodate a speckless October sky,/ the farmer, his head later severed by some lowflying pilot's wheelbrace,/ busy among the dead cornstalks/ clattering in a light breeze/.

> Since he spoke of pheasants,/ ground squirrels, rabbits, eyes/ squeezed shut against/ the exploding prop wash.[48]

These open spaces were not permanent, dedicated areas for aircraft or friendly to passengers. More often they were farmers' fields, racetracks, golf courses, polo fields, fairgrounds, or even roads. Observed Harris, "Humorist Will Rogers' description of the average landing field in the United States at that time was 'a small open space, surrounded on three sides by high tension wires, and on the fourth side by a cemetery.'"

It was not until 1928 that the first permanent, hard-surfaced runway in the United States was created at Newark, New Jersey. That same year Panagra's first flight—the Fairchild FC-2—took off from a Lima racetrack.

The fact that the first Panagra flight originated on a racetrack should provide a clue as to the primitive conditions surrounding early Panagra landings and takeoffs.

---

[48] The detail regarding the farmer's decapitation came from Harold Harris' memory of those early days.

"Landing fields," noted Harris, "were wherever the pilot felt he could land and take off with a load." In 1928 Peru "the only prepared landing fields were the Army Field at Las Palmas, (Lima), and the Navy Field at Ancon, a few miles north of Lima. Trujillo, 322 miles north of Lima, didn't have a landing field but it had a straight stone road, narrow but perfectly good until it got planes with wide landing gear. Fortunately, this road had almost no traffic and we never had an accident there."[49]

He continued, "The Peruvian Air Force let us use the facilities at their Lima Airport until Limatambo [Panagra's airport] was built in 1935, for which we were most grateful. One of the many modifications Panagra mechanics had to make in 1929 to the first Fairchilds because our landing areas were so gravelly, muddy or deep in dust, was to replace the standard tires with larger ones.[50]"

"Typical conditions", Krusen writes, outside the cities "were at best a bumpy cornfield, at worst, a pile of rocks." Designated landing fields were "even worse." With below-minimum weather at Tucuman, Argentina," noted chief pilot Frank Havelick, "I landed a DC-2 passenger flight at Cachi Yaco and quickly sank into the mud to the under surface of the wing. Besides being the designated alternate to Tucuman, Cachi Yaco was a cattle ranch, and it took all the gauchos, horses, and tractors on the estancia to extract me from the mud."[51]

As late as 1938 Panagra Captain Havelick described the runway at La Paz as nothing but loose gravel.

---

[49]   Harris memoir.
[50]   Ibid. Harris writes, "This was long before the U.S. Federal Government established standards for the equipment of an aircraft after they were put in service according to the requirements of their utilization."
[51]   William Krusen, *Flying the Andes,* 18.

There was no hard surface landing and at the east end of it, there was a drop off of about 1000 feet that went down into a canyon ... If you got off and then had engine trouble, you might end up going down into the canyon... Now at the west end of it, the Indians, under the supervision of our airport construction engineer named Peper, a Dutchman, had moved big rocks and boulders out of the runway area, which was delineated by white stone markings (they'd just paint stones and that was the limit of the runway.) At the west end of the runway they had piled up all these rocks that they had picked up out of the runway which were too large to leave [in place] and had piled them at the west end of the runway, not realizing that if something happened to a pilot on a take off in that direction and he couldn't get off and had to stay on the runway at a great speed, he would go piling into the rocks. In addition to that, we had frequent bands of llamas that would just cross the runway not knowing what they were doing ... and we had burros and donkeys running around free. Also during many periods of the year, there were wind conditions up there that would give rise to dust. We called them 'dust feathers.' [Modern parlance might call them 'dust devils' or miniature tornadoes.] These things would appear off the side of the runway and blow directly across it while you were taking off. You'd be attempting your takeoff in relatively good visibility when suddenly one of these things would blow across the runway in front of you and you'd lose any forward visibility momentarily... The runway was absolutely minimum because if our load was the maximum, when we got off, we'd just skim those piles of rocks.[52]

---

[52] Krusen, 64-65. For the "two bottles of Scotch" episode cited by Krusen, See pp. 156-7; See also Marylin Bender and Selig Altschul, *The Chosen Instrument*, Simon and Schuster, New York, 1982, 164-5.

"Aerial garages" were developed in the U.S. These forerunners of hangars and maintenance shops, included dry lakebeds in Nevada and roadside gas stations along early roadways. Some aviators built hangars using the packing crates in which early airplanes had been delivered.

Airport surfaces were spread with gravel or cinders to help drainage. The only equipment and buildings were typically one hangar, gasoline and oil storage, a wind indicator, a telephone connection, and a location marker, all well spaced in case of fire or crash. Fields ranged from about 70 acres to 100 acres. Non-postal airports copied the square design of postal air stations, though some built rectangles, T-shapes with a perpendicular landing strip, or L-shapes with a crosswind runway.

Most flying took place in daylight when pilots relied on the practice of writing numerals, messages, or symbols on rooftops or hillsides to direct pilots toward the nearest airport. This practice, called airmarking, from the 1930s was an important means of visual navigation until around World War II. Flagmen on the ground signaled to the aircraft to indicate correct landing areas.

The introduction of regular night service assured the granting of mail subsidies by the U.S. post office. In Europe Harris had already given night instruction in the Capronis at Foggia. At McCook his log book noted that his first night flight in the U.S. at least the first entered in his book was on January 26, 1920. "Night operations were piloted by me in the JN4H (the "Jenny"), the XB1A, and the Martin Bomber-2 on that night and the same planes were flown by me on the night of February 25, 1921."

The U.S. Post Office's patronage was responsible as well for the construction of airfields—essential for ensuring regular mail delivery. U.S. Postmaster Otto Praeger established five air stations at existing experimental airplane fields between New York and Chicago by the end of 1919, plus emergency stops consisting of a hangar, an extra airplane, relief pilot, and supplies and mechanics. At the mail station in Chicago, local businessmen donated a $15,000-hangar. The Federal Government tapped businessmen for airport funds because they stood to profit from passenger travel.

Post Office air stations usually had two runways set at right angles to each other plus a powerful light beacon revolving on a tower. The strength of artificial lighting is measured by how many candles it would take to burn as brightly, and the Post Office specified 500,000-candlepower beacons. By 1924, the most common design of airmail stations was a 2,000-foot by 2,000-foot (610-meter by 610-meter) square to allow for takeoff and landing into whichever direction the wind was blowing.

During this period Harold Harris, Don Bruner, and others played an active role in setting up and operating the first lighted airway, an 80-mile stretch of land between Columbus and Dayton, Ohio, thus allowing the introduction of regular night service.

This remarkable achievement had been made possible by "Henderson, [Paul Henderson, Second Assistant Postmaster General], [who] in 1923 managed to secure funds for lighting a portion of the transcontinental, though he found many a man who doubted that the project would ever succeed.

'Over 90 percent of the advice which came to me [wrote Henderson] was to the effect that it could not be done,' he recalled. He got contrary advice from two young Army lieutenants, Donald L. Bruner and Harold R. Harris, who had begun experimenting with night flying at McCook Field, near Dayton, Ohio, in 1921. The Army was an old hand at night flying; it had conducted night bombing missions during the war and had continued nighttime experiments after the Armistice. But, like the Post Office's 1921 experiment, the Army's wartime techniques depended too much on pilot skill and too little on ground organization. Bruner and Harris depended on ground organization.[53]

Safe night flight allowed—among other types of cargo—the mail to be carried on a 24-hour basis. Harris noted, "The idea of 'aerial lighthouses' of great power was unsuccessfully tried in Europe. Meanwhile, the U.S. Army's scheme, consisting of strong beacon lights set slightly above the horizon angle, supplemental blinker lights and emergency landing fields every 25 miles was adopted by the U.S. Post Office, moving toward the goal of safe and dependable night flight. Step by step, the lighted airway reached from coast to coast. By the end of 1926 all segments were in place."

In *The Early History of Air Transportation*, E. P. Warner noted, "Of all American contributions to the technique of air transport operation, this was the greatest… As late as 1930, European officials were still but fingering the hem of night flying, and the British government report could say of that government's attitude: Consideration has been given to proposals which have been made by the Federation of British Industries and by the Associated Chamber of Commerce to the effect that night air mail services to the Continent should be organized."

Warner went on to state the "lack of sums (in the United Kingdom) for this purpose has made it impossible as yet to make a definite start".[54]

---

[53]   Nick A. Komons, *Bonfires to Beacons: Federal Civil Aviation Policy Under the Air Commerce Act, 1926-1938*, 130.

[54]   E. P. Warner, *The Early History of Air Transportation* (York, Pennsylvania: Maple Press, 1938, 26-29.

Chapter 10: Carrying the Mail

In the early years of the 20th century the backbone, the seedbed, the mother of all future American aviation developments lay in the U.S. Post Office's subsidies. Without these, innovations such as the development of night flying would not have come about as quickly as they did. Initially Post Office subsidies were awarded to help speed the mail, with no thought of passenger service. That soon changed. In his unpublished memoir Harris noted that "the first official Post Office operation occurred on September 23, 1911, when Pilot Earle Ovington carried some U.S. mail as an advertising stunt... In 1917, even while engaged with our allies in a war against Germany, the U.S. Post Office Department received an appropriation of $100,000 for an experiment with Air Mail.

Late in the winter bids were requested for the construction of five Postal airplanes for a Washington-New York service. The Air Mail was to be 25 cents an ounce for this airmail trip. When bids were opened on February 21, 1918, three in number, they were by manufacturers who were currently building training planes for the Army and proposed a delay of 90 days in filling the Post Office bid. Since the Post Office wanted to get started right away, the Army furnished the airplanes, pilots and mechanics for the first operations.... Major Reuben H. Fleet, [another Harris friend], was given command of the Army group assigned to fly the mail.

Harris wrote:

> The Washington terminus was a polo field, and the New York terminus was the infield of the Belmont Race Track on Long Island. The official date of commencing service was May 15, 1928..." The President and members of his cabinet came to see the Postmaster General start the historic undertaking and found that the mechanics ordered to fill the fuel had not filled the gas tank of the Jenny that was to make the flight. By draining the tanks of other aircraft around the field, the pilot took off for New York but flew south, and landed on a farm in southern Maryland!
>
> The plane from New York did better. It transferred its mail load to another plane in Philadelphia and the whole flight was made from New York to Washington in only 3 hours and 20 minutes from Long Island.
>
> 'Start up' difficulties were soon overcome and by the end of the second week the operation had settled down to a reasonably smooth basis.
>
> At the end of May the Post Office could report that more than 1/3 of the total number of trips scheduled had been completed within 4 hours from field to field.
>
> It became evident after a short period that Military Aviation had plenty to do about the War without worrying about the Post Office operations, so on August 12, 1918, the Post Office took over and began to run its own service using six planes especially built for this purpose by the Standard Aircraft Corporation, using civilian pilots who had been flight instructors prior to going to work for the Post Office. The cost of sending a letter by air mail was 24 cents, which included special delivery of this service to the addressee. The average air mail income was less than $50 a trip So . . . this was a very uneconomic business.

Since the Washington—New York operation was too short to be commercially feasible, the more important attempt had to do with the New York to Chicago operation.

The Armistice freed the Post Office from any further interference with the military effort and on December 12, 1918, a number of Army observation planes attempted to make the flight between the cities. Every airplane but one crashed, and the one that didn't crash had a forced landing! It became obvious that contact flying in the winter over the Allegheny Mountains was impractical. On May15, 1919, a Chicago to Cleveland route was established and on July 1, 1919, this was extended across the mountains from Cleveland to New York.

The first U.S. transcontinental Air Mail flight was made on September 8, 1920, and on February 22, 1921, scheduled operations on a 24 hour day was commenced with two planes each from San Francisco and New York. From San Francisco one crashed in Nevada and killed the pilot. The other got to Omaha where the mail was supposed to be picked up by a plane from Chicago, which failed to appear. So the pilot who brought the mail to Omaha, Jack Knight, guided by bonfires in Iowa, landed in Chicago at daybreak. The balance of the trip to New York was normal and the mail arrived in New York in 33 hours and 30 minutes from San Francisco! Of the two planes from New York, only one reached Chicago but was grounded by weather there!

Various combinations of rail by night and plane by day were tried, but the saving of time was too small to be important. Night flying was required . . . Godfrey Cabot had an experimental twin-engined plane built to carry out his experiments for picking up mail sacks from the ground by a plane in flight. I flew the first test August 11, 1921, with the grapnel hook on the end of a flexible cable. The hook hit the mail bag support and looped over the plane, jammed the elevator and ended up in the left engine, tearing it from its mount. Although the plane was destroyed, I emerged undamaged. Later, when a rigid pole was substituted for the cable, everything went well as demonstrated. The idea was successfully developed and used for a few years where airports did not exist. The method is still available for special situations."

On September 1, 1927, the U.S. Post Office made its last flight.

Chapter 11: Crop Dusting

The origins of crop dusting from the air and ultimately of the birth of Delta Airlines derived from a single historical fact: In 1892 the boll weevil threatening the cotton crop migrated from Mexico into Texas.[55] By 1922 the resulting loss to farmers of the Southern cotton crop was estimated to be over $200 million.

Yet Harris observed, that as late as 1920 "practically the only use for aircraft in the United States was in the military services. A small amount of commercial photographic mapping was being carried out, but it was not a significant business. The United States had not made intensive efforts to develop commercial passenger use of transport aircraft, even though the Europeans had started immediately after WW I. A transcontinental air mail service was operated by the Post

---

[55] James John Hoogerwerf, *Roots: From Crop Duster to Airline; The Origins of Delta Air lines to World War II.* Ph.D. dissertation, Auburn University, 2010.

Office with surplus WW I aircraft, rebuilt for mail purposes, but proved very costly. The mail plane carried no passengers."

Most flying in the U.S. had centered around Dayton's Federal Aviation Experimental Station at McCook with its flight testing facilities. Besides testing for military purposes, records indicate that at McCook tests were also conducted for "manufacturers, private individuals and agencies that had aviation equipment or theories that lent themselves to study or experimentation."[56]

Ohio catalpa trees, grown for posts and poles because of their straight trunks, were being attacked by the larvae of the Catalpa Sphinx Moth causing extreme defoliation. Typically American farmers had applied substances poisonous to pests by hand, a time-consuming and labor-intensive task. Knowing McCook's generous testing policies, entomologist C.R. Neillie of the Ohio Department of Agriculture who saw in a nearby town the opportunity to prove his theory that insecticides might be advantageously applied to affected areas by airplane, managed to convince H.A. Gossard, chief of the Department's Entomology section to turn to McCook for help.

The Army engineers came up with a radical solution: a method of aerial spraying that would do away with the awkward, cumbersome, time-consuming hand spraying used to that point. "A crude metal hopper" writes Anderson, "with a capacity of roughly 100 pounds was built by a talented employee, Etienne Darmoy, which, when completed, was bolted to the side of a Curtiss JN-6H (Jenny) aircraft, alongside the observer's seat. This hopper had a sliding gate, operated by a handle at the rear, and a small hand crank mounted near the top. The observer was to sit, or stand, in the rear seat of the aircraft and crank the insecticide out over the trees as the pilot flew it across the grove at a low level. The material to be used

---

[56] Mabry Anderson, *Low and Slow: An Insiders History of Agricultural Aviation.* California Farmer Publishing Company, 1986, 5-6.

was powdered lead arsenate, about the only thing available that would kill most pests when ingested."

A catalpa grove ten miles north of McCook in Troy, Ohio, was selected for the experimental run which was conducted August 31, 1921, with John A. Macready at the controls and Darmoy in the rear seat operating the hopper. The dust was distributed by the propeller.[57] What would have taken months to do on land was easily accomplished in a few minutes in the air. With the aid of the attached hopper, John Macready had made the first aerial dusting flight ever in Aug. 31, 1921, a run of 54 seconds!

The news of this great success spread rapidly. The March 1922 issue of the National Geographic featured an article by C.R. Nellie and J.S. Houser: "Fighting Insects with Airplanes, An Account of the Successful Use of the Flying Machine in Dusting Tall Trees Infested with Leaf-Eating Caterpillars." A feature article in The New York Times for January 8, 1922, on the Troy success heralded a Congressional hearing on the possibility of aerial spraying.[58]

By 1922 the boll weevil, replicating itself in the cotton bolls four or five generations in one season, had spread across most of the Cotton Belt to the consternation of Southern planters. Seeing their crops ruined, they feared the result would be the mass departure of the Black laborers normally used for harvesting cotton.[59]

In 1909 the U.S. Department of Agriculture had set up the Delta laboratory at Tallulah, GA., for cotton insect control

---

[57] Hoogerwerf, 38: "The material was placed with precision and, carried by the wind, it dispersed throughout the grove. As assessment determined that less than 1% of the insects remained alive on the trees."

[58] Ibid.

[59] Hoogerwerf, 20.

research.[60] By 1919 calcium arsenate was discovered to be the most effective insecticide against boll weevils as well as other agricultural pests. The laboratory explored its use through various types of dispensers operated from the backs of mules. Both the powder and the dispensers were costly, however, and the times of dispensing limited by the fact that the poison appeared to stick only to dew-covered plants.

The Director of the Delta laboratory, Dr. [an honorary title only] Bert Coad, and his assistant C.E. Woolman, a young farm agent, entomologist, and—having flown since his first ride in 1910—aviation promoter, enthusiastically endorsed the new approach: the use of airplanes to distribute insecticides—specifically calcium arsenate—further and faster. To aid in this work the Army Air Service in 1922 provided equipment and personnel. From Tallulah extensive testing occurred on various plantations with old Jennies and other planes in at best rickety condition.

"As I watched," wrote Alan L. Morse, an aeronautical engineer assigned to the program, "a three-man crew prepared to swing the prop. Numbers one and three faced the aircraft while number two, in the middle, faced away. Then each man grasped his neighbor's wrist and they were ready. Number one then pulled the prop down and through, and as 400 horses came to life, the other two jerked him clear of the whirling blades. Then the D-H wobbled away to the end of the field, headed into the wind, and took off over the trees."[61]

The pilots who volunteered for crop dusting were highly skilled individuals who appeared to have a reckless disdain for high risks. Anderson writes, "They proved it often by demonstrations of low-level acrobatics and by rolling their wheels across the tin-roofed tenant houses that were scattered

---

[60]   Tallulah because the area appeared destined for the next weevil onslaught. Hoogerwerf, 23.

[61]   Anderson, 11.

throughout the large plantations [where they did their crop dusting.]

"One pilot, advised by his doctors that he was suffering from leukemia, which was then untreatable, decided to fulfill a longtime wish to fly his airplane down Washington Street, the Main Street in Vicksburg, Mississippi, just across the river from Tallulah. One day he did just that. The street was so narrow and the buildings so tall that he had to skid the aircraft sideways down the street, just above the streetcar cables!"[62]

In addition to the problem of developing both an adequate dispensing device and an effective spray was the problem of the inadequacy of the WW I aircraft for the job. Even more important was the fact that since the poison would only stick to dew-covered plants, the poison would have to be spread at night after the dew had fallen. This meant night flying at extremely low altitudes.

It soon became clear, however, that possibly thanks to the combination of static electricity and the air blast caused by the gas-emitting device—the hopper—the poison stuck to the plants even in the daytime, making night flying unnecessary. Early morning or late afternoon were proved to be equally as safe as at night.[63]

Fortunately, the pilots flying low and slow were skillful enough to avoid most serious mishaps. But not always.

Thomas Huff and Elliott Daland had formed a company to manufacture airplanes. In an attempt to sell planes to the U.S. Army Air Service, Huff had traveled to Dayton where he met

---

[62]   Ibid, 12.

[63]   "Low flying during the middle of the day was dangerous on account of rough air, and the air temperature was such that the motors overheat badly in a short time." Hoogerwerf, 40-47.

Harold Harris, a renowned test pilot, whom he subsequently recruited for his dusting company.

The story goes that in 1924, with no further contracts for his company's airplanes forthcoming from the military, Huff was casting around for something to energize his ailing business. Then by chance George Post, a former World War I naval aviator, who had aided Huff and Daland in securing contracts and, as a consequence, had become vice-president of the Huff Daland Airplane Corporation, ran out of gas while flying and made an unscheduled landing in Tallulah, LA. There he met the two entomologists: Woolman and Coad, who convinced him of the commercial importance of aerial crop dusting.[64]

Said to be impressed by Post's story, Huff persuaded wealthy friends to finance an Airplane Cotton Dusting company and to give the factory an order for the design and construction of twelve dusting airplanes. He then spoke to General Mason Patrick, the head of the Army Air Service, who agreed to give Harris, by that time a Captain, a year's leave to help organize a company to dust cotton. Harris came on board as vice president and operations manager of the Airplane Cotton Dusting Company.

"It was early in 1925," wrote Harold Harris in his Memoir, "that Tom Huff of Huff Daland, Ogdensburg, New York, who manufactured planes, asked me to leave the Army. He wanted me to join an airplane crop dusting company he was setting up. This unique field appealed to me and General Patrick, Chief of

---

[64]   Hoogerwerf, 61, calls this story "apocryphal." He notes that Coad pushed the concept of commercial dusting with Congress, and that George B. Post "a pilot with Huff Daland, traveled widely as he investigated commercial opportunities for his company." But Huff Daland was already attempting to manufacture planes specifically for dusting operations.

the Air Corps, gave me a year's leave of absence to see whether I liked it.[65] I resigned my commission a year later."

In a 1987 letter to Mabry Anderson, Harris wrote, "I was put in charge of the work of [what became] the Huff Daland Dusters Company because of my experience flying all sorts of aircraft in Italy, in the summer of 1918 . . . Considerable work had previously been done by other pilots at McCook Field in dusting clouds for rain-making."

Harris left the Air Service permanently in February, 1925, and immediately began recruiting pilots for the dusting company, soon known as Huff Daland Dusters. The company was formally incorporated February 27, 1925, with its business "the carrying and transportation of passengers, goods, wares, and merchandise, for all kinds of commercial purposes, including agriculture and forestry, such as dusting, seeding, planting and fertilizing, forestry patrol and survey, for aerial survey and photography, for any and all kinds of uses, for exhibiting or advertising purposes, at any place within or without the United States."[66]

George Post was named director and its general manager of a company whose "assets included eighteen aircraft, twelve pilots, and twenty mechanics, all under the direction of Harris who was also was in charge of hiring and firing pilots and mechanics."[67]

Although Harris himself did not fly the dusters, he developed specialized techniques for the duster pilots still in use today.

---

[65] Patrick, seeing this new area of interest as a boost to the Air Service was eager to have his pilots and planes participate in the dusting. Ironically, aerial crop dusting led ultimately to the demise of the small farmer who could not afford the expense involved in aerial dusting operations. Hoogerwerf, 42-3.

[66] Hoogerwerf, 67.

[67] Ibid.

Crop dusting, Harris noted, "was one of the earliest uses of aviation supporting an activity other than transportation and little was known about it. Naturally, one of the problems of this new outfit was to secure pilots, so I went to Kelly Field at graduation time, since graduates were not then retained on active duty with the Army. Among those I interviewed was a lad named Lindbergh. He listened carefully to my sales pitch and asked for time to think it over ... When he returned, he said 'No. I am not interested. I own a Jenny (Curtiss JN4D) and will barnstorm and make a lot of money.' And so he did, as we all know ..."

[In another version, Harris recalls that Lindbergh said he owned a Standard, a WW I training plane. but "wasn't going to tie himself down to this dusting business."]

C. E. Woolman, in the future a co-underwriter along with Harris of what ultimately became Delta Airlines (of which Harris became, at least on paper, a vice president) soon joined the company. He had been loaned to the U.S. Department of Agriculture by the Agricultural Organization of the State of Louisiana, for which he was working as a County Agent. [In Louisiana the job was known as Parish Agent.] Concerning Woolman, Harris wrote: "He had done quite a lot of entomological work with Bert Coad and was an extraordinary salesman."

Harris's memoirs recount his adventures with Woolman on the road to gather Southern business for crop dusting.[68] He notes

---

[68]   Harris memoir: ""Woolman and I made an automobile survey of Georgia and North Carolina to see whether we could drum up some business there ... But before we left Macon, Woolman and I made a trip into South Carolina that is worth recalling. We'd had a very unsatisfactory day trying to arrange some business and Woolman said, 'I know a fellow in Columbia, South Carolina, who has a fine house and would be glad to see us. He's got a lot of good corn liquor (remember, that was the days of prohibition), and we'll sit on the porch and talk about this.' So we went to see

that a decision was made to move dusting headquarters to Macon, GA. where he said he relocated from Dayton. Soon Huff Daland was claiming success in dusting both fruit orchards and cotton fields. By June 1925 the company had signed contracts in Georgia, Mississippi, North Carolina and Louisiana.[69] The move proved, however, not to be economically viable. The company had stretched itself too wide, and besides, Georgia, replete with small farms and low-grade cotton, was not a promising prospect for dusting.

Driving over roads that were sometimes barely cow tracks, Harris and Woolman moved on to the Mississippi Delta region. In Monroe, LA. the head of the local bank arranged to have the town build a small hangar for their use. This meant moving operations from Macon to Monroe, where they found a lot more business.

It had become clear that if a duster plane was to be used commercially, to become commercially viable, its design would have to be larger, with a larger dispenser that could cover a larger acreage.

When Harold Harris joined forces with C.E. Woolman and the Huff Daland Duster Company began crop dusting in Louisiana, it was with a plane specially designed for use as a duster that was larger and heavier than the Jenny. This plane (nicknamed "the Puffer") Harris tested in February 1925, "under difficult

---

his friend. Woolman wanted to wisecrack and said, 'Look, you've lived here in South Carolina for always. I just want to tell you that Harris and I have been all around this state today and we never saw a state that had so many crazy people in it.'

"'Well,' his friend said, 'yes, you're probably right. We have a lot of crazy people but when they get crazy enough, we send them down to Georgia to teach school.' Knowing that we had just come from Macon!"

[69] Hoogerwerf, 72.

conditions on the windy, ice-covered St. Lawrence River," a flight that was postponed till the weather cleared.[70]

Harold and Grace along with their small son moved to Monroe, LA., a tiny back—woodsy town. Shortly after installing his wife and child, Harris left for a job crop dusting in Peru, returning only periodically. How long Grace and Harold Jr. resided there is not clear. I assume they lived in Louisiana mostly without Harold Sr. for perhaps two or even three years. The rural South being what it was in the 1920's, Grace must have suffered from a sense of isolation and deep alienation from the backwardness and poverty of body and spirit of the local inhabitants. Further, she was concerned about Harold Jr.'s health. He had a bout of serious illness that was undiagnosed, whose symptoms included a high fever and the appearance of spots on his legs.

Wherever Huff Daland Dusters operated, the community was always invited out to the performance. Furthermore, the pilots were always ready to take children up with them—until the practice was stopped as being too risky. It was thus that the pilots won the hearts of the local farmers, a vital step in developing and widening a paying clientele. Soon the world's first dusting organization proved its worth.

Crop dusting is seasonal. When the company finished with cotton in the South, it moved its focus to California and the west coast of Mexico where the growing season comes earlier. In short order the dusting operation with 18 airplanes had become "the largest unsubsidized air fleet in the world at the time."[71]

---

[70] Ibid, 62. While he was still in the Air Service, Harris and Daland had tested a prototype in July 1924. I assume this was the "Petrel 5" mentioned by Anderson, 15. The model was replaced by the larger and heavier "Petrel 31" with a wingspan of 50 feet and a 400 HP Liberty engine. It was known as the Puffer.

[71] Anderson.

Chapter 12: The Morrow Board Testimony

"The general atmosphere of Aviation in America," a visiting British journalist wrote early in 1925, "impressed me as being in that state when something is just going to happen. Not so much the calm before the storm as the slump before the boom."[72] Although the U.S. was one of the few developed nations that still had no civil aviation policy, American citizens certainly were looking to the sky. Indeed, 1925 was a fateful year for American aviation.

Challenged by the establishment of small airlines started by entrepreneurs like Henry Ford, General Billy Mitchell pressed to have all air travel—commercial and military—brought under the umbrella of a unified military air service.

Mitchell was not currently popular in government circles, however. In response Congress passed the Kelly Air Mail Act in February, 1925. Named for its originator, Congressman Clyde Kelly (R-PA.), the act authorized the postmaster general to contract for domestic airmail service with commercial air carriers. It also set airmail rates and the level of cash subsidies to be paid to companies that carried the mail. As Kelly explained: The act "permits the expansion of the air mail service without burden upon the taxpayers...."[73] By transferring airmail operations to private companies, the government thus effectively helped create the commercial aviation industry.

Henry Ford and other entrepreneurs persuaded Calvin Coolidge (president 1923-29) to appoint a committee, known as the Morrow Board—headed by Dwight Morrow, a successful banker—to investigate and report the status of aviation in the United States.

---

[72]   Komons, 66.
[73]   Ibid, 66-7.

It was in no small part due to the September 1925 historic and visionary testimony of Harold Harris and others before this committee that the government became convinced of the growing significance of commercial aviation, and, even more important, the concomitant need for proper governmental regulation to ensure the safety of aircraft passengers.

After presenting his credentials as a pilot of recognized distinction who, during the previous year and a half, accrued more airplane records than any other man, Harris had launched into a brief history of airplane dusting to that point. He noted that continuing development by Department of Agriculture engineers had aided the material used for dusting and the dusting equipment's efficiency. He observed that, forced to operate initially with essentially obsolete WW I airplanes, the Huff Daland Company had decided to invest in developing airplanes specifically equipped for the dusting task. Huff Daland Dusters thus established itself as a commercial entity, utilizing twenty airplanes and the services of ten pilots, "as well as the necessary supervisory personnel entomologists, mechanics, etc." whose skills might otherwise have found no satisfactory outlet, and who through necessary continuing experimentation were essential for the continuing success of the commercial operation.

"So far this year," Harris testified," these men [pilots] have flown a total of 900 hours, and have applied 375,000 pounds of poison dust on cotton, peaches, pecans and sugarcane, with most extraordinarily satisfactory results to the planters. This, the first fundamentally sound commercial aeronautical venture in this country, has gone steadily forward without publicity and without any stock selling attempt. It has met with the most amazingly cordial reception from the planters for which it has operated."

Predicting the coming enormous shift from the domination of the air by experimental planes primarily for military use to future transportation serving the general public, he continued persuasively, "One ordinarily thinks of aviation and aviation functions as rather mysterious, and covered with a shroud of secrecy. There is no mystery to real service, no matter what agency is used to accomplish that service. Many of the men for whom we operated this year had never seen an airplane at close range before, and the aeronautic information in the regions that Huff Daland Dusters covered from Virginia to Texas was largely limited to the front page stories of the latest aeronautical accident. These men, it would seem, would be the most difficult in the country to convince of the ability of the airplane to accomplish a real service, but the entire background of the "Dare-devil aviator" was completely forgotten in the actual results obtained in a dollar and cents return from the Huff Daland Dusting Service. In other words, commercial aviation is fundamentally sound and needs no direct subsidy or other means of artificial support if it truly fulfills an economic need, no matter what task it may be called on to perform."

Harris went on to point out the labor-saving aspect of aerial crop dusting, not to mention "the relative advantages of speed, thoroughness of application, saving in money [etc.]" He noted that the planters serviced through aerial crop dusting were not impressed so much by the fact that it was done by an airplane, as by the fact that it was in every way an economic investment.

He continued by itemizing the exact cost to a planter of Huff Daland services: $75/flying hour. This price included cost of "depreciation, gasoline, oil, interest on investments, accident insurance and obsolescence," but did not include "any organization charges or overhead of operating personnel or supervising."

Harris then went into specifics to demonstrate the economic feasibility of the dusting operation. He noted that the price of each of the 14 specialized duster planes owned by the company—$14,000—was justified by the fact that each plane was able to carry 500 pounds of dust as compared with 200 pounds carried by the reconditioned WW I Jennies. Further, each duster plane was equipped so that the pilot alone could manage flying and the dusting apparatus, thus eliminating the need to include a second man.

He pointed out the juggling act that an aircraft company had to undergo to make money and concluded that "unless a commercial aviation venture is economically sound and properly engineered, it cannot be made to pay its way. Therefore, it was essential that "some form of United States" Government inspection and licensing of commercial aircraft and operators be instituted at once, "since the public at large, as well as the individual concerned, is likely to suffer from badly engineered, badly built or badly repaired aircraft equipment, whether new or in use as a result of being surplus wartime stock."

In this regard, Harris had a recommendation. "It is believed that the Society of Automotive Engineers Aeronautical Safety Code is the proper basis upon which to build such an inspection and licensing system, and that the necessary legislation be enacted as quickly as possible in order to avoid all available motor or plane failures such as have occurred so many, many times in the immediate past as a result of lack of competent inspections. This of course would also eliminate the large number of accidents which have been caused by unskilled operators of aircraft."

Harris concluded his presentation by pointing out once again that the planters employed Huff Daland "not because the company used airplanes but because it was an economically sound move."

Chapter 13: From Dusting to a Dream

The year following his historic testimony to the Morrow Committee, Harris and C. E. Woolman, the two vice presidents of Huff Daland Dusters, made separate trips to Peru to discuss the possibility of dusting Peruvian cotton.[74] In his memoir Harris noted that "The cotton plants in Peru were being ravished by army worms. Planters in Peru arranged with Pedro Beltran, an owner of a large cotton farm, to come to the States to see what the U.S. Department of Agriculture would recommend for dealing with the army worms. Dr. Coad suggested airplane dusting and said there was only one commercial outfit that did that sort of thing. He recommended that Beltran talk to us.

"As a result Woolman was sent down to Peru to secure a dusting concession from the Peruvian government and to contract enough business to warrant our shipping personnel, aircraft and equipment from the States in December, 1926.

"We found cotton dusting in Peru a very satisfactory experience. By the end of the cotton season there, I had learned the hard way how long it took to get any material or even any considerable amount of information by steamer mail. In Peru we were dependent on steamships as our sole connection with the outside world. The idea of air service began to take form."

---

[74] Hoogerwerf, 76-77, observes that the traditional explanation that Huff Daland went to South America to take advantage of the reversal of seasons between the U.S. and S.A. is overly simplistic; in the U.S. the off-season was normally used to repair aircraft, and there were winter dusting possibilities, not to mention the fact that it was an onerous task to ship aircraft by steamer through the Panama Canal. More important was the return of Augusto Leguia to the Peruvian presidency. Leguia advocated La Patria Nueva, the modernization of Peru. The use of modern techniques to combat pests was clearly high on his agenda.

Harris studied the maps showing the long, straight West Coast of South America. He noticed that the shortest air route—more than a thousand miles shorter—from New York or Miami to Buenos Aires was via the West Coast. This was because the East Coast route closely followed the undulant East coastline. On the basis of his map reading, Harris developed a dream of a West Coast airline linking South America and the U.S.

The dusting season over, Harris searched out additional business in South America. In 1927 as he stopped at each nation's capital to promote interest in crop dusting, he also "made careful inquiry into the thoughts of the people" he met regarding their ideas concerning a possible west coast airline that would connect them with the rest of the world and minimize transport time.

> I traveled by steamer from Callao, the port of Lima, to Mollendo in southern Peru, the point where the railroad starts up into the Andes. I took the train from Mollendo to Puno on Lake Titicaca, the northern end of the Lake. There I got a small steamer and made a night voyage to the Bolivian port, Guayaquil, on the southern end of the lake. I transferred to a railroad again and went down the short distance into La Paz, Bolivia. From La Paz I took the train south on the altiplano, the level plain which was more than 12,000 feet above sea level, to Uyuni, Bolivia. At Uyuni the railroad splits, the west branch going onto Santiago, Chile. I went via the east branch to Buenos Aires, Argentina. From Buenos Aires I took a night boat to Montevideo, Uruguay. From Montevideo I took the steamer to Santos, Brazil, the port for Sao Paulo. From Sao Paulo I took the train to Rio, and from Rio, the steamer to New York.

Huff Daland duster in Chile in 1926. Harris stands at far right

> My research and observations throughout this journey convinced me more than ever the great need for the feasibility of an airline down the West Coast of South America and across the Andes to Buenos Aires.

While Harris was making his survey trip, Huff Daland Manufacturing Company and its subsidiary dusting company, almost bankrupt, were taken over by the Wall Street brokerage house, Hayden Stone. The airplane manufacturing company was turned into the Keystone Aircraft Company. As for the dusting company, Harris noted that "The Huff Daland owners decided that Woolman and another chap and I would be given the dusting aircraft and whatever other material they might have for a windup of their debts to us. Actually 'Huff Daland Dusters' continued as a dusting company, but I had nothing further to do with it, having sold out my share to Woolman. Woolman carried it on as a separate company within an airline structure he built into what is now known as Delta Airlines."

James Hoogerwerf, a Delta airlines biographer, notes that Harris' memoir is too modest, that in actuality Woolman and Harris's investments bailed out the nearly-defunct company thus enabling the founding of what became Delta Airlines of which—on paper, at least—Harris was listed as a Vice President.

Chapter 14: The Challenge of Towering Mountains and Huge Deserts

One of Panagra's Ford tri-motors flying the Andes

On the basis of his map reading, Harris had developed a dream of a West Coast airline linking South America and the U.S. His landmark tour of the region for Huff Daland focusing on contacts with representatives of the governments on the West Coast of South America convinced him of the possibility of the dream's realization. Many problems, not the least the topography of the region, stood between his dream and its realization.

In his 1943 survey for a U.S. government concerned with the continued presence in South America of German-sponsored airlines, *The Struggle for Airways in Latin America*, William Burden observed that the geography of South America, particularly the fact that the continent is essentially split in two from north to south by the Andes mountain range, has a great deal to do with the problem of communication both along the coasts and across the mountains.

"That continent," he noted,

> has the smallest population and lowest density per square mile of any continent save Australia. The population is distributed in separate clusters around the margins of the land mass, and the few major hubs of dense settlement— Rio de Janeiro, Buenos Aires, Santiago, and Lima—are separated by great distances... High mountain ranges and great areas of jungle are serious geographic obstacles to the construction of highways and railroads. As a result, the ground transportation system is inadequate and fragmentary in the extreme.[75]

Burden observed that earlier exploitation of the east coast as compared with the west coast was due to the fact that the east coast, considerably closer to Europe, had a number of flourishing cosmopolitan centers that claimed cultural and historical ties with European nations. It is no surprise then, that when Juan Terry Trippe considered expanding his infant airline south from Havana, he thought in terms of the east, not the west coast of South America.

As Harold Harris discovered for himself, on the west coast there was no easy way to get around. He noted, "The only way to go up and down the west coast of South America was by steamer and steamer schedules were slow and infrequent; an airline was clearly the answer for the need for speedier transportation."

---

[75] William Burden, *The Struggle for Airways in Latin America.* Council on Foreign Relations, 1943. 5-7.

"In the first quarter of a century," he noted in his memoir, the situation in South America cried out for the speeding up of transportation between cities of commercial or political importance.

> As an example, it took from ten days to two weeks to go from the capital of Peru, Lima, to the important town of Iquitos on the Amazon River. Anything too heavy or bulky to be carried by mule would require 30 to 40 days of transport between Lima and Iquitos since such heavy transport had to be arranged by steamer from Callao (Lima) through the Panama Canal around the big out-thrust of the South American continent toward Africa and then about two thousand miles up the Amazon River to Iquitos.
>
> There had been some rail development for a few points on the West Coast of South American, into the interior but those were almost entirely to mines. The only rail route north and south in Ecuador was between Guayaquil and Quito. In Bolivia La Paz was rail-connected with Arica and Santiago, Chile, or Buenos Aires, Argentina. Chile had a rail connection from Santiago to Buenos Aires through the Uspallata Pass, (except at such time as avalanches closed the railroad during the winter.) La Paz had a connection to Peru through Lake Titicaca. There was no traffic, except by steamer, along the west coast to connect Buenaventura (Colombia), Guayquil (Ecuador) Callao, Mollendo, (Peru), Arica, Antofagasta and Valparaiso (Chile.)

This situation was exacerbated, noted Burden, by the fact that "agriculture and mining remained the basis of the [west coast] national economies and . . . nearly all internal lines of surface communication reach from the interior regions of agricultural and mineral production to the seaports from which the raw products are shipped abroad."[76]

---

[76]   Ibid, 3-8.

The geography of Peru typifies the communication problems of the region. In the middle of the west coast of South America, Peru suffers geographically. Most of its eastern border, with the exception of a small area that laps over into the Amazon Basin is flanked by the Andes. Prevailing winds across South America's midsection are from east to west. This means that Atlantic Ocean moisture from South America's east coast gets trapped by the high mountains and never makes it over as precipitation into most of Peru. So with the exception of what it gets from several huge rivers running westward from the mountains to the sea, most of Peru—although Lima in the winter is as damp as winter in southern California—receives no moisture, no rain or snow, indeed is basically desert.

A typical Andean highway

Hudson Strode describes Peru's "immensity of barrenness" and notes that "Pizarro seeking El Dorado had first dieted his gold-hungry eyes on this vast yellowish desolation—a desert as long as the distance between New York and Los Angeles . . . The coastal desert," averaging "forty to a hundred miles in width."[77]

Even more drastic, high ridges from the Andes running into the ocean historically made communication between the adjoining deep valleys almost impossible. Indeed, in pre-historic times entirely disparate cultures lived and died, each hardly knowing what existed outside of its own valley.

The Mochica culture, for example, that flourished in a northern Peru valley from about AD 100 to AD 800, was virtually unknown until the 20th century. Yet its elite culture is reflected in the rich iconography and monument constructions, elaborately painted ceramics, gold work, and irrigation systems.

The forbidding terrain of the High Andes as seen from a Panagra plane

So when alleged, as in *A Peru Reader: History, Culture, Politics* (by Orin Starn, Carlos Ivan Degregori) that unification of Peru and its indigenous populations could only have been

---

[77]   Hudson Strode, *South By Thunderbird*, (Random House, 1937), 71.

effected through autocratic control, I am inclined to agree. The text cites the "oligarchical" government of Pres. Pierola (1895-1899) as responsible for the "modernization" of Peru using the "top-down paternalism of the oligarchical state. Schools, hospitals, highways, and railroads were built by the government to accommodate the increasing takeover by foreign entrepreneurs of natural resources through mining and the creation of extensive plantations. 'Centralization' and 'national integration' were watchwords that perpetuated the essentially two-class system."

Chapter 15: Modernization: the Dream Fulfilled

Peruvian President Augusto Leguia   Pan Am President Juan Trippe

The cry for modernization was taken up by Augusto Leguia, Peru's president from 1908 to 1912 and again from 1919 to 1930. A violent Francophile and an even greater admirer of the United States—to the point in 1922 of appointing an American, Captain Walter Simon, as Assistant Director of Aeronautics for Peru—he welcomed American investment, promoted road building and railroad construction, as well as the growing of exportable crops. The concept of the development in Peru of foreign airlines did not disturb him in the least.[78]

Thanks to the ability of the dusting company to "spray anything that had bugs on it or fungus, not just cotton, but lettuce and

---

[78]   Hoogerwerf, 78-80.

tomatoes and the like," good relations had blossomed between the Woolman-Harris team, and Leguia.

Buoyed by the Peruvian president's enthusiasm for modernization, Harris pursued his dream. He writes, "When I got back to New York from Brazil, I called on Mr. Richard Hoyt." Hoyt was Senior Partner of Hayden Stone, a politically powerful law firm, who handled all their aviation business and who controlled the dusting company and became chairman of what was to be Pan American Airways with Trippe as president.

> In the course of the conversation I told him about the airline plan that I had worked up, showed him the map that I had drawn and the figures I'd put together, which showed what was possible with aircraft that were then available or could be ordered with quick delivery with the airline to start in Peru. We already had our foot in the door there. He was very much interested since the entire business world had decided that aviation was wonderful as a result of Lindbergh's flight to Paris early that year [1927].[79]

Hoyt responded readily to Harris's description of the potential of an airline along the west coast of South America crossing over into Argentina.[80]

---

[79] Robert Lee Boughton, Jr. *From Clipper Ship to Clipper Ship: A History of W.R. Grace &Co*, B.A. dissertation, Princeton University, 1942, 95. "It was fourteen years ago in a little hotel in Canete, Peru, that the vision of an airline connecting the West Coast of South America with the United States was sketched on a worn map by an American pilot."

[80] In a letter (Dec. 10,1972) to Capt. H.B. Grow of Pensacola, FL. Harris wrote: "When I reported to Mr. Hoyt, I showed him my proposed South American Airline... The plan called for the following operational developments: 1. Lima/Talara. 2. Lima/Mollando/Arequipa.3.   Talara/Guayaquil/Buenaventura/Canal Zone. 4. Arequipa/Arica/Santiago/Buenos Aires. 6. Brownsville/Central American/Canal Zone."

"He turned to his secretary and said, 'Get Trippe on the phone.' I had never heard that name before. He said, 'Trippe, come over here. There's a fellow I want you to meet. He's two years ahead of us. '

"I didn't know then", wrote Harris, "but Mr. Hoyt and the J.P. Morgan group were working with Juan T. Trippe to finance an airline from Key West to Havana, with plans to expand further into Latin America as opportunities developed.

"We met with Mr. Trippe and Mr. Andre Priester, who was Trippe's aviation expert. Mr. Priester was very knowledgeable about aircraft operations and attested to the soundness of my proposed program."

"Harris's plans," observe Bender and Altschul,

> came to grips with the reality of aviation technology. The farthest an airplane could fly with a useful payload was 600 miles. Pilots had no radio, meteorological services or aerial maps to guide them, a deficiency that made flying over water especially risky. On a map of the Western Hemisphere, the southern half of the Americas appears to be flung eastward into the Atlantic almost in an S-curve. When a ruler or a piece of string is placed between New York and Buenos Aires, the straightest, shortest route is seen to follow along the Pacific coast of South America to Chile and over the mountains to Argentina. Harris told Hoyt and Trippe that except along the northern stretch between Ecuador and Panama, there were numerous landing fields on the Pacific side. Indeed, said Clement Keys when Hoyt mentioned it to him, 'No big mountains, no big oceans, no big jungles, and a nice traffic center every thousand miles.'[81]

---

[81]   Marilyn Bender and Selig Altschul, *The Chosen Instrument, Pan Am, Juan Trippe, The Rise and Fall of an American Entrepreneur*, New York: Simon & Schuster, 1982, 117.

Thanks to Hoyt's close ties with Trippe, Trippe's political influence within the American government, and the enthusiastic backing of the Grace Steamship Line, that saw in a new West Coast airline an opportunity to curb Pan Am's expansionist tendencies, Harris' Pan American Grace Airways—sponsored half by Pan Am and half by Grace through Grace Shipping—would become a reality with Lima, Peru, as its base.

"The basic deal between Hoyt and Grace", Harris noted, "was that Grace would handle legal and business problems in South America and Trippe would handle the flying part."

W. R. Grace was the West Coast giant whose diversified interests traditionally included the production of agricultural machinery, fertilizer extraction, mining, and tourism. It had textile mills, sugar plantations in Peru and rubber plantations in Brazil, chain stores in Chile and, of course, its West Coast shipping routes. "If the east coast of South America was predominantly European in terms of industrial and transport development, the west coast was U.S.-dominated by virtue of the Guggenheims in mining, Standard Oil and W. R. Grace" wrote Bender and Altschul.[82]

They noted that Grace had already developed its own plans for a West Coast airline. So why did it agree to a half share with Pan Am? "Trippe and William R. Grace had the power and resolve to block each other's ventures in the area: Grace was influential enough to frustrate any Pan Am quest to fly down the west side of South America, and Trippe was able to use his lobbying powers in Washington to prevent the Grace Company from forming an air carrier with privileges to fly routes north of Panama. Thus, rather than competing, the only financially responsible solution seemed to be a merger although Trippe later had misgivings all along about the combination."[83]

---

[82] Bender and Altschul, 119.
[83] Ibid.

Harris gave another reason for the compromise. "They [Grace and Pan Am] were sure there would be no profits for a long time and so the deal was put together on the basis that they would share the losses. Actually no one was prepared to give up one percent, so fifty-fifty was the best compromise in the first instance."[84]

In fact, possibly much to Trippe's chagrin, Panagra became enormously successful in its entire existence, "both as to profitability and to the essential services it provided to a vast public."[85]

Yet, Bender and Altschul observe, "The partnership of Pan American Airways and W. R. Grace was flawed from the beginning. Fifty-fifty may be the ideal basis for a union of a man and woman, but in a corporate merger it is unworkable."[86]

A June 1952 Fortune article titled, "The Long Cold War of Panagra" focused on the core of the long—running dispute between Pan Am and Grace: what Pan Am called the "constitution of Panagra" based on a letter of August 31,1928, from Grace's Assistant Secretary to Juan Trippe. In the key paragraph Mr. Cogswell [the Assistant Secretary] said to Mr. Trippe: "You will have charge of the operation from the Canal to Valparaiso and our houses on the West Coast of South America will be the agents of the company on a reasonable compensation basis, such agency to continue during the life of the transportation projects undertaken by the company."

The implications of the letter were at the root of the problem. Pan Am saw Panagra as simply a branch of its line. Grace, on the other hand, "believes that it went into the Panagra deal

[84]   Libby.
[85]   Wrote John Leslie, Pan Am historian, "Over the 38 years of Panagra's life, its net earnings totalled some $20 million. Considering that each of the partners had originally invested $500,000, and that there had been no subsequent additions of capital, these figures rather refute the common belief."
[86]   Bender and Altschul, 120.

as an equal partner in an individual airline, set up to grow in competition with other lines, including any controlled by partner Juan Trippe."

Grace more than stuck to its part of the bargain, always providing advice and diplomatic assistance to the young airline. Pan Am, on the other hand, although initially providing both personnel and aircraft, did its best to control any expansionist tendencies on the part of Panagra, and denied its uniqueness, insisting always that Panagra routes were merely legs of the overall Pan American World Airways empire. Harris noted dryly that "It did not suit Pan American to pay for any special public relations activity for Panagra."

Pan Am historians Bender and Altschul note that the reason that Panagra was not allowed to have its own president was due to the fact that Trippe "wished to establish the impression that it was a division of Pan American Airways rather than an independent airline." In effect, Panagra was to be Pan Am's unwelcome stepchild created from "a marriage of convenience."[87]

"You don't expect that I would be as much interested where I have only fifty percent as where I may have a hundred percent in the operating company," Trippe is said to have observed to Grace vice president Patchin.[88]

Thanks to Trippe's close association with members of the Civil Aeronautics Board, the South American concession was divided. Pan Am would fly down the east coast to Venezuela, Brazil, and Argentina, while Panagra would operate the so-called "diagonal route" from Panama to Cali, Colombia, Quito, Ecuador, Guayaquil and Lima, Peru, La Paz, Bolivia, Asuncion, Paraguay, Santiago, Chile and terminating in Buenos Aires, Argentina. Pan Am's discrimination against the new airline is shown by the fact that

---

[87] Pan Am's unwanted stepchild was claimed by Grace that considered it "the latest addition to the Grace family." See Boughten, 95.
[88] Bender and Altschul, 121.

whereas Pan Am received six airmail contracts for the east coast operation, Panagra on the west coast was limited to one.[89]

As a result of Trippe's insistence on counteracting any possible challenge to Pan Am by Panagra, Panagra was required to conform to some stringent restrictions on its operations. Although a US airline, with corporate headquarters in New York City, its routes were confined to the area south of Panama. Its maintenance base was also off-line, in Miami, where half-owner Pan Am handled technical matters. To bring the operation into a more logical network a three-way "through plane" operation was organized. Panagra route licenses were used from Buenos Aires and Santiago up to Panama, then the aircraft continued as a Pan Am flight to Miami, as only Pan Am had route licenses for this sector.

Finally, as Pan Am was not allowed domestic flights within the USA, National Airlines route licenses were used from Miami to New York City. Local passengers were taken on all stages, which were just sold as normal flights of the operator with the relevant licenses for that sector, but the Panagra aircraft worked right through from Buenos Aires, or intermediate points, to New York, and passengers could ride right through but crews from each carrier changed over to operate the relevant sectors. The wrangling between Grace—that insisted on Panagra's extension to the U.S.—and Pan Am, that didn't want the competition, continued for many years, finally being resolved only with the sale of Panagra to Braniff.

---

[89] Libby bio. See also Krusen, 34. "Woolman, the consummate diplomat, sent initially by Huff Daland to investigate the possibility of dusting in Peru, made a favorable impression on government leaders of nations soon to be involved in the airline's development. Harold Harris's initial exploratory tour had a similarly favorable impact. In Ecuador, for example, hardly a friend of Peru, Panagra's home base, since Harris was personally trusted by the Ecuadorean government, he achieved the transfer of Ecuadorean national contracts to himself—contracts he immediately turned over to Panagra."

Chapter 16: The First U.S. Scheduled Flight South of the Equator, September 13, 1928

After a 100-meter run, the plane rose above the surface of the earth... made a spectacular turn to the right, flying directly above the numerous public in the field, and headed directly north, on its route, rapidly disappearing from sight in the sky...

El Commercio, Lima's newspaper.

Passage through Peru by means of ground or ocean transport typically had required days or even weeks of difficult travel. Under such circumstances the tremendous significance of regular reliable air service was evident to commercial and political interests, as well as to the press. If there ever was a magic bullet for Peru, a small but aspiring nation, it clearly lay in a future portended by the departure in a cloud of dust of this tiny single engine plane.

Harris' and Woolman's previous good relations with the Peruvian government had paid off. November 28, 1928, the Huff Daland concession was turned over to Peruvian Airways Corporation (PAC).[90] As Libby observed, "There were just two officers of PAC: Trippe as President and Harris as Vice President and General Manager. Yet only Trippe and Hoyt established policy." Noted Hoogerwerf, "Woolman returned to the United States to operate a mail route between Dallas and Atlanta that grew into Delta Airlines and Harris remained, to become chief pilot, mechanic, general manager and vice president" of the new airline."

The concession provided for domestic and foreign mail, passenger and cargo service. The route was soon extended to include passenger, mail, and express service to Guayaquil,

---

90   Hoogerwerf.

Ecuador in the north and Arequipa, Peru, in the south. The way was thus cleared for the purchase of one single-engine four passenger Fairchild.

Harris and John MacGregor, co-vice presidents of Panagra

Harris wrote, "I went to the Fairchild plant to have the plane constructed. Actually, this was a plane of the type that Sherman Fairchild had designed and built for his own aerial photographic company. It was very satisfactory in being able to carry four passengers and some small payload the 600 hundred miles required in my map set-up between refuelings. The plane had a 220 h.p. air-cooled radial engine and was a high wing monoplane whose wings could be folded for storage. I had a toilet built in, perhaps the earliest in a U.S. scheduled transport. The concession having been secured, the airplane was completed and shipped by steamer to Peru."

Since it was not considered safe to fly the Fairchilds over large expanses of water, Harris ordered at the same time a set of pontoons. Thus "A land plane would fly up to Talara from Lima. The load would be transferred to a pontoon-equipped plane which would be flown over the ocean from Talara to Guayaquil."

"At first," noted Harris, "there wasn't any real separation between the people doing the crop dusting and the infant airline. The Dusting Organization furnished the pilots and mechanics for once-weekly service, which started from Lima to Talara.

Fairchild FC-I with the Panagra logo

"The first scheduled flight on the West Coast of South America," he wrote, "occurred on September 13, 1928 from Lima, at the Santa Beatriz racetrack, to Talara, 600 miles to the north, with intermediate stops at Trujillo, Chimbote and Paita enroute. The pilot was one of the dusting pilots, Daniel Tobin. The passengers were Mr. Hanrott, representative of the British Marconi Co., which had the Post Office concession with the Peruvian government, and Mr. Benjamin Romero, a representative of the Lima newspaper, 'El Commercio'".

Translation from "El Commercio", Lima, Thursday, September 13, 1928

INAUGURATION OF LIMA-PAITA AIR SERVICE

The First Passenger Plane of the Huff Daland Dusters, Inc. Left This Morning Also Carried Mail

Air Message from "El Commercio" to Northern Newspapers:

Taking advantage of the kind invitation extended to "El Commercio", for one of its editors to fly in this first commercial flight between Lima and Paita, we have sent the following message to the northern newspapers:

"El Commercio" takes pleasure, on this memorable day in which a new and transcendent era of progress in the republic's commercial transportation has just begun, to send its cordial greetings through Mr. Benjamin Romero, bearer of this air message, to its esteemed colleagues of the press in northern Peru and, through them, to the towns called upon to receive the great benefits of the modern and rapid means of communication inaugurated today, which offers so many promising hopes toward the development of national commerce and industry by bringing the capital of the republic [Lima] closer to its valuable dependencies of the northern coast, binding them more closely, and with solidarity, for the better satisfaction of their common destiny and interests.

[signed] The Editor of "El Commercio".

Background details followed:

Two months ago, we informed our readers of the establishment of an air navigation company which would operate permanent passenger, freight and air mail service between the United States and Peru. This company, Huff Daland Dusters, Inc., after a few trial flights in Lima and nearby towns, accomplished, not long ago, its first flight with a "Wright Whirlwind" engine, piloted by Mr. Dan E. Tobin, who flew to Guayaquil—principal port of the neighboring republic of Ecuador—carrying the vice president of said organization [Harris? Woolman?] as passenger, together with another American financier.

This flight was achieved with complete success, in spite of being only a test run, and actually represented the definite establishment of regular service by the Huff Daland Dusters, Inc.

Last Sunday, we witnessed the test flight of the new and modern passenger aircraft "Fairchild"—6853—"Wright Whirlwind" engine which has a capacity of five people, is equipped with rest-room compartment, and with all the trimmings of a perfect limousine.

On that occasion I also gave detailed information in "El Commercio" concerning the various flights made by the pilot, Mr. Tobin, around Lima that day, carrying passengers, much to their satisfaction.

It was announced then that the plane's first flight to Paita (first stage of air service to Ecuador, Panama and the United States) would take place today, Thursday. In accordance with this announcement, the airplane "Fairchild" departed this morning for the northern districts of the republic, thus giving start to scheduled service (as these flights will operate every Thursday, from now on) to those important regions of our national territory, which, will in turn place us in rapid and direct contact with the northern republics of South America, with all the Central American countries, Mexico, and the United States of North America, as the planes of The Huff Daland Dusters, Inc. will have established connecting air service for passengers and mail with those of the Pan American Aircraft Corp. and the United Fruit Aircraft, which have established service between the United States and principal points in Central American and the Canal Zone.[91]

Mr. Woolman, Vice-President of the Huff Daland Dusters, Inc. distributed invitations for this morning's ceremony and, according to these, numerous persons of diplomatic, official, political, commercial and social circles of the republic met at Santa Beatrice field (racetrack inner

---

[91] Since there is no evidence in the texts I consulted of the existence of "the United Fruit Aircraft", I cannot comment further on this reference.

grounds) at ten o'clock, anxious to witness the departure of the initial flight of this important air service.

At 10:10 A.M., the president of the republic arrived, accompanied by the minister of the government; the chief of the army, Colonel C.J. Bazo, and the chiefs of the aide-decamps, Commander Mendivil and Major Castillo, and aide-de-camp, Captain de la Rive Aguero.

The representatives of the aforementioned company, Mr. Woolman, Doctors Alfredo Alvarez Calderon and Antenor Fernandez Soler, greeted the Chief of State. Already in the field were the Ambassador of the United States, the British Minister, the Mayor of Lima, American businessmen and financiers, high officials of the Post Office and Telegraph services, some members of the national parliament, and several ladies, who lent grace to the ceremony. Also present were the American writer Mr. Halliburton, recently arrived from Panama, and all the American embassy personnel.[92] A large crowd filled the private and public grandstand and, also, the field in the proximity of the airplane, brought out, moments before, by the expert pilot, Mr. Tobin.

Mr. Leguia chatted during twenty minutes with many of those present, and examined the airplane in the company of Capt. H.B. Grow, Director General of Aeronautics; of Commander Megar, Director of the Army Aviation School, and of various pilots, officers or our armored forces.

At 10:30 A.M., one of the mail trucks arrived carrying the correspondence to be transported by the plane to its various points of destiny in the north. This permanent air mail service carried five bags of correspondence to Casma, Chimbote, Trujillo, Pimental, Palta, and Talara.

---

[92] Richard Halliburton, a world famous adventurer, was on a fund-raising tour of South America.

These were brought to the plane where Sr. Leguia was standing, in the company of Ambassador Moore and Pilot Tobin, next to the aircraft, whereupon our Chief of State took three of the bags and deposited them in the plane's special cargo compartment; a fourth was placed there by the American Ambassador, and the last and most bulky, by Pilot Tobin.

Following, the Ambassador of the United State spoke the following words:

'I am pleased to be able to be present at a ceremony such as this, when we are celebrating the inauguration of permanent passenger air service in this great republic. For the present time, the service established by Huff Daland Dusters, Inc. will only be between Lima and Paita; but it will soon be extended to Guayaquil, in the neighboring republic of Ecuador, and the ports of that of Panama, in order to make connection with the planes going to Central America and the United States, thus making air communication between your country, Mr. President, and mine, a reality.

'My sincere wish is that nothing may stop the route established today and that the best of fortunes may accompany the pilots of Peru who have crossed these skies with their planes.

'It must not be forgotten, Mr. President, that the airplane is the best means of communication between the capital city and the most remote regions of your vast and rich territory. I sincerely hope this will be so, owing to the great drive shown, in all respects, by the present President of the Peruvian republic, Sr. Leguia.'

Sr. Leguia thanked him in a few short phrases, and immediately proceeded to inaugurate the new Lima-Paita air service, declaring the 'Fairchild' plane ready to commence its flight.

Sr. H. G. Hanrott, Postmaster General, and Senor Benjamin Romero P. of the "Commercio" newspaper, the first two passengers of this interesting flight from Lima to Paita and Talara, immediately entered the cabin. Senor Leguia bid farewell to each passenger and them to the pilot, and wished them good luck on their trip.

Mr. Tobin then carefully closed the cabin door, and started the engine. A few minutes passed, in which could only be heard the muffled roar of the powerful engine, until the aircraft rapidly began to move across the field. After a 100-meter run, the plane rose above the surface of the earth, it being then 10:45 A.M. The plane headed directly south, and then made a spectacular turn to the right flying above the numerous public on the field, and headed directly north, on its route, rapidly disappearing from sight in the sky.

The 'Fairchild' airplane is a limousine-type monoplane, with capacity for five persons, including the pilot. It is all painted dark green, except for the wings, which are canary yellow ... It was specially constructed for this service ... and is equipped with all the comfort required in a machine which will be used to transport passengers a great distance. It has glass windows on each side of the cabin. It had two great doors, one on each side of the fuselage, in the center of the cabin. It is also equipped with a complete restroom. At the front of the cabin, a sliding door gives access to the pilot's compartment, which is roomy, and fully equipped for command. It is shut in by the windshield and the roof of the compartment, which fully protects the pilot from wind and rain, without obstructing his vision. Other technical characteristics of the airplane are those corresponding to the most perfect machines of this type since this is one of the most modern aircraft.

After the aforementioned ceremony was over, Senor Leguia and his retinue, also accompanied by all the other guests, went into the Jockey Club, where they were feasted with champagne by the representatives of the Huff Daland Dusters, Inc. and many toasts were drunk to the success of the new national air service.

A communication was received from the central telegraph offices of the States informing that the 'Fairchild' airplane passed over Pativilca, and continued its trip to the north.

At 12:50 the plane landed at Casma Airport, in order to leave mail destined for that point.

Krusen's account of the departure of this soon-to-be famous maiden flight highlights the momentousness of the occasion "that ushered Peru into the aviation century. The remainder of the South American west coast would soon follow."[93] What Krusen failed to mention is how much Harris's Panagra ultimately "did more than its share in the development of today's air transportation system . . ."[94]

"When Panagra started," Harris wrote, "we had one single engine Fairchild, of alleged 220 horsepower. It carried four passengers and the pilot . . . It had windows in the cabin which could be opened by the passengers if they desired to have

---

[93] As Krusen observed, p. 5, both C.E. Woolman and Harold Harris were on hand for the historic flight. Yet "neither the racetrack attendants nor Daniel Tobin, [the pilot, loaned from Huff Daland] nor even Harold Harris, had any idea that one day that same aircraft would hang, as Panagra Aircraft Number P-1, [the first U.S. flag airplane to make schedule anywhere in the world south of the Equator] in the Smithsonian Institution's National Air and Space Museum in Washington, D. C. "

[94] Harris, memoir: The entrance to the toilet in the rear of the plane was guarded by two swinging barroom doors, the type you see in western movies, providing, I am sure, only a minimum of privacy!

additional fresh air. "At my insistence'" he continued, "a toilet was installed, the first in any U.S. commercial airplane."

The craft "depended upon its one engine. It had no brakes, no controllable propeller, no flaps and no reverse thrust. It had a cruising speed of perhaps 85 miles an hour, could not surmount high mountains and was forced to remain at low altitude since it had no oxygen system or cabin pressurization."

"In those early days," Harris notes,

> cruising altitude was about 2000 feet above the ground [and range about 600 miles.]. The air can be very rough at that altitude particularly over the desert, which comprises much of the Peruvian coast. Anachronistic though it now seems, the windows of this plane could be lowered in flight. One day a lady passenger became airsick and made a real mess of the cabin (we hadn't graduated to airsick bags yet). On landing the pilot asked her why she hadn't used the toilet. She's forgotten about it. And why hadn't she lowered the window? 'I was afraid I would lose my false teeth!'

> The cabin vibration was uncomfortable and seats were poor. The cabin was so low that the average passenger could not stand erect.

> The lack of a public address system was not a problem since the pilot was in the same compartment with the passengers and he could carry on in a loud voice over the noise of the engine and propeller, although he had no assurance that his passengers were able to hear him. There was no cabin attendant. The limited fuel supply required refueling at least every 600 miles. The only prepared landing fields were unpaved military airports. The actual landing fields used by our early fights were generally some cleared space near the town served, such as a soccer field for the local team.

A characteristic of early flight—the onsite repair of some structural item preliminary to takeoff—was not missing from this flight. "Tobin said to us, 'I've got a bit of a gas leak here, right over the cabin door, but I don't think it's much,'" William Howell [then a stenographer with W. R. Grace] recalled. "He rolled some soap up with a band of tape, covered the leak, stepped back to survey the results, and said, 'That's got it.'"[95]

Howell, Panagra's first employee, remembered "'While a speech was being made to the new device, I think at Pimental, a drunken Indian walked into the propeller since the engine was not shut off. The engine didn't even stop. It just killed the guy and right on going. They got the blood and guts off the airplane and kept on going with the first flight anxious to reach Talara before dark!'"

Why Talara? Harris explained: "The northernmost possible place in Peru just before you got to Ecuador, Talara was the headquarters where all the Peruvian oil was being shipped out. There were wells there. Peru has an enormous amount of oil, but it's mostly back in the Amazon where you can't get at it. But they have big wells right there in Talara. Never made a pipeline as far as I know across the Andes. Talara was one of the reasons for getting the airline started in the first place, because there was a great deal of traffic between Talara and Lima . . ."

Howell reminisced, "'When I joined the company, we flew 1200 miles a week, one four passenger plane, no instrument flying, no radio. When I left the company, we had a daily DC-8 in each direction between Buenos Aires and New York. Quite a development.'"[96]

That same year, 1928, before his inauguration as President, Herbert Hoover [1929-1933] made a trip down the west coast of South America on a U.S. Navy cruiser in order to determine

---

[95] Harris memoir.
[96] Ibid.

for himself the viability of an airline located there. He was not just convinced; he was enthusiastic. "He assured me," Harris wrote, "he would give us full support in our efforts to grow and expand internationally.[97]

> So we bought several larger Fairchilds (400 h.p. engine) carrying six passengers, plus pilot, a fine out-growth of the smaller airplane with which we had started service. I piloted the first of these larger airplanes from Lima to Guayaquil and talked with the Grace people there. The agreement between our owners was that Grace would represent the new aviation company wherever Grace had an agency and Pan American would specialize in the operational aspects of the airline. The Grace people in Guayaquil pointed out to me that to call it "Peruvian Airways Corporation" was unwise from the standpoint of trying to get any concession from the Ecuadorian government. I piloted the first Round Trip by air from Guayaquil to Quito, and took the President of Ecuador for his first airplane ride. Consequently, the concession in Ecuador was issued in my personal name with the right to transfer it to a corporation.

> Shortly after the receipt of the Ecuadorian concession, I received a cable from New York advising of the formation of a new company called Pan American Grace Airways Incorporated. I had the initials of this name, "PAGAI" painted in the fuselage and had baggage tags made up with

---

[97] Bender and Altschul, 119: "Hoover was on a pre-inaugural journey to Central and South America to signal the desire of the United States to 'be a good neighbor.' He made a point to discuss aviation rights with every President he met and elicit support for a U.S. commercial air service. Harris flew to meet the battleship Maryland, as it steamed into Guayaquil with Hoover aboard to deliver a letter of welcome from the President of Peru. 'You go right ahead with your plans,' Hoover told him. 'We'll make sure you get your airline.'"

that name. Shortly thereafter, New York advised me that the name Panagra would be used.

Since the Ecuadorean concession could be transferred to a corporation, it was transferred to Pan American Airways, Inc.

This corporation was created in the same ownership as Peruvian Airways Corporation had been, that is, half owned by W. R. Grace Co. and half owned by Pan American Airways.

Astride the uneasy union were two vice presidents: Harold Harris, Operations Manager, based in Lima, and John MacGregor, General Manager, based in New York. Since Trippe wanted no Panagra president, until the appointment of Harold Roig in 1939 there was none.

Chapter 17: Air Mail Subsidies: Panagra Blossoms

Without the guarantee of subsidies by the U.S. Post Office, the development of U.S. airlines both domestically and abroad would have been impossible. In the case of Panagra, its very existence depended on the certification by the Postal Department of F.A.M. No. 9, a route from Cristobal, Canal Zone, down the West Coast and over the Andes to Buenos Aires, Argentina.[98]

Backed by Pan Am and Grace, Harris's pre-Panagra Peruvian Airways Corporation had gained Peruvian government authorization to operate a mail and passenger service throughout the length of Peru. This authorization was quickly handed over to what became Panagra. The historic departure from the Lima racetrack that began air mail and passenger service to Talara via Paita, Pimental, Pascamayo, Trujillo, and Casma was under the aegis of PAC. Shortly, however, Panagra air mail and passenger service extended to Guayaquil, Ecuador in the north and Mollendo in the south.

A portion of Panagra's "Diagonal" route

---

[98] F.A.M. refers to the Foreign Air Mail Act of 1928 that made possible the systematic planning of air routes to Latin America. See Boughten, 97.

Boughten writes: "In May, 1929, the company began air mail service, on a frequency of once weekly, between Cristobal, Canal Zone and Mollendo, Peru, a distance of 2,400 miles. A flying permit through Chile had been granted early in 1929 and in July, 1929, the first United States airmail arrived at Santiago, at the scheduled hour, approximately 6,000 miles from New York.[99]

"The scheduled hour"... Today it is difficult to appreciate what feats of skill and daring by those early Panagra pilots lay behind the delivery of the U.S. mail "on schedule." Over and above all was the difficulty of ensuring continuous unbroken air mail service over some of the worst topography in the world which frequently demanded makeshift adjustments by pilots whose skills and nerve were tested again and again.

Reminiscing in the 1980's, Tom Jardine mentioned one such incident that involved a local farmer.

> There was a revolution in Chile, a big one. I hadn't been down there very long. I went through three or four layers of clouds. No one told us you had 130-140 mile an hour winds through there and I was flying about 9,000 feet I guess. I figured I'd better get down and I went through another layer, and I finally ended up by a little farm about 10 miles north of Santiago. Torrential rain, and I was going around and around this house. This was a Fairchild. The farmer was very nice and he got out some horses and we got on the horses and took the sacks of mail with us. I think we went through about 10 barricades. Actually, we got into the Grace office about one or two o'clock in the morning with the mail and, of course, the farmer. They didn't show much courtesy but being with me and the international mail, boy, that was better than a passport. We went right through all those barriers. Nobody stopped us, and finally [we] got into the office with the mail. If it hadn't been for the U.S. Mail, we'd be there yet.

---

[99] Boughten, citing Grace Log, March-April, 1931, p.50.

He remembered flying a Fairchild from Arica, Chile, to Lima, Peru, on a make-up mail flight that had to be flown at night. "I had no weather reports or radio," Jardine recalled. I took off from Arica at midnight, following the coast north underneath the overcast. The glow from the engine exhaust stack eliminated any forward visibility, so I looked over my right shoulder to see where I was.

> At Chala I had to go up on top of the overcast to about 5,000 feet. My first gas tank ran dry just then. It must not have been full. I switched over to the second tank, but now I knew I didn't have enough gas to reach Lima. But I did have two five-gallon tins of gas, which we always carried.

> I crossed the Nazca and Ica Deserts, and about abeam Pisco decided I had to get down soon. Rather than descend through the fog, I headed for the mountains and landed uphill on an old trail. I was out of fuel; it was just getting daylight, and the fog was rolling in. I walked up the hill and took a nap.

> When I woke up, I looked over towards Lima and saw that the fog had lifted. I poured the gas from the two tins into the fuel tanks. I didn't have anything else on board except possibly ten kilos of international mail. I fired up, held the brake, lifted the tail, and just got off.

> I figured I had just about enough gas to get to Lima. I came into Lima, landed, rolled up to the hangar, and the engine just stopped. I was out of gas. This was at 11 A.M. and I had been due in at 6:30.

Next came authorization in October to extend service to Buenos Aires, with the final leg to Montevideo added in November.

Boughten explains that "Under contract with the United States Post Office until1938, Panagra received payment for carrying the mails twice weekly between Cristobal and Buenos Aires and, in turn was obliged to carry up to 800 pounds of United

States mail on each trip. The United States Post Office was reimbursed a substantial part of this amount (the cost for subsidizing the airline) by the sale of stamps in the United States and by the payments by South American governments to the United States Government for all mail from each respective country destined for the United States. However, the Post Office was to pay the airlines, according to that rate, for the services rendered. This is still the method used for subsidizing Panagra and the other airlines."[100]

Writes Boughten, "The enthusiasm with which the business interests in the United States and in Latin America seized the opportunity for rapid postal inter-communication even at high surcharges, prompted a further study of the situation. From all countries came the request for lower surcharges, increased frequency and speedier schedules. Therefore, in six months' time the postal surcharge was reduced to 25 per cent, the frequency doubled, and the flying time cut two days between Cristobal and Montevideo. On July 1st, Panagra started making two round trips weekly between Cristobal and Buenos Aires."

Fueling the "San Fernando" at Las Palmas airport, Lima, Peru

---

[100] Boughten, 100.

As soon as one region responded to the service offered by
Panagra, another region presented itself as a proper one in
which to operate. On the whole it was evident that Panagra
fulfilled a great need. Panagra planes had flown as many
as thirteen times in one day across the Andes between
Santiago and Buenos Aires. As fast as the best equipment
obtainable at that time was purchased, it became
insufficient for the constantly increasing passenger, air
mail, and air express traffic. In 1934, as soon as they
were available from the factory, Panagra bought a fleet of
14-passenger Douglas DC-A Monoplanes, followed by the
purchase of the larger 21-passenger Douglas DC-3's.

Thus in only six months Panagra had instituted airmail service
over a route 4,500 miles long, entailing half a million miles
of flying annually, possible only with the "frenzied activity of
engineers, radio operators and construction gangs dispatched to
the deserts and mountains ... Captain Harris' dream was coming
true and growing with almost the swiftness of argosies."[101]
Indeed, by January 1930, the routes that Panagra was to use for
the next 47 years were essentially established with the exception
of a later extension into Bolivia and northern Argentina.[102]

The vital importance of the U.S. government subsidy for Panagra's
ability to extend its airmail traffic and therefore its area of
operations was true even as late as 1941. In his Trip Series
32, Harris wrote: "I hope that by the mail which I shall receive
tomorrow (the South bound mail is over-nighting in Lima tonight
rather than making Arica as scheduled for a reason with which
I am not familiar), that you and Mr. Patchin [a Pan Am executive]
have had a satisfactory meeting with the Post Office and CAA
officials in Washington on the question of securing an additional
service between Cristobal and Guayaquil or Lima. I hope that you
have been able to get this authorized as one additional service all
the way through to Buenos Aires by way of the Diagonal ..."

---

[101] Ibid, 97-98.
[102] See Krusen, chapter 4.

Chapter 18: The Diagonal

THE *Panagra* ROUTE

1942

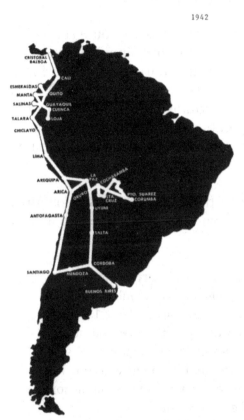

At the time of the original agreement between Pan Am and Grace, the South American concession had been divided. Pan Am would fly down the east coast to Venezuela, Brazil, and Argentina, while Panagra would operate the so-called "diagonal route" from Panama to Cali, Colombia, Quito, Ecuador, Guayaquil and Lima, Peru, La Paz, Bolivia, Assuncion, Paraguay, Santiago, Chile and terminating in Buenos Aires, Argentina.

The development of the famous Panagra "diagonal" route—through Bolivia and northern Argentina to Buenos Aires, with stops at La Paz, was due in large part to the threat of competition created by the French and German interests on the West Coast. German interests planned an enlargement of their services into this interior section of South America. This threat from foreign sources gave added incentive to Panagra's diagonal route; a mail contract granted by the Inter-departmental Committee on Aviation in Washington made this route a reality and on July 23, 1937, it was initiated."[103]

---

[103] Boughten, 99.

Harris: "After the diagonal operation was going well, we were flying from Buenos Aires to Lima with DC2's. The plane had dump valves on the gas tank so we could reduce the total weight of the aircraft to be flown on the remaining engine in case of one motor failure. Hopefully to get us to an intermediate airport for an emergency landing."

The diagonal proved so popular that it was the route chosen by members of an investigating committee appointed by President Roosevelt and led by future Supreme Court Justice Hugo Black (and known therefore as the Black Mail Committee). The committee's mission was to determine the essentiality to the U.S. of the entire Pan Am operation with a focus on Panagra's diagonal from Buenos Aires through Bolivia and the main line between Lima and Panama.

Recalled Harris, "I met the investigating group in Buenos Aires and went with them in a DC2 from Buenos Aires up into Bolivia and Uyuni.

> We fueled and took off for La Paz. Shortly after leaving Uyuni one of the engines failed. I remember that the ground altitude at that position averaged about 12,000 ft. above sea level. So the pilot dumped the fuel and headed back to Uyuni. We were gradually descending in spite of full power on the good engine to a point where it was a touch and go situation whether we'd make the airport. Finally the pilot did make it, landing downwind at the airport altitude of something like 12,000 ft. and when we got there found the bad engine was in such shape that we had to have a new one. The only engine available was in Lima, some twelve or fourteen hundred miles away, with only direct air transport available. The only way you could get an engine, unless you flew it as cargo, was by way of sea from Lima to Mollendo. Train and lake steamer from Mollendo to La Paz, and from La Paz to Uyuni by train. The train people in Uyuni were very fine to us and offered to put us up for the night in the manager's home, but since

the group was traveling on a time schedule, it was decided that rather than stay there overnight, we would get an auto carril, which is a railroad car with an automotive engine.

We would make the rail trip from Uyuni to La Paz where we would have a plane pick us up from Lima and carry on. The British manager and his wife at Uyuni, who were most solicitous in looking after us, prepared the necessary sandwiches, coffee, all the fixings and got the auto carril ordered from wherever they had one; it might have been sent from La Paz. In more or less the middle of the night, we took off in this auto carril on the single track railroad from Uyuni bound for La Paz. The auto carril had no heat, and at this altitude and in the middle of the night, it was mighty cold. We were bundled up with blankets, sweaters, and the Bolivian driver of the auto carril, who spoke no English at all and in fact was more of an Indian than a Bolivian, didn't like the idea of having to do anything with airplane people, even under emergency circumstances. He apparently didn't like anything about any big business. I presume he was a member of the Communist party, although I didn't ask him. He was damn annoyed at having to make this special trip. After we'd been en-route for two hours, it seemed to be a good idea to break out the hot coffee and if we gave him some hot coffee, maybe he'd feel better. One of the members of the investigating team, Sam Gates, volunteered to fix a big cup of coffee for our driver and present it to him with our compliments, which he proceeded to do. The only trouble was that in packing all these goodies, the sugar and the salt were put in exactly similar containers. Sam got the salt by mistake, instead of the sugar, and sprinkled plenty of it in the driver's coffee. The driver took a gulp of the mixture and was then sure he was being poisoned and didn't want to have anything to do with us! The atmosphere finally got settled down and we carried on.

They had a very interesting way of running their single track operations there. They have apparently switched blocks at an intermediate stop every so often and the driver carries a special kind of key which was good for his block, (southern block for instance), and for the next block north, he had a new key which made it possible for him to be the only one to travel on the single-track line. Since the key was in his possession, no train could come south on the same track on the same block.

The net result of the trip was that we finally ended up in La Paz in the early hours, completely tired out, worn out, glad to get in the airplane to take us the rest of the way.

Chapter 19: Flying Across South America in the Twenties

Crew of the "San Fernando"; from left to right, M. Vargas, R. Ewing, T.F. Jardine, C.H. Pursley, J. Sosa

> *This was the era of 'those daring young men in their flying machines,' when almost no one had flown. To fly was glamorous, rare, maybe even a bit dangerous. In South America it was macho. Not surprisingly, every dictator on the continent wanted to do it or to be seen shaking hands with those who did.*
>
> (William Krusen)

Even taking into account the skill and courage of the pilots Harris hired, in the face of challenges posed by route and topography, not to mention the primitive state of commercial flight, Harris' proposed airline probably seemed to many a most foolhardy undertaking. To others, however, it posed an unparalleled adventure.

"Think back," Harris wrote, "to the middle 1920's when land based aircraft carried a small load for very short distances before requiring landing to refuel, without the ability to communicate by radio with the ground or to climb over intervening mountains. There were no landing fields anywhere in most of the world except those provided primarily for military purposes. Competent designers of aircraft, aircraft engines, propellers and other specialized experts now available in large numbers were extremely rare in the middle 20's.

"Almost no international agreements, with respect to laws of the air, existed."

> A start toward commercial aviation development had been made in Europe where the distances were relatively short but almost no long range routes had been planned and considered. Night flying was almost non-existent. "Commercial flying of any kind was still in the earliest stage of development. Weather forecasts were rudimentary and the communication between various ground points, by wire, cable or radio was still in early stages of development.

An early Panagra radio shack

"In laying out my program for Latin American operations [regarding Harris' proposed route from the U.S. down the west coast of South America], I was well aware of the limitations of the equipment then existing or anticipated to be available in the immediate future. At that time, it was felt to be unsafe to attempt to operate across large bodies of water unless the aircraft was able to operate on water as well as land . . ."

Unloading the San Fernando at Huanaco Tampa

Operating standards regarding overhauls, inspection, servicing, etc., still had not been established. The specialized experts in flight operations, maintenance, communications and passenger services had to be trained and gain experience in order to give assurance of satisfactory performance. An unexpected difficulty arose thanks to the discovery that the vagaries of local conditions or faulty aircraft and equipment engineering necessitated equipment modifications. "For instance," wrote Harris, in August 1929, when the first Fords arrived, because our landing areas were so gravelly, muddy, or deep in dust, we found that the standard tires were too small, and we had to increase their size… We also put NACA cowling on the engines of the Fords… and found it to give about 10 miles an hour more speed and better cooling of the air-cooled engines."

The Panagra hangar at Limatambo airport

A Panagra FC-2 parked next to one of the new Douglas DC-2s.

When the first DC-2 came to Lima in September 1934, we arranged a courtesy flight for the appropriate folks in Lima. As the passengers were being loaded, the landing gear suddenly collapsed and the plane settled to the ground long before the engines were started! It was found that there was a factory engineering mistake in the landing gear control mechanism. If the plane sat on the ground for a considerable time, it would build up a good deal of hydraulic pressure in the retracting mechanism and would automatically retract the valve that would retract the gear. In this particular instance our faces were red, and our spirits were really low since a considerable amount of damage was done to the airplane, and the important people who had been invited to go along had been unceremoniously dropped onto the ground, without ever having flown in the new aircraft!

The Douglas Company was very proud of the fine engineering that they had done throughout the development and construction of the DC-1, and rightly so. However, they also erred in the installation of the controllable pitch propellers in that they had only one lever that controlled the pitch simultaneously on both engines. If you had an emergency and wanted to shut down one engine, you would want to have that engine propeller in high pitch but the propeller on the good engine in low pitch. I had a separate control rigged up for each propeller and advised the Douglas Company of what I had done. They sent Eddie Allen, their very fine test pilot, and a couple of engineers, down to Lima to observe what had been done and to run tests on how it worked. I believe that the arrangement that we built into the first Douglas DC-2 in Lima, was subsequently installed in all DC-2's that the factory turned out.

Then there was the problem of establishing passenger facilities. "There was no passenger terminal at any point. The local airline representative would know that it was time for him to crank up his automobile and drive to the landing spot when he heard the airplane fly over his place of business. There were no passenger buses, no amenities for the passengers, not even a drink of water. If it was not raining, and the wind happened to be blowing, the dust was so bad that it was most uncomfortable when the engine was started. Bystanders got an even more severe dusting. It was a real adventure to travel by air in the early days!

> It was of course necessary to have adequate capital and a keen political understanding to arrange operating rights, have access to the necessary landing facilities, passenger stations, hangars, shops, etc, to assure the safety and convenience of travelers, mail and cargo.
>
> Pressure had to be kept on the designers in all the various special fields of communications, power plants, etc., to assure comfortable, safe and efficient aircraft in all respects, with a maximum of speed at minimum cost in order to make air travel affordable to a large enough number of people to achieve commercial success.

Harris went on to discuss the specifics of starting an airline from scratch in a foreign country containing some of the most forbidding terrain in the world, which he proposed to fly over on a regular basis with what appeared to be woefully inadequate vehicles, landing fields, and personnel.

Ultimately, everything came down to the skill and adaptability of the pilots who had to contend on a daily basis with the weather surrounding and generated by some of the world's highest mountains. The pilot had no contact with the ground since aircraft radio between various ground stations and the aircraft had not yet been developed. "Ground fog," noted Harris, "very low clouds close to the ground or rain might prevent the pilot from visually sighting the normal landing area. The pilot would then search elsewhere in the vicinity for an emergency landing field within the range of his reserve fuel."

He had no indication of wind direction, which he needed to properly effect a normal landing. If he landed with a tail wind, he might over-run the available space and if he landed with a strong cross wind, his drift sideward might wreck the landing gear. The pilot had no maps except those he developed himself. And there were only rudimentary landing fields except for military use.

Harris wrote,

> The Murphy Law application is of course very much in evidence in the airline business. For instance, coming out of Buenos Aires for Mendoza and Santiago on regular schedule, one of our pilots observed that some of the cowl fastenings on the left engine cowling were loose. He consequently radioed Villa Mercedes, an intermediate emergency landing field, to have a ladder ready at the airport, so that he could climb up to the cowl fasteners and fix them. When he reached the Villa Mercedes field, he found no one on the field at all. Obviously, this message had not had the desired result. Consequently, it was necessary for him to unload a quantity of the passengers' baggage, which he stood on in order to reach the cowl fasteners, made the necessary correction, returned the baggage to the plane and took off again not ever seeing anyone on the ground!

Chapter 20: Lima

As Harold Harris soon found out, politics in South America were often turbulent. Augusto Leguia himself was certainly aware of the prevalence of revolutions. Elected President of Peru in 1908, he was kidnapped a year later by members of the opposition party and only rescued by the police after a fight that took at least 100 lives. In 1919 he again sought the presidency of Peru and launched a successful military coup, which led him to succeed the incumbent as an interim president. He then proceeded to dissolve Congress, whereupon the new parliament elected him constitutional president of Peru.

Limatambo airport in 1935

Rabidly pro-American and dedicated at least initially to the modernization of Peru, and, more particularly of Lima, Leguia was enthusiastically in favor of the new airline which Harris asserted would peacefully revolutionize Peru by creating a new and rapid means of communication.[104] Located strategically on the Pacific coast of South America, Lima, the logical epicenter of the new airline, was founded by Spaniard Francisco Pizarro and his conquistadors on January 18, 1535. They called it La Ciudad de los Reyes, or The City of Kings because the date of its foundation was January 6, the feast of the Epiphany. However, 'Lima' became the name of choice for what soon became the most important city in the Spanish Viceroyalty of Peru. After the Peruvian War of Independence, Lima was made the capital of the Republic of Peru. Today a third of the Peruvian population (7.6 million) lives in the metropolitan area, one of the ten largest metropolitan areas in the Americas. Lima's seaport is Callao—and includes the valleys of the Chillón, Rímac and Lurín rivers. From the Rimac River, whose dams provide hydroelectric power, Lima gets its drinking water. The name "Lima" may have derived from the Spanish attempt to pronounce "Rimac", that in Quechua means "Talking river".

Harris and Grace with their daughter Alta Mae holding their wire-haired terrier "Whiskey"

---

[104] Hoogerwerf, 76. Quoting from Peter Flindell Klaren, *Peru, Society and Nationhood in the Andes:* "Such was the extent of Leguia's Yankeephilia that he ordered a portrait of President James Madison hung in the presidential palace and actually declared July fourth a national holiday in honor of the United States."

The population consists of mixed racial and ethnic groups. Traditionally, Mestizos of mixed European (mostly Spanish) and Amerindian descent are the largest contingent. Second in numbers is the group originating from Europe, mostly of Spanish descent, but also Italians, Germans, Jews, and Middle Easterner. Afro-Peruvians, initially brought to the region as slaves, are yet another part of the city's ethnic quilt, and Asians, an even smaller one. Unlike other ethnic groups in Lima who speak only Spanish, most of the peasant population that migrated to Lima speaks primarily Quechua or Aymara.[105]

The Harris family moved to Lima in 1928, a few months before I was born. This was our home base until 1939 when Harold Harris was transferred to Panagra's New York office, and we moved to New York.

Due to the huge disparities between the Peruvian socio-economic classes, Harold and Grace Harris encountered two types of Peruvians: the upper classes, fair-skinned, proud of their links to Spain; and the lower classes, Indians and those of mixed race, in our day both generally lumped into the one category of *cholos*. We children dealt mostly with the latter; our parents, with a mixture of both.

There were also the foreigners who came, made their fortunes, and, a generation later, called themselves Peruvian. The (originally German) Gildermeister family, responsible for creating a huge plantation, Casa Grande, that produced 45% of Peru's sugar crop and which formed the backbone of a coastal plutocracy of bankers, entrepreneurs and land-owners, is one example.

---

[105] During the 1950's Lima's population ballooned as Andean Indians seeking relief from the near-starvation conditions of their mountain villages, created on Lima's northern and southern periphery some of the largest barrios, [slums], in the world. Housing the majority population of Mestizos (locally known as cholos)—only a few of whom manage to escape to middle class status—these shantytowns often lack electricity and running water.

Nowadays the baronial style in which many expatriates lived in Lima during the decade 1928-39 may be seen as evidence of their crass exploitation of the innocent Peruvians. Certainly the Harris family was not alone in regarding most of the Indians and *cholos* as dirty, backward, irresponsible and immoral. What all foreigners overlooked, however, was the fact that they themselves had simply bought into an already corrupt system: a colonial-style government by the elite whose power to repress an impoverished minority was reinforced by foreign corporations, the latter relying on what was politely known as the *regalo*, gift; locally, *the llapa* or bribe, in all transactions.

From the moment Harold Harris found that all the detachable gadgets—hood ornament, mirrors, cigarette lighter—had been stripped from our car some time between when it was lowered from the ocean liner and when it arrived at our door, we expected that the servants, indeed, all members of the lower class, would steal. Friends warned Grace to keep the drapes closed at night to prevent potential thieves from seeing the ornate silver coffee urn and other valuable pieces on the sideboard. She soon took for granted that the servants would steal small things, food, etc.

Thus in Peru there existed a sort of implicit compact between the haves and the have-nots. According to the terms of this compact, both groups subscribed to a sort of interdependency. The haves exploited the have-nots through denying them adequate wages, a decent education, and economic opportunities. The have-nots retaliated by stealing, cheating, and expecting the haves to provide some of the social services denied them by the government.

The compact was universal. Once Panagra had obtained the mail concession, complaints from would-be recipients of airmail started coming in. It was discovered that the clerks in the Lima post office were stealing the stamps and destroying the letters. When confronted, the Lima heads of the Marconi Company were, as Harris noted, "perfectly frank". By way of explanation they said, "We don't pay these people enough money to live on so they have to do that to maintain their families."

"They refused to do anything about it," noted Harris, "except to tell us that the only way this could be eliminated was to have all of the air mail that was dispatched from Lima registered, paying an extra fee for the registration, in which case there was no chance of thievery without it being detected."

Lima Social Life

El Presidente de la República
y la Señora de Benavides tienen el agrado de invitar al

León H. R. Harris y *Señora*

al banquete que, en honor del Excelentísimo Señor Secretario de Estado de los Estados Unidos de América y de la Señora de Hull, ofrecerán en el Palacio de Gobierno, el jueves 11 de enero, a las 9 de la noche.

UNIFORME

R. S. V. P.
Servicio del Protocolo
Ministerio de RR. EE.

Invitation to a Presidential reception for Secretary of State Hull

Grace Harris was pregnant with me when in late 1928 she and her son Harold Jr., using a Grace Line ship to Panama and PAGAI (Panagra's early name) from Panama to Lima, joined her husband Harold Harris in Lima. The couple soon plunged with energy and enthusiasm into an all-engrossing social life. Their reception was helped by Grace's beauty and warmth,

Harold's black hair and bristling black moustache—he could easily be mistaken for a Latino—and their active, sociable, and fun-loving natures. They quickly merged with the American and British diplomats and families of the Panagra pilots. In Lima, a small and relatively unimportant national capital, our father's position as the head of a new and prospering airline became both politically and diplomatically important. As a result, our parents were soon introduced to the elite of Peruvian society, as well as those members of various diplomatic corps who spoke English. These, along with Panagra pilots and their families made up the bulk of their new friends.

British Ambassador Bentink, Harold Harris, the Prince of Wales and others at Lima airport

In the late 20's and early 30's there was quite a fad for traveling by the new means of transport around South America. Women aviators, authors, celebrities of all sorts, came to Lima and were wined and dined by our parents and friends. Along with the new Ford Trimotors, popular in South America, came requests from national leaders and businessmen for free trips for themselves and friends. Ross Allen Harris, a widower, who had become reconciled to his son's precarious lifestyle, with his daughter Jessica, was among those who traveled to Lima in 1929. Two years later, on February 15, 1931, it was the turn of Edward, the Prince of Wales, and his party of ten.

For the British crown prince Harold Harris arranged a special trip from Lima to Arequipa aboard Panagra's new Trimotor, the *San Jose*. The journey actually required two planes, the first for the Prince and his entourage, the second for the baggage. In his "Memorandum of dates and incidents with Panagra, 1931", Harris described the event.

> February 10th, I arranged for the Prince of Wales and his party to fly in a Panagra Ford from Lima to Arequipa.

> February 15th, Prince of Wales and party actually flew in a Panagra Ford, *San Jose*, Lima/Arequipa. This flight by the Prince of Wales was directly opposite of what Mr. Bentinck, the British Minister, had told me ahead of the Prince's arrival in Lima, that his Government had told him that the Prince was to do no flying during his South American trip.

Although he was privately worried, Harris acceded to the Prince's request to make the trip. As Krusen points out, "Airplanes weren't that safe, and Harris didn't want Panagra to be responsible for the killing or injuring the future king of England. But, aside from Pan Am's relations with England, he had to consider Panagra's relations with Peru. To refuse the Prince would be to embarrass the Peruvian government, which would surely retaliate."[106]

Harris continued, "My query to the British Minister as to whether we could have some alcoholic beverages aboard the Prince's party of ten was turned down by Mr. Bentinck. I felt

---

[106] Krusen, 44.

that the Prince would prefer liquor, so put in a considerable assortment for the flight. After the flight the steward told me he had run out of gin before they had got 135 miles south of Lima.

The Peruvian Air Force was upset that Panagra was handling the Prince's flight but the Peruvian Air Force had no passenger airplane except one single-motored six passenger Boeing. So they offered to carry the baggage. After the Prince and party had taken off and the Peruvian Air Force Boeing was loaded with all the baggage it could carry, there was still a mountain of baggage on the ground and the Peruvians had no aircraft or pilots available to do anything about it. At this time, we were using a hangar at Los Palmas, the military base where the party had departed from, and I saw one of our Fairchilds sitting in the hangar.

All my people had gone home but I saw an American Vice Consul and got him to help me push the plane out, and loaded the baggage in the plane. Then the Vice Consul, who had never flown before and had often hinted he would like to go aboard and I took off for Arequipa with the balance of the baggage. Six hours later we landed in Arequipa and turned the baggage over to the Peruvians at the airport. I doubt if the Prince of Wales ever knew how close he came to being shy of much of his baggage on the balance of his South American trip.

Chapter 21: Border Wars and Revolutions

 "Doing business in foreign countries" observed Harold Harris, "is not always easy, even if some of the wars and revolutions are not really well-organized." From the very outset Panagra had to face the fact that operators of an American airline passing through fractious South American nations required skillful diplomacy in all their dealings.

Harris was up to the task.

> As the Ford Trimotored aircraft began to arrive to improve the Fairchild fleet in the early days of Panagra, 1929-30, we decided to have each aircraft named for the saint of each of the countries we served by the appropriate Catholic representative of that country. This went very nicely but we had one problem. Ecuador, at that time, did not have any Ecuadorian then sanctified enough through the highest rank. Ecuador did have a lady, Sister Marianna, who had gone through all but the last stages of promotion. So we asked the Archbishop of Ecuador if it would be appropriate to use the name, "Santa Marianna" since she was obviously about to be made a saint. He agreed that it would be perfectly acceptable, and carried out the necessary rites in a public christening of that name.

The people of Ecuador were not taken in by this 'jumping the gun' and the local name for the Santa Marianna became Santa Manana![107]

---

[107] Krusen commented on the brilliance of Harris's choice of names for his aircraft. "Panagra's first Trimotors instituted a new tradition.

It was essential to Panagra that it make powerful friends. In a letter to the Panagra directors dated December 29, 1938, Harris lamented the fact that the new Chilean administration had removed from office "many of the persons with whom we have had amicable relations in the past."

By dealing personally with Government officials and powerful landowners, Harris was thus able to achieve a high degree of cooperation in regard to landing rights, the establishment and/or development of landing fields, radio and weather stations.

In a 1939 letter from Buenos Aires to the new Panagra president, H. J. Roig, Harris wrote that he had met with Mr. Patron Costas, Vice President of the Argentine and also the owner of the Tabacal sugar estate, "upon whose landing field we are planning to put our radio station. He is very much interested in our plan to make an emergency and possibly a flag stop and is also interested in helping us eliminate the Jujuy stop. He promised to discuss this matter confidentially with the Minister of the Interior and the President of the Republic... I took the opportunity of our visit to thank Senator Patron Costas for the real help he and his organization have already been to us."

Both border wars and revolutions routinely broke out between and within South American nations. Krusen notes, "Coups were

---

Pan Am's early planes were often named after local dictators... But dictators and postmasters-general were temporary phenomena. Dictators had the added liability of having enemies, both within their own country and abroad. Privately, Harris could work politicians with the best of them, but publicly he wanted neutrality. One thing South American countries had in common was the Catholic Church and a host of saints. So on August 11, 1929, Harris invited the archbishop of Peru to christen the first Ford the Santa Rosa. On September 2 the San Cristobal was baptized in Santiago, Chile, and on December 8 it was Ecuador's turn, with the Santa Mariana. It was a tradition that was to prove useful over the years; the aircraft were interchangeable between nations and didn't need repainting with every passing revolution."

common. In just six months in 1930 the governments of Argentina, Brazil, Chile, Bolivia and Peru were overthrown, largely as a result of economic upheaval caused by the worldwide depression."

If the airline was to continue to grow, these disputes had to be addressed diplomatically. Then there was the further challenge of operating an airline at extremely high altitudes with aircraft in no way specifically equipped for the test. These two factors were frequently intertwined.

Ecuador, the first leg of the rapidly expanding airline, and Peru, Panagra's home base, were not on the best of terms. The former, not happy to give a concession to a foreign airline based in Peru, gave it instead to Harold Harris personally who then forthwith turned the concession over to what became Panagra and flew the first ever round trip between Guayaquil (Peru) and Quito (Ecuador).

Shortly after the Harris family arrived in Peru, they were confronted in 1930 with a revolution led by Sanchez Cerro, a high-ranking Peruvian army officer that threw out the then-current president, Augusto Leguia. Sanchez Cerro flew to Lima and served as provisional president until the military with whom he had effected the coup forced him into exile after six months in office.

Harris recalled, "After he [Sanchez Cerro] had been president long enough to make the people of Peru think that he wasn't very good either [than Leguia], he decided that, in order to take their minds off their economic troubles, he would pick a quarrel with Colombia. He claimed the Colombians had taken over a small town in the interior of Peru called Leticia. This was such an unexpected thing to all the business people of Peru that the first day it was announced that Peru was at war with Colombia, the business men I talked to were all aghast and couldn't imagine what was going on or why it was so important that Peru should go to war about it... The power of propaganda is so enormous that by the second or third day the same business people who had been startled by this activity were now convinced that the Colombians had done the Peruvians a dirty trick, had failed to live up to border treaties, and the only honorable thing for Peru to do was to go to war.

The Peruvian air force was sadly lacking in aircraft, particularly transport aircraft and since the 'war' was to be carried out in the Amazon Valley, which meant an unsatisfactory transport of supplies and men overland to the battle grounds, Sanchez Cerro decided that he would take over the Panagra fleet of aircraft, since Panagra was based in Lima. I didn't know anything about it until one evening I had a call at my house to appear at the palace at 9 o'clock that night for a meeting with Sanchez Cerro. I didn't know what this was about, and my Spanish was so poor that I felt very uncertain about making the trip alone, so called my secretary who was British, and who had been working for the Grace Company when I first came to Peru. He was a good stenographer and knew both languages. I called on him to go with me to the palace. I advised the U.S Embassy about the call I'd received and my concern that they might not be able to find me the next day. They'd better know where I had last gone. At the appointed time we arrived at the palace and were taken in to Sanchez Cerro who gave a speech on how important it was that the Peruvian army have transport and that he was going to take over the Panagra aircraft to carry out his war activity. I told him that didn't seem the right thing to do, and we had a discussion about how terrible it was that it seemed impossible to carry on without having to interfere with foreign business, particularly the day-by-day operations of the *airmail* airline. Finally we made a compromise. I made a gift to the Peruvian government of one Fairchild airplane . . . out of, I suppose, four or five Fairchilds. Our main fleet at that time was Ford, trimotor Ford. So while Sanchez Cerro wasn't very happy about the deal, I guess he figured he didn't want the U.S. to get mad at him, so he accepted. Obviously, I had no time to tell my superiors in New York about the problem. I had to do it on my own, so there it was. We turned the airplane over to the Peruvians very quietly and within a few days the plane flown by a Peruvian army pilot cracked up—I guess fatal to all the people aboard. I don't know about that, but that's my impression.

This was a very ticklish thing because obviously Panagra had to have its fleet of airplanes to carry on the international business it was doing from Panama to Buenos Aires or else we were out of business. Furthermore, we had to land in Colombia, which was at war with Peru for our refueling on the regular route for the distance was too great to overfly Colombia. They (the Peruvian pilots) had to refuel in Barranquilla, so there would have been quite a black eye for Pan Am if word had gotten out that part of the Pan Am system was furnishing

airplanes to the Peruvian government. Fortunately, nothing of this came out publicly. We had no problems with Colombia. In due course the war was settled.

That was not the end of the problems with Sanchez Cerro. True to form, revolutionaries sprang up intending a military coup. "Arequipa is some 600 miles south of Lima," noted Harris. "The military garrison at Arequipa decided to rebel against the Lima Government, so when our southbound Ford carrying the U.S. mail landed at Arequipa Feb. 21, 1931, to refuel, the pilot, Byron Rickard,

Peruvian President Sanchez Cerro

found a company of soldiers with guns lining the landing area. They seized him and his plane. The telegraph line to Lima was functioning, and we learned that our plane and pilot were in the hands of revolutionaries.

We made vigorous protest about the seizure and the delay of the U.S. mail, and they finally agreed that we could send a single engine plane, a Lockheed, to pick up the mail for onward flight, but the revolutionary forces retained the Ford and its crew for the few days that the revolution lasted. The leaders of the unsuccessful coup then boarded our plane and in what was surely one of the earliest political hijackings, had themselves flown to Arica, Chile, where they would be safe from reprisal. And all ended well, as we got our plane and crew back unharmed.[108]

The Chaco War (1932-35) between Bolivia and Paraguay, both landlocked and both seeking access to the sea, killed over 100,000 soldiers, and also gave rise to one of Panagra's more hilarious anecdotes. Writes Harris:

As we expanded across Bolivia, from Peru to Argentina, we encountered difficult but soluble problems for the airports at La Paz, Oruro, and Uyuni are all above 12,000 feet above sea level.

Our Bolivian concession had a time limit before which we had to start service. All landing fields, radio installations and passenger stations were for our account and had to be constructed by us. Uyuni is the junction of the railroads between Chile and Argentina from Bolivia. The field at Uyuni and the station and radio had to be built and operational before the deadline. The Chaco war was in progress between Bolivia and Paraguay and no manpower

---

[108] Krusen comments, "Arica was something of a staging area for disenchanted Peruvians. A dispute over the Atacama Desert between Peru and Chile had commenced in 1879. Shooting broke out and Chile occupied Lima from 1881 to 1883 when Chile ceded back to Peru the town of Tacna and gave Peru access rights to the port of Arica, on the new Chile-Peru border. Now the cafes of Arica were filled with losers of political battles across the border, and the air was thick with plots."

was available; however, one of our airport engineers was assigned the job.

Nerves were getting a bit frayed as we heard nothing from him until the day before the deadline. Then his radio station went on the air advising us to proceed with the planned flight schedule for the next day.

When he returned to Lima, I asked him how much the Uyuni job had cost. "Two bottles of Scotch," he replied. When he arrived there he had sought out the Chief of Police, handed him a bottle of Scotch, and outlined his airport problem. The Chief got out his truck and started across the pampa, lassoing every Indian man he saw. He brought them back to a barbed wire enclosure—the site of the new airport. Indian women followed their men with all necessary cooking gear. The women parked outside the wire and fed their men through the wire. All day the men picked up rocks from the airport surface, piled them in the truck, and picked more rocks as an empty truck arrived. With a few days the field was cleared and the Indians were turned loose. Whereupon the Chief of Police received the second bottle of Scotch!

There were many encounters in the high mountains between Panagra pilots and planes and hostile Indians. Tom Jardine recalled another explosive incident.

We went back to Tacna—it was the regular stop. One of my passengers turned out to be President Leguia's new prefect for Tacna or some such. Since the town had been taken over by rebels, I knew we were in for some business. I didn't even shut the props off. I went back to the door and let these fellows out, and they had a duel right there, guys shooting at each other. I just slammed the door and ran up and jumped into the pilot's seat and took right off for Arica.[109]

"Farther south," writes Krusen, "at Antofagasta, Chile, Jardine picked up Harold Harris. Harris had been trying the reassure the New York office that the aircraft, personnel, and mail, were all okay. He had come over from Buenos Aires to see for himself."

'Things seemed to be back to normal,' Jardine recalled. 'We got out of Arica and picked up gas at Arequipa. When it came time to take off for Lima, the agent and five, six, seven people were standing in the back. The aisles were full of luggage and every seat was taken. I wondered why there were so many people on the airplane. I forget the name of the agent, but I told him to get the excess people off.'

'They won't get off,' the agent said. 'And I won't get off either.'

'Well, why not?' I asked.

'He pointed through the cockpit windows and said, "Look down the road." I looked and several hundred drunken Indians were coming at us.'

Harris was sitting right behind Jardine, who turned to him for advice.

'Captain,' Jardine said, (using Harris's military rank at the time), 'We're in a helluva fix. Here we've got an overload with all those people and they won't get off.'

Harris stood to get a better view down the road. Then he sat back down and buckled himself in. 'Well, let's go,' he told Jardine.

---

[109] From Jardine's journal.

Needless to say, they made it. Knowing the quality of the man in the seat next to him, Harold Harris never doubted they would make it back to Lima safely.

Occasionally, it wasn't just revolutions or border clashes that Harris had to deal with. Now and then problems came up with the relatives of ruling men. Harris wrote:

> In the cotton dusting season of 1927 in Peru, A. B. Leguia was President of the Republic. He had a son named Juan, who could drink a good deal and then do some very outlandish things. Juan Leguia sought me out from time to time. We were in the bar of the Lima Country Club one evening with Colonel Recavaron of the Peruvian Air Force and an ex-British officer, who was an instructor with the Peruvian Air Force at Las Palmas, their Air Base in Lima. Juan Leguia had taken flying training in Great Britain with the Avro airplane, the same type plane that was used by the Peruvian Air Force in their training. He felt no pain at this particular time and began to make remarks about the ex-British officer's flying ability to everyone's discomfort except Leguia's. Finally it got so nasty that the ex-British officer told Leguia that he didn't know anything about flying. Leguia challenged the ex-British officer to an air duel. Colonel Recavaron was to be the second for Leguia and I was the second for the ex-British officer. The arrangement was that we would pick out any two airplanes at the field, try them out, flight testing if necessary. A coin toss would decide which plane was to be piloted by whom. At the starting signal each would take off and try to run the other plane into the ground! This didn't sound very delightful to me, but it's what they wanted to do, at least what they wanted to do that night, and I worried about it all night long. I called Recavaron the first thing the next morning and said, "Hey, how about this?" He had had plenty of experience with this sort of thing and said, "Just forget it." He said, "The two people that were in the argument last night are going to forget it anyway, and

we'll just forget anything ever happened." Sure enough, that was how it turned out but it really had me concerned. Actually, my guess is that Leguia talked a better flying game than he flew!

Chapter 22: The Germans are Coming, the Germans are Coming!

Our whole future is in the air. It is by air power that we are going to recapture the German empire. To accomplish this we will do three things. First we will teach gliding as a sport to all our young men. Then we will build up a fleet of commercial planes, each easily converted to military operations. Finally we will create the skeleton of a military air force. When the time comes, we will put all three together—and the German empire will be reborn. We must win through the air.

Hermann Goering talking to Eddie Rickenbacker, 1922.

At the end of WWI, the U.S had sat comfortably in the shelter of the Monroe Doctrine that appeared to insulate the Americas from foreign, i.e., non-U.S. intervention. Growing European interest in creating airlines in Latin America attracted little American attention. Besides, it seemed too early for the U.S. government to engage in intergovernmental negotiations regarding air traffic; there just wasn't enough of it and an airplane capable of carrying pay loads had not yet been invented.

Thus few specific regulations existed regarding U.S. carriers in Latin America. The State Department had "tolerated" private individuals and governments making their own deals with Latin American governments, in competition with each other and with freebooters of other nationalities.

In this lax and permissive atmosphere, Juan Trippe, with rich social, political, and financial connections, who initially ran a mail route between the Florida Keys and Havana, dreamed of extending his airline, Pan American Airways (Pan Am), throughout Latin America. Toward this end Pan Am developed what Bender and Altschul termed "a special relationship" with the U.S. State Department, the Department of Commerce, and the U.S. Postal Service—all run by Juan Trippe's Yale friends and business associates. In any conflict of interests, these men consistently favored Pan Am's hegemony over either indigenous Latin American airlines, airlines owned by Europeans, or other US airlines seeking Latin American routes.

Shrewdly Trippe acquired concessions through the purchase of national companies like Compania Mexicana. He dispatched agents like John MacGregor—a veteran negotiator and Trippe's choice later as co-vice president of Pan American Grace Airways—to dispel any injured nationalist feelings and to lock up operating rights and contracts to carry mail back from foreign countries to the United States—all before the bids in the U.S. Postal Service for Latin American mail routes were opened. In this manner Trippe extended his airline all the way down the east coast of South America.[110]

By 1927-8, the War Department was obsessed with the potential threat to national security posed by the airplanes of foreign nations cruising over the Panama Canal Zone.[111]

---

[110] Because of its secret and devious methods, Pan Am was hated and distrusted throughout Latin America. "As a consequence", note Bender and Altschul, "the Latin American airways were secured in political ambiguity and confusion as to whether the Yankee imperialist or the good neighbor was approaching from the skies."

[111] Already a year earlier (1926) Congress had passed the Air Commerce Act that "provided that foreign aircraft, even of non military character, had to have permission from the State Department to fly through the airspaces of the United States, including that of the Canal Zone, and then only if reciprocal

Pressures were mounting for the American government to intervene by assisting in the development of air service by U.S. carriers to Latin America.

The Kelly Act of 1925 had provided for the U. S. Congress to allocate funds for the U.S. Post Office's subsidy for U.S. based airlines. The Foreign Mail Act of 1928 subsidized foreign air transport expansion by American carriers and, as Harold Harris wrote, "made possible the systematic planning of air routes to Latin America."

Stirred into action, the U.S. Post Office Department, run by another of Trippe's friends, let it be known that it was ready to award mail routes—and their corresponding rich subsidies— to any U.S. airline that could fly Central American and South American routes.

In November, 1927, President Coolidge (1923-29) had appointed an inter-departmental committee of subcabinet officers to assist in the development of commercial aviation to Central and South America. The chairman was Francis White, Assistant Secretary of State, Yale '13, and, along with a number of committee members, a good college friend of Juan Trippe. White, convinced by Trippe's persistent emphasis on the danger of "certain German interests" in the region, promoted his friend's proposals for an American airline extending from the U.S. to both coasts of South America.

Trippe simply re-issued a plan he had proposed to his board of directors a month previous: Two routes to Latin America, one from Havana to the west coast of South America via Mexico, Central America, and the Canal Zone; the other from Key West to Havana, Trinidad and Venezuela, where it might connect with SCADTA, the Colombo-German Air Transport Society,

---

privileges were accorded American planes would it be granted."
Bender and Altschul, 141.

(Sociedad Colombo Alemana de Transporte Aereos), at some point secretly purchased by Pan Am.

During the following Hoover administration, thanks to continuing U.S. governmental concern about the takeover by Europeans of Latin American air routes, the U.S. decided to subsidize the expansion in Latin America according to these previously proposed routes of a single all-American airline.

NYRBA Commodore

The award of course fell to Pan Am. As result SCADTA was barred from operating flights to the US and the Panama Canal, although it continued to maintain a broad route network in the Andes region.

NYRBA (New York Rio Buenos Aires) was a bidder for the east coast route. Incorporated in March 1929 under the leadership of Ralph O'Neill, NYRBA purchased four flying boats and had them in Rio, ready to initiate a service on the East Coast of South America. By that time, however, predictably, Pan Am had tied up the U.S. mail concession.

O'Neill's bitter book, *A Dream of Eagles*, gives an early taste of the desolation wreaked on American entrepreneurs by Trippe's growing sway over US government policy regarding US air carriers abroad and their potential competition. Unfortunately, O'Neill's insistent revelations in his book regarding NYRBA's pilot failures and lack of overall planning lead me to conclude that perhaps in this case replacement by Pan Am may have saved some lives![112]

Harris had intended that Panagra's route down the west coast should extend across the Andes, across the Argentinean pampas and into Buenos Aires. "This fit well," notes Krusen "with Trippe's ambitions. With the acquisition of NYRBA's east coast routes and with the purchase, in 1928, of SCADTA, the Austrian-run Colombian air-line, at the same time, Trippe could now tie his Pan Am routes to those of Panagra at both Panama and Buenos Aires. This was especially important in securing air mail concessions because the route down the west coast and across the Andes was two days shorter in flying time than was the east coast route."

Pan Am had been favored by the U.S. government over competitors in South America such as NYRBA, Aereo Boliviano (LAB), and SCADTA, along with a number of small startup airlines by France and Italy. LAB in Bolivia and SCADTA in Colombia survived Pan Am's onslaught because the Germans who had either organized them or provided them with airplanes had wisely made them national airlines.

Before Juan Trippe's Pan American Airways started its apparently inexorable march through Latin America, an earlier Pan American Airways, Inc. was founded in 1927 by a group of U.S. Army Air Force officers concerned with the growing presence of German aviation activities in Latin America. The purpose of that airline was, as Krusen points out, "to beat them

---

[112] Ralph A. O'Neill. *A Dream of Eagles*. Boston: Houghton Mifflin Company, 1973.

to the commercial markets."[113] The officers were primarily concerned with the activities of SCADTA.

Although the first Pan American Airways did not survive, replaced by Trippe's line down the east coast of South America, there is good reason to think that one of the prime motivators leading to early acceptance of Harris's dream of an airline down the west coast may have been U.S. government realization—exacerbated by Trippe's propaganda of a German takeover of airlines and airline routes in Central America and the Caribbean—that a forward-thinking German air arm was quietly installing itself throughout South America. In this climate of U.S. suspicion and fear of potential damage to the nation's hegemony, the establishment on South America's west coast of Pan American Grace Airways (Panagra) was accomplished with a minimum of fuss, seemed, indeed, almost inevitable. Complicating the situation was the fact that by the 1920's all nations claimed exclusive rights to their airspace, and "jealously guarded their rights to internal traffic from outsiders. Some Latin American countries willingly extended such privileges, known as *cabotage*, to foreigners in the absence of native companies able to perform the services, but many withdrew them as soon as national airlines were organized."[114]

Germany had been forbidden by the Versailles Treaty from developing aircraft for military purposes, but nothing had been mentioned in the treaty about commercial aircraft. During WW I, Germany, along with most other western nations except the U.S., had mapped out extensive airline programs particularly for other continents.

The Germans, noted William Burden, "found South America an unusually favorable field, for added to its natural potentialities

---

[113] Krusen, 13.
[114] Bender and Altschul.

for air transportation it was free of French and British domination . . .

> Though appearing somewhat haphazard on the surface, the German air transport projects in South America give evidence of having followed a carefully worked-out plan. Between 1920 and 1929 the Germans sponsored several local operations as national lines of their respective countries—a type of organization that they had been forced to use in Europe because of postwar restrictions. This method of organization had certain advantages in that nationally incorporated companies were regarded sympathetically by local governments which granted concessions to them more freely than to foreign-incorporated lines. The German-sponsored companies were not national in the true sense. Resident Germans occasionally contributed funds, and there was little if any genuine Latin American capital involved.[115]

Burden wrote that whereas the early German airline incursion into South America was initially commercial, "In 1926 . . . the Reich took over German commercial air transportation through

---

[115] Burden,11. "When the Second World War broke out," wrote Harris, "the axis powers had established air transport systems for this hemisphere which threatened out security. Considerations of national defense then demanded that the airways of the western world should not be operated on policy dictated by Berlin or Rome. Mr. William A. M. Burden was appointed a special consultant in aviation to the Coordinator of Inter-American Affairs. He wrote a confidential report for the Coordinator, which in 1943 he used as a basis for his book published by the Council on Foreign Relations in New York called *The Struggle for Airways in Latin America.* [In this book] the valuable conclusions reached by Mr. Burden helped the government of the United States to take a firm and successful hand in the various maneuvers that were required in order to eliminate the German and Italian attempts at controlling commercial air activity of Latin America."

the government-owned Deutsche Lufthansa, and it was not long before the propaganda element came to the foreground in all German airline activities. By 1932 Germany was making thorough plans for the domination of South American air transportation." In that year, he continued,

> W. Bley, a leading German writer on aviation, advanced the idea in his history of Deutsche Lufthansa that any single European nation would be too weak to oppose single-handed the United States and the British air policies in South America, and that the only solution was a Pan-European air transport combination under German leadership. Other German writers on the subject frankly admitted that German commercial aviation was being used as a weapon in the struggle for *Lebensraum* and a means of strengthening the ties uniting the *Auslanddeutsche* in South America to the Reich.[116]

Harold Harris, who had over the many years participated actively through diplomacy and skillful dealing in the push by the American government to eliminate foreign air competition in South America, wrote: "Between 1920 and 1939, German and Italian air interests were strong with their governments' backing and acquired control of 10,000 miles of air routes in Latin America, and in addition, established two airlines linking South America with Europe. This development had obvious political and strategic possibilities and caused the United States to watch with increasing concern, particularly after 1934."[117]

Although the danger to the Canal and to the U.S. hegemony over all of Latin America had been well publicized and utilized

---

[116] William Burden, *The Struggle for Airways in Latin America*. New York, The Council on Foreign Relations, 1943.

[117] Bender and Altschul's chapter "Imperial Diplomacy" provides a good summary of Trippe's moves to alert the government to the German threat and in so doing, promote U.S. backing of Pan Am's preeminent claim to Latin America.

for their own purposes by Trippe, his friends in Government, and his business associates, the danger was real.

SCADTA, (the modern Avianca) the first commercial airline in the western hemisphere and one of the first airlines in the world, operating from 1919 until World War II, was established in Colombia in 1920 by a private Austro-German group "with no support from the German government yet with German pilots."[118] It was based in Colombia within 100 miles of the Panama Canal.

Panagra pilot Captain A. W. Dubois in "Memories of Panagra" calls SCADTA "the spearhead of the German airline penetration into South America."[119] This designation William Burden would have challenged, pointing out that despite allegations that SCADTA represented the initial threat by German-led airlines to US hegemony, it did not come under the suzerainty of Lufthansa, as a creation of the Third Reich, as did LAB and Kondor.[120]

---

[118] Burden, 11. Burden points out that the line was successful because it connected Bogota, Bolivia's isolated mountain capital, with the seaport of Barranquilla.

[119] Indeed, by 1925-6 SCADTA's expansionist dreams included extending the line through the Caribbean and Central America.

[120] Burden, 24. See also A. W. DuBois, "Panagra—The Beginning", 14, in Captain Paul Willey, Memories of Panagra, Pan American-Grace Airways. Blurb.com. See Burden, Chapter 3.

SCADTA Junkers Ju-55 floatplane on the Magdalena River

Initially a small airmail carrier in Colombia, SCADTA was run by Austrian Peter Paul von Bauer, its principal share holder, and utilized German WW I pilots flying Junkers hydro-planes capable of landing in Colombia's Magdalena River. The product of German businessmen, it utilized along with Colombian capital, war surplus airplanes and personnel from the WW I Luftwaffe. By the end of 1920 SCADTA had an exclusive airmail contract with the Colombian government. The contract, which lasted eleven years, included the right to print and sell their own SCADTA airmail stamps.

"Everywhere Harold Harris and C.E. Woolman turned, in Peru, Ecuador and Bolivia," said Bender and Altschul, "there was SCADTA vying for the same concession . . . In South America, von Bauer seemed to be hatching a scheme for a continental system. He was causing mischief in Peru, trying to get Harold Harris' concession annulled, and [presumably to encourage competition with the new airline]," he was negotiating with other Americans"...[121] It was SCADTA's aggressive expansion throughout South and Central America during the 1920s that led to the Foreign Air Mail Act of 1928.[122]

Harold Harris, noted an article in *the American Aviation Historical Journal*, "had been influential in obtaining flight concessions as early as February 1929 from the Ecuadorian government in order to compete against that German enterprise which had begun survey flights along the Colombian-Pacific coast in 1927 and regular service to Guayaquil from Ecuadorean cities on 30 July 1928. Perhaps to hide its German connections SCADTA was known in Ecuador and later, inspired by famous German pilot Herbert Boy, flying Junker F-13 seaplanes, in Bolivia as Bolivariano de Transportes Aereos. The hard bargaining government in Quito did achieve some important stipulations in its negotiations with Harris including restrictions in carrying munitions, photographic gear, passengers not certified by the Ecuadorean government, no outgoing mail without government postage, and certain routes were disallowed.

> Nonetheless, Harris gained sizable concessions from the
> government although they could be considered standard

---

[121] Bender and Altschul, 142,144. This concession originated November 28, 1928, when on the strength of the Peruvian government's association with Harris personally and commercially, the Huff Daland concession was turned over to Harold Harris' Peruvian Airways Corporation (PAC). One is left to wonder which "other Americans". Could this mean Pan Am?

[122] The history of SCADTA deserves a book of its own. Pan Am secretly owned a major part of the airline, which it had acquired with help from the U. S. Secretary of State during the early days of the Depression. This ownership led to Pan Am ownership of 65% of AVIANCA formed from SCADTA when it was nationalized by the Colombian government of President Dr. Alfonso Lopez in 1934. (It has been said that Von Bauer secretly sold his shares to the United States in an attempt to protect acquisition of the airline by the Nazi Government.)

contract provisions including the right to fix charges to establish postal and ticket facilities, freedom from non-duty port charges, radio and telegraph privileges, free use of government transportation as well as freedom to purchase the rent lands. The contract would be in force for twenty years. Previously Woolman had failed to obtain this agreement but Harris, with persistence and spurred on by the threat of SCADTA and German interests in the country was successful.[123]

There is no doubt that the formation of Panagra, able to fly to more locations and more swiftly, in 1928 eroded SCADTA's position in the market. In 1941, following the Japanese attack on Pearl Harbor, SCADTA was forced to cease operations and its assets were merged by the Colombian government into the state owned airline SACO, forming the modern Colombian national carrier: Avianca.

SCADTA was just the beginning. A report by Panagra to the Civil Aeronautics Board, Panagra's *Confidential Report to the Civil Aeronautics Board reference Elimination of Axis Airlines in South America during World War I, 1943*, revealed that Nazi-controlled airlines (under the overall Lufthansa umbrella) were operating in Peru, Ecuador, Bolivia and between Chile and the Argentine.[124]

Alerted to the threat, Harold Harris, (until 1942 when he left Panagra for military service), became a vital actor in what the *Confidential Report* described as "colorful chapters in this country's fight against fifth column activities."

He promoted negotiations and operations aimed at eliminating all of the German airlines along with airlines operated by France and Italy. Traveling the line, he reported back to

---

[123] "Pan American Grace Airways: Silver Ships of the Andes", *the American Aviation Historical Society Journal*, LIV, Spring, 2009.

[124] See Appendix.

Panagra's New York base efforts and suggestions regarding cooperation with leading political figures, the condition of German-operated airfields, as well as recommendations for improving and enlarging the line.

In various trip reports and letters to the New York office, Harris revealed the breadth of vision and prescience that helped Panagra wake up both the American and Bolivian governments to the importance of the Nazi threat.

There is not a complete record of Harris' many achievements in dealing with various foreign airlines in South America. Some of his Trip Series (reports to the home office) do exist, however, many involving dealings with and about the Bolivian-German airline, LAB, during the crucial period of 1938-1941. These reveal not only the breadth of his knowledge regarding practical matters, such as the need to replace airfields and to build up communications, but also his astuteness in dealing with local politicians. Profiting from his SCADTA experience, Harris knew that the only way to beat the Germans was for Panagra to provide better and faster service over most of the territory covered by its rivals. This was his goal and—with the help of many others—his ultimate achievement.

Bolivia, land-locked, has no coastline and in the past has been a very isolated region. The development of its commerce and trade depends to a large extent upon connections with the outside world through air transportation. In 1925 Guillermo Kyll founded Lloyd Aereo Boliviano S.A., (LAB) South America's second commercial airline. The airline's first airplane, a Junkers F-13, came as a present from the German community in Bolivia. It was set up as a national airline, but with the Bolivian government holding only a minority share of the stock. Furthermore, the operations were largely carried out by German personnel.[125] The line was a creature of Lufthansa, with "a substantial part of the stock held by Germans.[126]

LAB's initial fleet of Junkers F.13 aircraft in 1925

Wrote Burden, "LAB was, like SEDTA, [The Sociedad Ecuadoriana de Transportes Aéreos] used to further German propaganda. The pilots and other officials of the line were active agitators for the Nazi cause. Propaganda leaflets, motion pictures, illustrated booklets and other material were repeatedly flown by LAB to its main base in Bolivia and from there distributed throughout the country. LAB had active connections with the German legation in Bolivia and attempted to develop good-will by offering cut rates and giving free service to Bolivian officials. The company was much more firmly entrenched than SEDTA because of the great interest which many native Bolivians or Bolivians of German extraction

---

[125] *Confidential Report* to the CAB: "The company was, . . . entirely German controlled. The planes flown were German Junker planes, the pilots were either German pilots or Bolivian pilots many of whom were sympathetic to the German cause, and the executive management was German controlled and German dominated."

[126] Boughten, 100.

had in the company's activities through their ownership of its shares."[127]

LAB first flew internationally in July 1930, with planes used by the Brazilian airline. During 1932, as a good will gesture, LAB loaned its planes and personnel to the Bolivian government, to help during the Chaco War (Guerra Del Chaco) with Paraguay.[128]

LAB focused on flying routes away from the coasts and into the interior. In these villages and towns "the latent industrial wealth of Bolivia and the northern agricultural resources of Argentina... [made] a lucrative reward for the first venturers. German interests planned an enlargement of their services into this interior.[129] Bolivian business interests quickly utilized the opportunities offered by the new airline. As the *Report* noted, "The effect of the LAB operation has been in no manner better demonstrated than by the nature of the cargo carried by air into the region north of the altiplano since the operation commenced. This cargo has included such things as salt, flour, sugar, toilets, wash basins, rice, potatoes, anvils, slices, cement, carbonated water, cloth and hats."

The company operated its main route from La Paz (Bolivia) to Corumba (Brazil) and made connections between Corumba and the east coast of South America through arrangements with Condor, another Lufthansa operation, which was very active in Brazil.

Panagra began operating in Bolivia in 1935, at that time establishing an operation from Arica (Chile) to La Paz (Bolivia). From the *Confidential Report* we learn that "it was necessary to obtain permission from the Bolivian government to operate in and out of La Paz and a Panagra representative was sent

---

[127] *Confidential Report.*
[128] Ibid.
[129] Op. cit.

to Bolivia to make the necessary arrangements."[130] Panagra's official report never singled out individuals. However, since he had a long history of successful dealings with governments in the region, this individual must have been Harold Harris.

As LAB continued to expand, Harris called the attention of the State Department to the LAB operation and concomitantly to Panagra's own need to expand.[131] Harris' Trip Series 32 emphasized the gains to be had from Panagra's expansion and increased contacts with the rich Bolivian interior.

Harris Trip series #32, no date [italics mine]

I hope that... you [the new Panagra president Harold Roig] and Mr. Patchin [Grace Company Vice President] have had a satisfactory meeting with the Post Office and CAA officials in Washington on the question of securing an additional service between Cristobal [Canal Zone] and Guayaquil [Ecuador] or Lima. I hope you have been able to get this authorized as one additional service all the way through to Buenos Aires by way of the Diagonal, and must confess that I can see no reason why they should not do this on the basis you suggest of giving us this third service at a rate subject to an adjustment to be advised when our rate hearing is held.

If we do not get a third trip by way of the Diagonal and if Dr. Guzman Tellez [the Bolivian government official who acted as a sort of liaison between Panagra and his government] can work out with those concerned *the question of Panagra's taking some interest in the Lloyd Aereo Bolivian picture*, it might well be that this additional Diagonal service could operate La Paz, Oruro, Cochabamba, Yacuiba, (all in Bolivia), and Salta in Argentina, instead of duplicating our present operating

---

[130] Ibid.

[131] Op. cit.

between Oruro and Salta via Uyuni. *Such an alternate for
the Diagonal would tap a rich part of Bolivia, which we now
contact only indirectly."* [Italics mine.]

In 1937 the Diagonal, thanks to a mail contract granted by
the U.S. Interdepartmental Committee on Aviation, became
a reality. The development of this famous route—through
Bolivia and northern Argentina to Buenos Aires, with stops at
La Paz, Oruro, and Uyuni, (all in Bolivia); Jujuy, Salta, Tucuman,
and Cordoba, (all in Argentina), in large part a response to the
challenge created by the French and German interests in the
interior regions, had been strongly promoted by Harold Harris.

Once the Diagonal was operating, as the *Confidential Report*
points out, there was "Strong opposition from LAB but there
was little the company could do at the time to effectively
check Panagra. Through the good auspices of the W. R. Grace
Company officials in Bolivia, it was possible to convince the
Bolivian government that it stood to make tremendous gains
by having a direct air connection with the [West] Coast and
Argentina."[132]

Recalled to Panagra's main office in New York City in 1939,
Harold Harris moved his family to Scarsdale, N.Y. He continued
to travel ceaselessly, monitoring the airline's operations.
These travels resulted in a series of running reports (Trip
Series) to Roig at the New York office during the intense
period 1939-41 when Panagra and the U.S. Government were
primarily concerned with the effect of developments in Europe
on the operations of Bolivian-based LAB and other Lufthansa
operations. In that period Pan Am and Panagra fought to
eliminate all foreign airlines, particularly those involved in
Lufthansa, the Nazi umbrella.

---

[132] *Confidential Report.*

#10 Trip Series (August 25, 1939)

Harris, impatient, lamented the delays to his proposed expansion of Panagra to combat this threat.

> It is indeed most unfortunate that our entire expansion program upon which we commenced intensive work as a result of the request of the Civil Aeronautics Authority has now bogged down, apparently because of their inability to find ways and means of pushing it. As a result of my trip to date, and I have been over the entire line, I am more than ever convinced that the most important single thing that can be done to solidify the American general business position in South America is to increase the American air service to all points. At every point where I stopped, not only our own people, but American businessmen and important local Nationals have told me the same thing. The remarks have been without regard or reference to the more immediate problems from our own standpoint of promptly increasing American air service in order to combat the European competition which is every day increasing in both paralleling and shortcutting of American air service.

Conversely, in a letter to Mr. Roig dated September 1, 1939, Harris predicted the potential benefit to Panagra from the Nazi-led war in Europe. This benefit would be due to the imminent failure of all European airlines in South America cut off by the war from their European suppliers. He itemized how each foreign airline operating in South America would suffer and ultimately fail because of lack of fresh personnel and equipment from Europe.

> It is now apparent that the European war cannot be avoided. It may easily develop that not only the Lufthansa but also the Air France services from Europe to South America and those services in South America may and probably will be suspended for a considerable period.

Studying the various points where such services parallel our service, we find first, Ecuador, where the Sedta subsidiary of Lufthansa is operating.

My guess is that this operation will be continued as a local company as long as they have either of their aircraft in flying condition as long as there is any war in Europe since the planes cannot be returned to Germany while war is on and presumably the one or two pilots required would be spared from the German air force if local pilots could not be utilized. My guess is that this service could not be continued for more than six or nine months in view of the necessity of replacing parts and materials for the equipment which presumably would not be available.

Also regarding LAB he noted that "While I was in Bolivia last week I was informed that the Lloyd Aereo Boliviano planes are so old and in such unsatisfactory condition that the two Peruvian licensed Lufthansa planes are used all the way from Lima to Corumba. It would therefore seem that it is only a question of a short time when the LaPaz/Corumba operation will have to suspend, since presumably the only important cash income which would be available to Lufthansa would be for the services between La Paz, Arequipa, and Lima, and this service should be able to continue for a good many months without difficulty, provided that pilots and German ground personnel are not recalled to military duty. Any increase in their service in this area in time of European war is unlikely."

Fortunately for Panagra, LAB's experiencing "several spectacular accidents due to the poor condition of landing fields and inadequate communications" made a bad impression on the South American governments involved with its operations.[133] By contrast Panagra's assumption of the expense associated with the development of and/or improvement of landing fields and radio control towers made a crucial

---

[133] Burden, 75.

difference in the attitude of the host governments as well as in the line's ability to penetrate further into the hinterlands.[134]

Increasingly, the Bolivian government, concerned and disgruntled by LAB's performance, turned to Panagra. Even so, Harris trod on shaky ground when discussing any extension to the Diagonal. He noted that Guzman Tellez had warned Panagra (Trip Series #38) not to get involved in any Bolivian government-LAB dispute. To avoid it, Tellez had suggested a second Diagonal service within Bolivia, "from Oruro to Sucre, and Sucre to Yacuiba, then Yacuiba to Salta." This route, avoiding Cochabamba, a provincial capital, would not antagonize LAB.

In a letter to Mr. Roig September 13, 1939, Harris recounted the exchange at a luncheon arranged by Grace agents for Colonel Britto, general aide to the President of Bolivia and Panagra's good friend. Discussion focused on the Bolivian Government's plan to improve the LAB airports and communications by expropriating LAB-owned property

---

[134] Harris Trip series #49, Oct. 6, 1939 described the condition of LAB landing fields, fields that Panagra ultimately took over and renovated. "With regard to the LAB Oruro Airport, Nelson made a close study of this situation from the air, and finds it very satisfactory as far as it goes. The one runway is apparently 5,500 feet long, and can be extended for another 200 meters without difficulty. The airport is on high ground and the low hills in the vicinity do not obstruct the takeoff or landing. According to Nelson, the runway is probably cross wind, but he says that a cross runway can also be constructed without an interference for either approach or takeoff from surrounding obstructions. I hope that Brookshire will be able to get up to Oruro soon, but it looks now as if his work in Quito will take longer than was anticipated. I doubt very much whether LAB will respond for any further expenditure on the Oruro airport. Since we really should have an all season airport in Oruro, I suspect we will be stuck for this expense, too, however, there is no reason in the world for our La Paz agency not attempting to get LAB to share in the cost. "

in LaPaz. A proposal arose that LAB and Panagra, working together, develop this property into a proper landing field.

"At this luncheon," wrote Harold Harris,

> Colonel Brito also mentioned the fact that the Government was considering the necessity of reorganizing LAB in view of its bad accident record, its unsatisfactory economic condition, and the impossibility of replacing or repairing its current German equipment from Germany. He stated that what the Lloyd Aero Boliviano needed was a better organization and a couple of American aircraft, preferably DC-2's. Late in the conversation he indicated to me privately that he felt that perhaps some of the Lloyd Aero Boliviano operations could well be turned over to Panagra. I told him that Panagra would be interested in any proposition that the Government or Lloyd Aero Boliviano cared to make to us, that, of course, the bringing into the picture of Panagra would depend entirely upon the actual propositions, which would have to be passed upon by our directors.

> It might well be that it would suit us to take some interest in the Lloyd Aero Boliviano picture, either directly or indirectly presumably upon Dr Guzman Tellez's return to Bolivia [when] this situation may develop to the point where some actual propositions may be presented to us, through him.[135]

---

[135] In regard to Panagra's struggle against LAB, in <u>Trip series #11,</u> August 25, 1939, Harris recounted the loss to Panagra of Colonel Britto a key Bolivian employee. "Our Personal situation in Bolivia is acute, since immediately upon the death of President Busch, Colonel Britto was recalled to active duty by the Army and I now understand from Dr. Guzman Tellez that he is in command of the Presidential Guard at the Palace. Guzman Tellez does not believe that Britto will again be available for our work for a long period of time. This is a most disturbing loss just at the time that we were ready to develop services of this trained man along many lines."

Two years were to pass before the dialogue between Britto and Harris bore fruit.[136]

In 1940 the State Department requested that Panagra look into the matter and see what could be done to supplant LAB with an American flag line. Noted Harris, "I was sent as an officer of Panagra to Bolivia to eliminate any German activity in Lloyd Aero Boliviano. I spent from the end of October 1940 to December 6th at the headquarters of LAB in Cochabamba, making sure that the LAB activity from there on would be only such as made sense to the general picture of eliminating the enemies of the Western powers."[137]

The *Confidential Report* confirms that "Early in January, 1941, a Panagra representative while in Bolivia, made an extensive investigation of certain files relating to LAB." [It is not known whether this person was Harold Harris. It is worthwhile noting, however, that Panagra's actions reflected and were undoubtedly based on his concerns.]

These files the Panagra representative obtained, thanks to the assistance of W. R. Grace Co. Information gleaned from them essentially spelled out the end of LAB's hold over Bolivian air space. They disclosed, for example, that during the war between Bolivia and Paraguay [the Chaco War, 1932-35] the Bolivian government had, in effect, taken over LAB because of its military importance. During this period the operation of the line was financed through advances from the Bolivian government, and it was understood that at the end of the war a settlement would be made between the government of Bolivia and LAB, *at which time the Bolivian government would obtain an interest in LAB which was proportionate to the amount of money it advanced.* [Italics mine.]

---

[136] Boughten, 100.
[137] This is one of the very few references Harris made in his memoir to his involvement with Panagra's dealings with LAB and the Bolivian government.

After the war had ended, the report noted, the Bolivian government had appointed a commission to work out a settlement. The commission reported in favor of an arrangement that would give the government a 64% interest in LAB. "This arrangement, of course, placed the Germans in the minority. Accordingly, they immediately took steps to counteract the government's move. They refused to accept the report and arranged that the matter should be arbitrated before the La Paz Chamber of Commerce."

But the arbitration panel was tainted. The La Paz Chamber of Commerce was definitely pro-Nazi. Indeed, the entire arbitration was "engineered by the Germans in an underhanded effort to counteract the move on the part of the government of Bolivia. "The award," the *Report* continued,

> of the arbitration panel gave the Bolivian government a 48% interest and the German group a 52% interest. It was further shown that the Germans had protected their position by giving the government its 48% in Class B shares, which had no voting power, and in giving the Germans their 52% interest in Class A shares, which held the sole voting rights. As a result, the German group remained thoroughly entrenched in LAB's management from 1937 to 1941. *The Bolivian government did not challenge the arbitration award.* "[Italics mine.]

In view of this circumstance, Panagra's unnamed representative "disclosed the above facts to high officials in the government of Bolivia and urged that the government take immediate steps to set aside the arbitration award. On May 14, 1941 he was successful."

That same day Bolivia issued a decree stating that the arbitration award had been illegal. The government acquired all the shares that had been issued to non-government shareholders. Giving the government some leeway, the decree said that further study was needed before the controversy's final resolution. However, it did set up a three-man commission, pro-American and anti-Nazi, to reorganize LAB.

For some years LAB had been receiving a monthly subsidy from the Bolivian government, essential to its continued existence. When, not to be outmaneuvered, the Germans called a stockholders' meeting with the aim of enforcing the status quo, Government representatives appeared and announced that the Government would discontinue its monthly subsidy in the event there was any effort on the part of the LAB stockholders "to obstruct the execution of the decree or to have it set aside."

In view of the fact that this long time subsidy was essential to LAB's continuance, the German resistance folded. They "were forced to recognize that they must accede to the decree in order to keep the line in operation."

The Bolivian government, aware for some years of the extent of LAB's shoddy performance or the threat to its own sovereignty, decided to throw its full support behind Panagra. Panagra was asked by the Bolivian and United States Governments "to reorganize LAB's company and its operations and to undertake management of the company for five years". On May 24th another decree by the Bolivian Government authorized Panagra to operate twice a week between La Paz and Corumba with Panagra operating one trip to Corumba immediately. An additional trip "stopping at more intermediate points" would begin upon renovation of the airport and landing facilities throughout the former LAB routes."

This decree was of great significance since it eliminated LAB's exclusive rights to operate between these points in Bolivia. Panagra started its first trip from La Paz to Corumba early in June, after survey flights in May which revealed "grave inadequacies in existing airports and other facilities."

Wisely, Panagra did not advocate for the immediate replacement by Panagra of LAB's routes and service. Instead protection was offered the "bona fide" Bolivian stockowners with the understanding that for its services Panagra would be reimbursed in the form of stock and stock options, in other words, would own a substantial portion of LAB.[138]

Under that arrangement," noted Boughten,

> the United States provided Lloyd Aero Boliviano with some fresh capital (long term, low interest loans) and the Bolivian government agreed to pay them operating subsidies. Panagra then moved in and re-equipped the line with American equipment (Lockheed Lodestar planes) and proceeded to entirely revamp the base at Cochabamba, improve the airports and passenger facilities over the route, and entirely reorganize the operation and procedures and personnel. However certain Bolivian pilots who had served on the old Lloyd Aero Boliviano line were retained and others are being trained today. Top key men (technical and commercial managers) and many of the pilots are Americans but otherwise the business is carried on by Bolivians.[139]

Harris made sure that "One of the new services undertaken was between Lima and Oruro and was flown by Panagra voluntarily without mail pay, from June 3,1941 to August 26, 1941." No claim," wryly observes the *Confidential Report*, "is being made for payment on this mileage."[140]

---

138 Ibid.
139 Boughten, 100. See also Burden, pp. 74-5: "The complete removal of German influence from all air transport operations on the west coast of South America reached its final stage in May 1941 when the Bolivian government proceeded by decree to nationalize Lloyd Aero Boliviano... LAB's service had been very unsatisfactory and the company had experienced several spectacular accidents in recent years.
140 Panagra's Confidential Report

LAB reorganization required a great deal of maneuvering by both Washington and LaPaz. Loans were made and money transferred, enough to replenish the LAB fleet subject, however, to the condition that LAB would enter into a management agreement with Panagra. As a preliminary to the final execution of a management contract, all Germans in the LAB organization were paid off, their contracts canceled or allowed to expire, and all German influence thus eliminated.

"On July 31,1941, six further steps were taken to complete the elimination of German influence in LAB."[141] These included important details regarding the distribution of stock shares, new bylaws under which the Bolivian government was assured control of the chairmanship and a majority of the Board of Directors of LAB, the redistribution of routes to be flown, allocation and increase of postal revenues, and, perhaps most important, the creation of a management contract that effectively shut LAB employees out of the management of the line.

Naturally, these arrangements met serious opposition. Among other things, the Germans, appealing to their local Bolivian shareholders, generated a good deal of controversy through their efforts to take their complaints to the courts. When all else failed, in July 1941, they decided to generate a revolution, hoping to gain the support of the Bolivian Army.

Observes the *Confidential Report,* "While full details of the plot are not known, it was unsuccessful and some LAB pilots and the LAB manager were jailed the next day. It is known that Ernst Wendler, German Minister to Bolivia, had for some time worked in close cooperation with Major Ellas Belmonte, a pro-Nazi official who served as Bolivian Military Attaché in Berlin. A letter written by Belmonte from Berlin to Wendler disclosed that a revolution was planned for July. When this

---

[141] Details of the six contracts are included in the complete Confidential Report in the Appendix.

letter was made available to the Bolivian government, a
Cabinet meeting was held and Wendler, the German Minister
to Bolivia, was expelled. The letter indicated very clearly that
the revolutionists had planned to make use of LAB to bring
about the revolution. It was apparent from the text of the letter
that revolutionary activities were to centre at Cochabamba,
where the main office of the airline was located, and that
the planes would be used to further the purposes of the
revolution. The letter, which was later released to the public
read as follows:

Legation of Bolivia in Germany
Berlin, June 9, 1941.
His Excellency
Dr. Ernest Wendler, Minister of Germany
La Paz

Dear Friend:

I have the pleasure to acknowledge receipt of your
interesting letter in which you inform me of the activities
of yourself and your personnel in the Legation and our
Bolivian civil and military friends, which are being carried
out in my country with such success.

I am advised by friends in the 'Wilhelmstrasse' that
according to information received from you the moment is
approaching to strike our blow to liberate my poor country
from a government that is weak and with completely
capitalistic inclinations. I go still further and think that
the action should be fixed to take place about the middle
of July as I consider that the most favorable time. And I
repeat that the time is propitious as from your reports to
the Ministry of Foreign Relations in Berlin I am pleased
to note that all of the Consuls and friends of the whole
Republic of Bolivia, and especially our most friendly
centers such as Cochabamba, Santa Cruz and the Beni

Province have prepared the way and have organized our forces with ability and energy.

There is no doubt we shall have to concentrate our forces in Cochabamba as preferred attention has always been given to this point. I have learned from friends of mine that the meetings are continuing without any interference from the authorities and that the drills by night are continuing. Furthermore I see that a good quantity of bicycles have been accumulated which will facilitate our night movements as autos and trucks arc too noisy. I therefore think that during the coming weeks the activities should be carried out with much more care than before in order to dispel all suspicion. The meetings should not be held and all instructions should be given from person to person in place of giving them at meetings. Of course, the iniquitous transfer of the L. A. B. to the Yankee imperialism is an inconvenience as I had in mind taking over control of this organization immediately upon my arrival at the Brazilian border, but this I will solve with my friends here as I will make my flight accompanied by another plane which will follow me all the way. We have received the detailed maps showing the most favorable sites for landing. These show me once again that you and your staff are making excellent preparation for the realization of our plans for the welfare of Bolivia. I have taken particular note of what you write me with reference to the younger element of the Army. I have always counted on them and they are no doubt the ones who will best cooperate with me in the great work which we will carry out to fulfillment in my country. As I have already said, it is necessary that we move rapidly as the moment is opportune. We must undo the tungsten contract with the United States and cancel or at least substantially modify the tin contracts with England and the United States. The handing over of our airlines to Wall Street interests is treason to the country. As concerns the Standard Oil, which is working actively for an 'honorable' solution in order to 'reestablish

Bolivian credit', it is criminal. Since my brief affiliation with the Ministry of Government I have been fighting this.

What eagerness to deliver the country to the United States under the pretext of financial aid which will never come! The United States will follow its old policy of obtaining great advantages in exchange for small loans, which we would not even be allowed to have a voice in. Bolivia does not need American loans. With the victory of Germany, Bolivia will need work and discipline. We must copy, even though only modestly, the great example of Germany since National Socialism assumed power.

The 'famous' treaty of Ostria with Brazil is truly a crime. Once we are in control of the situation, this will be one of the first things we will change. The government with the aid of my good friend Foyanini did whatever was possible to prevent the execution of this treaty. It is clear that the famous 'give-away' Chancellor, Ostria, is completely influenced by capitalism and if it were up to him we would already be an American colony.

I await your final word in order to leave from here by plane to start the work which will first save Bolivia and later the whole South American continent from North American influence. Soon other nations will follow our example and only then, with one purpose, with one ideal, and with one supreme leader will we save the future of South America and start a new era of purification, order and work.

(signed) Elias Belmonte P.'[142]

---

[142] The *Confidential Report* continues. "It was to the developments indicated by this letter that President Roosevelt referred in his historic speech of September 11, 1941, when he discussed several outstanding examples of Axis penetration in South America."

As a result of the exposure of the Nazi plot to win a revolution with the use of bicycles (!) all the Bolivian airline schedules were ceded to Panagra. The fight was over.

Once Panagra took over actual management of LAB's operations, both the operation of express service in Panagra's name between Oruro and Corumba and supervision of the remaining LAB local Bolivian services, it was confronted with the enormity of the task of re-organization of an airline that had operated under what Harris had always considered absolutely primitive conditions. The setup was extremely chaotic. To Harris' dismay, it was discovered that LAB had only four radio stations operating on its main line. Most of the stops had no facilities "of any sort except a marginal airport, which were unusable in rainy weather." (*Confidential Report*). LAB had operated "without any semblance of orderly control and far below American standards of safety and efficient service. No flight maps, details of airports, radio, meteorological facilities or fuel supplies were available. The tariff structure of LAB had to be revised, Bolivian pilots replaced or retrained."

As early as 1934 Harold Harris had urged that Panagra take steps to nullify the danger of the expansion of German airlines in South America. He had worked diplomatically toward this end. By 1941 thanks to World War II, the exposure of a Nazi plot, and the undoubted superiority of services provided Bolivia and surrounding nations by Pan Am/Panagra, LAB's iron grip on Bolivian transport was eliminated. It had been achieved without armies or revolutions, simply—as Harris had noted—through the development of effective communications, improved or new landing sites and passenger facilities, reliable scheduling based on meteorological improvements making for better weather forecasting, and with faster turnaround times and overall faster and more frequent service.

In all this great drama Harris was indefatigable. In truth the ultimate triumph of Panagra over its opposition was due in no small part to Harris's relentless push to fulfill his dream.

Chapter 23: "An Airplane and [Ocean] Liner Race Against Death"

Shortly after Harold Harris' death, I discovered among his papers a collection of his father's letters written in 1932-3 from Los Angeles to his much loved and admired son in Lima. Also included was correspondence from Harold's sisters, June and Jessica, who in 1933 cared for the dying widower. In the depths of the Depression, these years were the last of Ross Allen's life. Increasingly desperate in tone, they revealed a lonely Ross Allen confronted with sickness, old age, and—his medical practice sadly reduced—penury.[143]

Reading these letters, I realized that regardless of his condition, to almost the end Ross Allen admired the ladies, invested in property he couldn't afford, dreamed of regaining his youthful vigor and, in a rush of optimism, asserted the possibility of actually selling his writings to pay off his debts.

Wise to his father's spendthrift ways, Harold balked at any plans involving a large investment on his part, although he did send money for immediate needs, e.g., back taxes, to his sisters to pay for the care required for the dying man.

March 9, 1933. Jessica wrote "Father is very ill and I thought yesterday that he would surely die... Of course there is no money to speak of, and no cash so I have been using my money (what there is of it!) Mrs. Marshall hasn't drawn her salary for weeks and Mrs. Clark is due $5.00. Father told me that in a recent letter you had sent him $700 for his taxes. Thank you, Harold, I'm grateful to you. Arthur [her husband] and I couldn't help him out there as Arthur is now supporting his folks and has had so many salary cuts that we have to go carefully. The banks being closed of course complicates matters. We'll

---

[143] See Appendix A for details of Ross' letters to Harold.

manage some way until they open again. I am going to stay here two weeks or longer if absolutely necessary . . .

"Mrs. Clark is going today and I will take her place house-keeping . . . Will write later. Please write to Father. He asks every day about you."

Harold continued to send checks. June replied—"Jessica and I fell on your three airmail letters yesterday. They were swell Harold and we think you're one good guy! The checks are highly appreciated also. Your $50 to me was a big surprise and thank you a lot but I have enuff money to get home all right."

June stated that she deposited all monies in a separate account in order to pay off bills, including the mortgage.

She said that the sisters did not believe Harold should come to Los Angeles, but at the same time she wanted to know his plans, since the sisters could delay the funeral." It is the indefiniteness of the whole matter that is troublesome . . ."

March 27, 1933. An unsigned cablegram to Harold: "Consultation of specialist think brain tumor possibly live month or more come if wish but unnecessary."

April 18, 1933: The Los Angeles Times: "L.A. Man Loses an Airplane and Liner Race against Death. Wings of a speeding South American airplane and the wave-cutting new Grace liner, Santa Elena, today had failed in a race with death in which Major Harold R. Harris of Lima, Peru, sought to reach this city before his 70 year-old father Dr. Ross Allen Harris of 623 Bonnie Brae Avenue, died. Dr, Harris died yesterday afternoon.

"Major Harris, his wife and two children, arrived last night on the liner. Major Harris, a native of Los Angeles, was a World

War ace in France and now is vice president of Pan American Airways.[144]

In later years Harold's younger sister, Jessica, confided that Ross Allen's fatal illness was perhaps due to Valley Fever, a sometimes deadly fungus infection that he may have caught from inhaling the spores of nasal and lung secretions of patients from one of the several petri dishes Ross used to collect and store in the family ice box. Since he died long before the invention of the MRI machine, we are left as were his physicians with no concrete diagnosis.

(From a letter to Harold Ross Harris, from Jessica, April 21, 1980).

"I am also sending you all the copies of Father's poems that I have. Perhaps you already have them? Poor father, he was always soul searching and trying to fortify his own beliefs. At the time of his last illness he had me read the Psalms over and over to him, knowing that he was dying and needing to hear the beautiful words of the bible to boost his morale. In many ways he was a great man but like all of us he had his flaws. I would say that mother probably had one hell of a life with him."

---

[144] So much for truth in the media! Harold Ross was to my knowledge never in active combat in France or anywhere else and was certainly not an "ace" (implying a fighter pilot.) He piloted so-called "heavy bombers" and was the first pilot to fly one of these across the Alps. Although much later he was a vice-president of Pan American Airways, at the time of his father's death in 1933 he was a vice-president of Pan American Grace Airways. As far as I know, until much later, there was no president of Panagra.

Chapter 24: Not all Mountain Flying Was Fun and Games: The Search for the San Jose

Investigators examine the remains of the "San Jose", washed down from the high Andes

In the mid-1980's Harold Harris, involved in writing a history of Panagra, wished to have further documentation on the one fatal Panagra crash in the Andes with which he was directly connected. Besides directing the search, he and two other pilots had actively participated.

He (and I) traveled to Birmingham, Alabama, for the purpose of interviewing Mary Alice Beatty, widow of Donald Beatty, a former Panagra pilot, who had been one of the three pilots who had searched for the lost plane. Once we were there, lodged in her comfortable home, Mary Alice and Harold Harris became immediate fast friends. She and her husband, both from wealthy families, had flown throughout Central America during the period of the late 1920's and 30's when newlyweds Charles Lindbergh and Anne Morrow Lindbergh, (sponsored by Juan Trippe with a view toward promoting his infant airline), popularized flying in Latin America. Inspired by their example, Donald and Mary Alice essayed the same sort of Central American junket. Subsequently, not satisfied with that taste of adventure, Beatty enlisted as a pilot with Panagra and the couple moved to Lima, Peru. Don Beatty had joined Panagra as a lark, deeming it to provide a path to adventure. He was hardly prepared, however, for the true adventure posed by the challenge to the fragile Panagra aircraft of the time by 20,000 foot high uncharted peaks with their attendant violent up and down drafts, the whole enshrouded by unpredictable weather.

The year was 1932. Harold Harris had hired Donald Beatty because of the latter's unique capabilities as both pilot and radio operator. This last was vital if he was to participate in a search for a lost Panagra aircraft and still maintain contact with Lima. Beatty's account years later of the search that he, Harris, and Tom Jardine conducted over the Andes for the *San Jose* poignantly reflected the perils of this Panagra route.[145]

The Andes, lying along the western coast of South America, form the world's longest continental mountain range, and except for the Himalayas are the highest in the world. The

---

[145] In going through the HRH archives at Dayton's Wright State University recently, I discovered the reports of their vain searches for the lost craft by Harold Harris, Captains Donald Beatty and Tom Jardine. I include the reports of the two latter because they emphasize different aspects. Beatty's account, written many years later, provides a graphic picture of the terrible risks involved in flying—without additional oxygen and with little communication with the ground—a small, lightweight plane amidst unpredictable weather at heights far above the estimated capacity of the craft amidst the violent up and down air currents perpetually sweeping the enormous mountains. Jardine's account reveals the thoroughness of the search.

range is over 4,300 miles long with an average height of about 13,000 ft. Split into two great ranges, named the Cordillera Oriental and the Cordillera Occidental, it extends over seven countries: Argentina, Bolivia, Chile, Colombia, Ecuador, Peru, and Venezuela. The highest peak, Aconcagua, rises to 22,841 ft above sea level. This is what Harold Harris' airline using planes initially completely unsuited to high altitude flying proposed to tackle on a routine basis.[146]

Ensuring continuous unbroken airmail service across these forbidding mountains frequently demanded makeshift adjustments by pilots initially anyway lacking adequate weather information or ground contact. Under these conditions their skills and nerve were tested again and again, occasionally with disastrous results.

The Uspallata Pass or Bermejo Pass, the shortest pass providing a direct route between Santiago, Chile, and Buenos Aires, Argentina, although weather-prone, was the one favored by early Panagra aircraft. Reaching a maximum altitude of about 12,500 ft, the pass runs between the peaks of the 22,841 ft Aconcagua to the north and the 21,555 ft Tupungato to the south. Today a monument, Christ the Redeemer of the Andes ("Cristo Redentor de los Andes") is located at the Chilean entrance to the pass.

---

[146] Krusen, 7, writes, "Rising in the fjords of southern Chile and climbing immediately to towering heights near Santiago, the Andes continued north all the way into the fringes of southern Panama. At the modern junctions of Bolivia and Argentina and Bolivia and Peru, the massive mountains divided, as a stream divides to flow around an island, and that island was the altiplano or high plain. The flow of mountains merged again in central Peru and continued northward as three parallel ranges into and through Colombia, where the ranges fanned out, like the fingers of a hand, before running to the ocean. The towering mountains utterly dominated western South America; you could never avoid their climatic effects, and only rarely were they not visible. "

Because of Uspallata's uncertain weather, on his initial investigatory flight to determine the best route for Panagra aircraft, Harris had chosen a more northern pass between Antofagasta, Chile, and Salta, Argentina. He noted:

> The only special equipment we [he and MacGregor] took were a few bottles of soda water and some sandwiches. The plane had no oxygen although the maximum altitude on the flight was probably 18,000 feet. This was the first flight ever made over this route—and it turned out to be quite a problem. As I climbed above the clouds after take off from Antofagasta, bubbles began to form in the compass liquid and the compass-card spun as each bubble hit it. No compass! In those days no radio, no direction finder, and no aviation maps. So I estimated my progress by time and sun direction. Gingerly, I let down through the clouds on what I hoped was the east slope of the Andes. I was lucky—it was, but I was far south of my goal so, following the railroad line, headed north to Salta.[147]

"When claims are made," Beatty wrote in his memoir of the search,

> that flights over the Andes and particularly 'flying the hump,' as the highest point of the Uspallata Pass is called, are 'the toughest flights in aviation', one visualizes the fog-covered Alleghenies, the blizzard-swept passes of the Sierra Nevadas, the Rockies and the Cascade Mountains. Uspallata Pass with its highest point at the Cumbre near the famous Christ of the Andes statue is the granddaddy of them all! Like a funnel at both ends the Pass narrows in places to a jagged granite-walled gorge less than 300 feet

---

[147] October 5, 1929, Krusen noted, "the first air mail destined for Buenos Aires left New York. There was a problem: the Santiago-Buenos Aires leg of the trip was over Uspallata Pass where the aircraft had to fly at altitude of at least 14,000 feet. It was all the Fairchilds could do to get themselves and their mail over the Pass. Passengers were too heavy. It would have to be for the time being a mail only route. "

wide! It has everything known in the weather line—ice, snow, storms lasting for weeks, thin air, cold air, fog, rain, and clouds, plus a terrific turbulence. While the Uspallata Pass provides a shorter route between Chile's capital city Santiago and the great wine center and port of entry into Argentina at Mendoza, it is considerably higher and a lot more rugged than the other somewhat easier pass, Paso du Maipa, some one hundred miles to the south. The latter was completely devoid of habitation even in its lowest approaches and consequently Uspallata was used at all times except when emergency conditions prevailed.

Despite the risks, passengers were eventually added to the perilous mix. Wrote Harris, "Panagra had to install its own radio stations, an act that made the governments of the nations it was flying over very suspicious. At first the only radio ground station was in Panama… On August 13, 1931, Panagra's passenger route opened from Lima down to Santiago, using radio-equipped Ford Tri-Motors. By the middle of October Panagra had passenger service, and even an express freight service established down to Chile. Passengers were flying across the mountains and even into the Argentine, using Fords without radios to save weight."

Beatty noted that "Every pound counted in the Uspallata Pass. The Andes, a massive wall of rock jutting four miles above sea level had been an impenetrable barrier arresting the political, social, and economic development between Chile and Argentina. Uspallata Pass was one of several notches in the wall. But because it was not a deep notch, the air at the summit of the pass was too thin to breathe comfortably, and early aircraft did not have pressurized cabins. Stewards circulated portable oxygen bottles to ease the passengers' discomfort at the higher altitudes."

The *San Jose*, a Panagra trimotor Ford, was lost July 16, 1932 in the Uspallata Pass. Since it simply disappeared mysteriously, it was assumed by Panagra that all passengers and crew, a total of 15 persons, were dead.

For emotional, political and legal reasons, it was essential that the status of the airliner, its crew and its passengers be verified as quickly as possible. As Donald Beatty observed in his search log, "Argentine law required that persons missing as a result of a catastrophe could not be declared legally dead nor could their estates be settled until after a period of twenty years from the date of such a tragedy. Bank accounts and other assets of those aboard the San Jose were thus frozen by law, which placed great hardship on some of the families of those missing. Salaries of flight crews were continuing and the company provided funds to financially—distressed families of those listed on the passenger manifest. Locating the lost plane and establishing the status of those aboard was thus a paramount objective."

The Search for the San Jose

"Panagra's first fatal accident and the report of Capt. Donald C. Beatty on his special search flights, 1932-33.

"This was Panagra's only fatal accident in the Uspallata Pass in the 38 years of operations on this route. As soon as jet-powered airplanes were available this trans-Andean crossing was scheduled at an altitude higher than the highest of the mountains."

Beatty continued:

> Why the search flights? The missing *San Jose*, a trimotored Ford airliner with 15 persons aboard, had flown into oblivion during a regular scheduled trans-Andean flight on July 16, 1932. It had taken off from Santiago without incident. Destination was Montevideo, Uruguay, with an intermediate stop at Buenos Aires. The route from the capital of Chile to the Argentina port of entry at Mendoza was via the famed Uspallata Pass through the highest ranges of the Andes Mountains. A few miles to the south of the

pass is Cerro Tupungato which rises in a jagged snow-clad cone almost 23,000 feet above the sea. Rough ranges of over 20,000 feet connect Tupungato with the famed monarch of the Andes—Mount Aconcagua, spotlessly white, sharply cut against an azure sky and towering almost 24,000 feet above the sea. A somewhat narrow 'V' in the ranges between the two giant peaks is 'La Cumbre' the summit of the high point of the Pass. Width of the bottom of the "V" is approximately 250 feet—both sides rise steeply to the crest of the jagged ranges at the 20,000 foot-plus level. The gorge on the Chilean side of the Cumbre is almost vertical—terrain drops down abruptly for several thousand feet from the Cumbre while it is somewhat less on the Argentine side.

The Uspallata Pass with Mount Aconcagua in the distance

The veteran pilot of the ill-fated flight was Captain Robinson, who had great experience in the trans-Andean operations and was in fact Manager of that Division. He was a thoroughly seasoned airman and had frequently captained similar trans-Andean flights.

The prevailing weather condition in the mountain pass was unknown to Captain Robinson at the time of his takeoff from Santiago. The important meteorological station had not yet been installed near the statue of Christus of the Andes at the Cumbre. His visual observation from Los Cerrilos [a village at the entrance to the Pass] indicated satisfactory weather conditions in the 'hills.'

The only other source of essential weather information was an occasional telephone contact over a substandard circuit with someone living in a small village in the rugged pass on the Chilean side of the Cumbre. When such a contact was made, the person at the other end of the line usually turned out to be someone without knowledge of weather conditions or other helpful information. It so happened in this case—Captain Robinson was unable to make such a contact.

The apparent flyable weather in the 'hills' began to rapidly deteriorate as the flight entered the Pass. Atmospherics in the high mountain are anything but stable—change with the rapidity of an electric light bulb responding to the flip of a switch. Shortly after Captain Robinson entered the Pass, he radioed to Santiago that a sudden and extremely heavy snowstorm had been encountered and which appeared to be rapidly increasing in intensity as the flight neared the Cumbre. Shortly afterwards he advised that both sides of the vertically-walled canyon Pass had disappeared from view, that both of his outboard engines and the nose of the plane were almost entirely obscured by the swirling mass of driving snow. A moment later a further report said that the storm had forced him to abandon his attempt to cross into Argentina and that he was returning to Santiago. Captain Robinson's final report stated that the return route to the west and safety was also blocked by the storm—that he was 'on instruments' and thought his position was on the Argentine side of La Cumbre. There was no further report.

Panagra management had originally planned for the search plane to be crewed by but one person—an experienced 'instrument' pilot familiar with flying in unmapped areas but who also was expert in radio telegraphy. I fulfilled the requirement. The search plane? . . . a model 71 Fairchild monoplane, arranged similarly to a Navy-type aircraft, and its wings could be folded back over the fuselage. Power plant? A single Pratt Whitney Wasp engine arranged for high altitude flight. Equipped with a 'tooth-pick' or flat-pitch propeller, the installation permitted high RPM with an instant application of power, an absolute essential for low-level flight among the rugged peaks and glaciers of the high Andes. Instruments for 'blind-flying'? . . . turn and bank, rate of climb and an air speed indicator, the basic minimum requirement. A sensitive altimeter and compass were also installed—period! Communications? . . . a radio telegraph key would be attached to a leg clamp that would fit just above the knee of the pilot!

It took but one flight over the proposed search area to convince me that the plan to use a single crew member for the search plane just simply would not work. I found that the ever-present clear air turbulence during low level flight in the mountains was terrific. I needed one of my hands on the 'stick' one on the throttle, (the engine would over-rev from sudden tail-wind type turbulence), one to hang on with, and one to make 'the sign of the cross' while negotiating at low level most of the canyons, glaciers, and peaks of those TALL hills!

Instrument flying was essential, even in perfectly clear air. Looking down into treeless canyons of the mountains, the eye is inclined to make the slope of the hills the horizon line. Lakes in the bottom of some of the canyons appear to be definitely 'slanting' whether they are ice-covered or not. The down drafts often accompanying clear air turbulence seem to cause the mountainside to seem to rise up before you. There was no sudden jar but a sensation as in a rapidly descending elevator. Sometimes in less than 20 or 25 seconds the altimeter would show that the aircraft had dropped 4,000 to 5,000 feet in that time . . . again, even with throttle closed, a similar turbulence would cause the aircraft to gain that much altitude in a like period of time.

Since the objective of the search flights was to locate a downed aircraft and not to endanger a second, two additional experts were added to the search crew—a flight radio operator and a professional photographer/observer. Thousands of photo-graphs of areas that appeared likely to hold remnants of the lost San Jose were subsequently made during the many months of the search. These were projected onto a large theater-type screen back at the Santiago headquarters and scrutinized thoroughly for any sign of the wreckage.

It would be difficult to record, in chronological order, the many details of the many 120-odd search flights I piloted. I suppose that the best manner of describing the usual flight would be in the form of a composite. Clear air turbulence was ever present, the severe low temperatures over the glaciers and snow fields at high altitudes could always be depended upon. Last but far from least was the difficulty of just remaining alert to the requirements at hand—the low cabin temperatures—my wrist watch would frequently stop during flight—(its small amount of lubricant would more or less solidify and freeze its movements) and oxygen deficiency had a most telling effect upon alertness. Many times during search flights I've observed the outside air temperature gauge to register more than minus 60 degrees Fahrenheit—the indicating thermometer needle resting against the stop-pin and apparently almost bending to register an even lower temperature!

I began each search flight at dawn. The takeoff would always be without incident from the sod-covered Los

Cerrillos airfield, which served Santiago, Chile as an airport. I would hold the aircraft in a steep climbing attitude on a northeasterly heading toward Los Andes, a small town in the foothills at the Chilean entrance to the 140 mile-long Uspallata Pass through the mountains separating Chile and Argentina, the 'dividing line' or bench mark as the individual search flight was programmed to be conducted either to the north or south of that line.

The flight was a repetition of many I had undertaken over a period of more than seventeen months. Each time I believed, as did my radio-operator and the observer/cameraman, that on that particular occasion the wreckage of the lost airliner, *San Jose,* would be spotted. The search area was large, doubly so when the high altitude and the rough terrain of the area was taken into consideration. It covered more than 30,000 square miles of jagged, vertically-walled gorges, peaks and dry river canyons, glaciers and snow fields of the highest ranges of the Andes mountains. On a horizontal scale the area stretched for over 200 miles north and south and somewhat less east and west. A large portion of it had never been explored even from the air nor had human eyes previously viewed it.

It may be asked, 'Why did the search flight always begin at dawn?' The reason was a practical one. From my first such flight I soon detected a pattern, which indicated, among other things that clear air turbulence over the Andes was at a minimum at dawn. The increasing sun heat with advancing daylight hours appeared to be a major catalyst which added greatly to the severe air invection eddies. The high velocity westerly winds usually encountered at the upper altitudes during daylight hours were minimal during the early pre-dawn period. As the day progressed, so did the Westerly winds, which, upon encountering the high Andes, were deflected upward in irregular columns of tumbling turbulent forces. The persistent high altitude clear air turbulence resulting from such conditions happens to be the most universal characteristic of the high Andes together with the perpetual glaciers, jagged, granite peaks, and instantaneous snow storms which sometimes do last for weeks! Trans-Andean flights were scheduled insofar as far as possible toward early morning hours as an aid towards safety in the flight and to the comfort of the passengers and crew of the scheduled airline trans-Andean operation.

No search flight could, by any stretch of the imagination, be characterized as a 'joy ride'. Emergency situations were always injected. Extremely severe clear air turbulence, CAT, was always there and on several occasions rolled the aircraft I was flying over on its back. On at least three occasions the lead weight at the end of the trailing radio antenna (about 63 feet long) was dragged off by contact with the earth—glacier or mountain top—resulting from encountering a severe but invisible down-draft which forced the aircraft within feet of the earth. Once or twice the trailing antenna was wrapped around the fuselage of the aircraft as it rolled over—it remained there until the landing back at Los Cerrillos airfield!"

Tom Jardine's Search Log

Tom Jardine, a veteran Panagra pilot, in 1981 sent the following log entries back to Harold Harris for use in the latter's book on Panagra—as yet unpublished and excerpted by Alta Mae Stevens in this book. In his log Jardine notes that Harris, too, was searching. The San Jose crash was, after all, the very first Andes crash of the infant airline. The fact that it attracted a lot of publicity was reason enough to exert all efforts to locate it and collect whatever could be recovered from the site.

July 17, 1932—(P-18) Lima/Arica; Night flight leaving Lima 12:15 A.M. Mr. Harris, Robbitale, special trip to Santiago to search for San Jose.—carried mail #114 (15:00) Lima/Santiago.

7/18/32—Santiago/Mendozsa—1 hour searching in east pass of Christo.

Note: Since we left Lima on 7/17, I would assume that the accident occurred on the A.M. of the 16th.

7/18 Searched all the pass from Christ to Uspallata, all peaks, valleys, pampas, etc. at altitudes 21,000 feet down to bottom of pass. East slopes of range, Mt. Jual to Mt. Plato—south slope of Cdr. de Tigre and foot hills into Mendoza. (4:30 flight P-18)

7/19 covered all the pass, dove down all the canyons to search pampa secos, etc. covered all peaks for 20—miles south of pass, around Aconcagua, north slope of Tigre Range and all valleys high peaks and Pampas of the Tigre—all peaks south (3:15) P-18.

78/19 Special search to Mt. Tupengato and country NE-SE. This search at request of Governor of Mendoza who was a search passenger. Searched Uspallata south. (I-30)

7/19 Mendoza/Santiago—from Christ, Mt. Plomo, Las Leones (I;50)

7/20 Attempted search N-NE and east Andes including Rio Artiga Arrayon, San Francisco, Yerba, Loco Monzano, Del Afo, Mt. Pasquero—SW El Plomo, Pt Cartachera, Bismarck, Los Andes to Ro Olivares thoroughly.

7/21 E. Patrerillos and all tributaries of Rio Olivares as far as Rio Colorado and 10 miles east of Rio Colorado. Returned darkness. P-6 Fairchild.

7/20 P-16 attempted search 0:40

7/22 P-16 Thoroughly searched slopes of Altar, Bismarck. This location suggested by Don Bate.

7/23—P-6. Mts close in. searched foothills south for 100 miles, snow all canyons.

7/23 P-9 Santa Mariana Night flight to look for San Jose fire signals, south of Maipo Pass and returned at alt. 21,000 feet to Mt. Plata. Ran out of oxygen at alt. HRH wrote note. Wish I had kept it.

7/25—p.6, searched East slope—attempted crossing to Santiago.

7/26—p.6 (3:20) Mendoza/Santiago, Mr. Harris searched thoroughly south side of pass, east of Christ on west slope Rio Blanco, Rio Rieullos, NW side of peaks and Los Leones Mts.

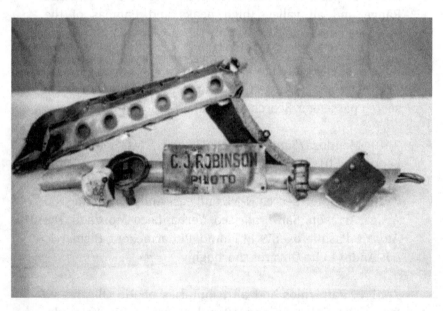

Part of the wreckage from the ill-fated "San Jose", including the nameplate of the pilot

Beatty noted that "Many other search flights for the *San Jose* with other pilots and planes were made, all without success. The wreck was finally located two years later, as reported by the then Panagra Manager for Chile, Argentine and Uruguay, Mr. John T. Shannon, a former Naval pilot also recruited by HRH [Harold Harris]. Shannon observed that 'Bobby [Robinson] in the trimotor Ford *San Jose* was lost on July 16, 1932. We had to assume at the time that he had crashed in the vicinity of the Christo [the statue of Christ of the Andes] and that is where the remains were discovered about two years later. Herders found the baggage piecemeal and word finally got to us that the police had questioned them and found that they were working on the baggage from the wreck."

Harold Harris noted that portions of the plane's wreckage, washed downstream in the spring glacier meltoff, were also discovered. Included in this discovery was a gold wedding ring belonging to a passenger whose widow, wanting to finalize her husband' s business affairs, was finally successful in having him declared legally dead.

From John Shannon's log: "In the summer of 1932-33, [probably as a result of the *San Jose* crash] Panagra established the first weather station at La Cumbre, alongside of the statue of El Christo. At first it had a telegraph connection to the Santiago office. Then later radio was installed so that it could communicate with both Santiago and Mendoza and the aircraft."

Chapter 25: Communications

Radiotelegraph lines in the Uspallata Pass, Chile. Statue of Christ of the Andes in left background

The Uspallata Pass tragedy highlighted the critical inadequacy of what theretofore had been the only source of weather communication in the area: a lonely shepherd. Amid much laughter, Chilean Purser Noel Chaytor told the story of this shepherd/ weather forecaster at a gathering of former Panagra pilots I attended with Harold Harris, a story that was repeated by Bill Krusen's *Flying the Andes*.

> Chaytor described his early morning calls to the airfield outside of Santiago: There was no operating manager at the airport, just a hangar mechanic named Stiles, whom I called Shoto.
>
> 'I'd get up at three,' Chaytor continued, 'and I'd pick up the passengers to whom I had sold tickets the day before. But before doing this, I'd call up the airport to find out what

the weather was like. I'd say, 'Shoto, what do I do?' Do I wake the passengers or not? 'And he'd say 'Wait a minute,' and I'd hear him shouting, 'Gerardo!' Sometimes Gerardo would say 'No, no. Don't wake them up. Let them sleep at least another hour.' I'd call the captain and tell him that Gerardo at the airport says the fog is so thick that the birds are walking.

In an hour I'd call again, and Shoto would call again, and Shoto would call, 'Gerardo, *que pasa?*' And I'd hear him say, *Dos estan libre.* [Two are free.] Call the passengers.' I was new, but I said to myself, this Gerardo, he must be high up. He was the man of the last word. He was the man who dispatched the airplanes and I had never met him.

Chaytor, Krusen notes, was in for a surprise. 'I went out to the hangar early one morning and ran into Stiles. There were some sheep grazing on the runway—in fact it was the best fairway in Chile—and I said, 'Hey, Shoto, I didn't know we had sheep.' He said, 'That's why it's cut so nicely. And that's Gerardo over there. You know, 'the fellow you used to call.'

Well, Gerardo was a small man with a big hat and no shoes on his feet. He was the shepherd. 'How does he have such an influence on all this?' I asked Stiles. 'Oh,' he says, 'when it gets rainy or is going to rain, the sheep move towards the hangars. They always move towards the buildings. Gerardo counts his sheep. He has three hundred, you see, and if none is missing, this Ford's [airplane] not moving. When they start moving out, he calculates how many move per hour or per minutes and that's how he knows what the weather's going to be like.'[148]

While Harris was Chief Test pilot at McCook Field in Dayton, Ohio, he and Donald Bruner were instrumental in creating

---

[148] Krusen, 52-3.

lighted airways that helped solve the problems of pilots navigating at night. However, for commercial purposes, the possibility of night flights alone would not be enough. "The lighted course," noted Komons, "was merely an extension of contact flying. It was, in short, a fair weather technique."[149]

In 1926, he observed, "a pilot was fed information concerning weather, wind velocity, the position of other aircraft and other pertinent details just prior to takeoff. This information was accurate enough insofar as it reflected conditions on the ground at departure time. But if weather conditions changed while the pilot was en route, the ground organization was powerless to warn him of the fact. Thus, instead of avoiding a newly developing storm area, he would unknowingly head into it. Conversely, a pilot encountering unexpected conditions could not pass on this information, which would have been of interest to other pilots, to the ground organization.[150]

To ensure reliable air transport that could compete fairly with trains, steamships, or buses, Harris noted that "it was essential that there existed" dependable communication between pilot and the ground". Further, if "commercial airlines were to operate successfully, they would have to assure customers of an economically viable air transport system that flew *by day as well as by night on a regular schedule.*"

Initially, the radio stations inherited by the Aeronautics Branch from the U.S. Air Mail service were capable of only point-to-point transmission via radio telegraph. Radio navigation did not exist from ground to pilot. Nor did voice communication. When the plane carried a radio operator, pilot and radio operator could not communicate with each other. Weather forecasts were given the pilot just before departure, with no possibility of predicting how or when the weather over the proposed route would change.

---

[149] Komons, 147.
[150] Ibid, 148.

The same year, 1926, encouraged by the Bureau of Standards, the Army flight branch developed improved radio devices. Within a year, both radiotelegraph and radiotelephone systems were operating, the latter allowing for two-way conversations up to distances of 50 miles.

"Science Comes to Air Transport" from "The Story of Air Transport" by Jim Ray, 1947

The Watres Air Mail Act of 1930, providing a premium for airmail contractors employing two-way radios encouraged the rapid proliferation of their use. Teletype circuits blossomed throughout the nation like mushrooms after a rain. The Weather Bureau cooperated, encouraged by the 1926 Air Commerce Act fostering the development of devices such as weather balloons to provide more accurate weather forecasting.

Harris recalled: "At the time that the aircraft and its operating devices were being developed, so was radio. Until air travel became feasible, the radio had been largely tailored to the requirements of ships at sea. Panagra, where the flying conditions varied greatly from the tropics to the frigid winters in the Chilean mountains, gave new dimensions to the radio requirement development being carried out by Pan American

Airways. Since the aircraft payload was severely limited, any radio device on board would have to be minimum in size and weight and dependent on a small antenna unless a trailing antenna was utilized. A good deal of work was carried out with a trailing antenna but eventually it was decided that the possibility of damage to ground property, if the operator neglected to properly reel in his antenna when near the ground, or the possibility of loss because of antenna breakage, made it evident that further developments were required.

No ground radio station existed at any of the airports, except at the Canal Zone. Consequently, it was necessary for Panagra to install, at its own expense, its radio stations secured from P.A.A. [Pan Am] at each landing point, and also other key points, for weather observations in the mountains or for radio direction-finding services.

"The various governments," Harris recalled, "were much concerned about having ground radio installations manned by foreigners in their countries. Fortunately, we were able to secure the necessary authorizations to install, at our expense, native radio operators for our constructions, utilizing equipment which we purchased for that use... Eventually all the multi-motored aircraft in the Panagra fleet were equipped with radio telegraph and remained so until the U.S. government insisted on transferring to voice telephone, rather than telegraph, during WW II."

"We first put in the radio telegraph", he noted in conversation with Mary Alice Beatty. "In the Fairchild airplanes; the pilot did the telegraphy work, too. It wasn't any problem for John Shannon because he was a Naval Academy graduate... We got this order and after he'd made one of these flights and found that flying an airplane fairly close to the ground and running a radio key at the same time was not the easiest thing in the world, [he complained.] He wrote me a note saying, 'Hey, why do I have to send this position report every fifteen minutes. It doesn't make any sense; I know where I am.'"

Years later Shannon noted, "I used to fly loads of lobsters over "the Hump"[the Uspallata Pass] alone in the FC2's because I was a half-baked radio operator from my Navy days and thus could carry more lobsters."[151]

Radio telegraph installation, said Harris:

> aboard aircraft required the utilization of competent radio operators as part of the crew in each multi-motored aircraft. Sporadic attempts were made to install radio telegraph in various single motored Panagra planes, but this was abandoned, since the average pilot was not competent in radio telegraph operation and the additional weight of a radio operator, with the single motored plane would be uneconomic.

> As soon as the ground station network had been accomplished, we employed competent meteorologists and furnished necessary theodolites, weather balloons and other necessary paraphernalia to establish good meteorological reporting points at various key spots throughout our routes. No such service then existed in any of the countries with which we were doing business, except the United States.

> This made a much more complete operational advantage for the management and the crew, since information of the weather conditions at the various destinations and en route was available prior to any flight and the pilot, while in flight could receive instructions and information as to changes of the weather in his path.

> After the installation of radio and meteorological stations by Panagra, almost no accidents occurred in its airline operation. Prior to such a valuable addition to our know—ledge, we had had a number of accidents, which presumably would have

---

[151] Thus allowing room for one more passenger.

been avoided had radio contact and meteorological data been available to and from the flight crew.

Weather problems were often severe on the run between Santiago, Chile, and Mendoza, Argentina through the Uspallata Pass. It was finally arranged through the Cable Company, whose cable ran through the Pass, to permit us to tap into that line at the highest point in the Pass. We put in our own building alongside the statue of El Christo with a radio operator, who would report on weather. He could look to the Chilean side and part way into the Argentine side of the Pass, with a reasonable chance to give a good report as to whether or not the flying conditions would permit the plane to pass. The first radio we installed at La Cumbre was Leuteritz telegraph—voice came later.

Since this area was snowed in, sometimes for weeks, and no one else was there, we arranged for a Chilean operator, who was married to a Chilean woman, who was also an operator, to pass the winter in this isolated location. We gave then plenty of provisions and other commodities, so they would not be too uncomfortable and wished them farewell. The wife, coming down to Santiago in the late Spring to have her child, had been pleased with the arrangement and she and her husband spent the next winter there. I hesitate to say how many children were the result of this situation.

Hugo Leuteritz, the radio engineer who developed all the radio installations for PAA [Pan Am] and Panagra, many years later provided Harris with a summary of his part in the development of communication between pilots and the ground.

The original equipment designed for R.C.A. as a result of a study I made beginning in 1926, of air operations and the future demand, called for 3 types. 1 for small aircraft—1 for Commercial service and the third for Dirigible service. The reasons being the weight factor. These were capable of operating on C.W. and voice. The equipment developed for Pan Am in the beginning was for Operator used only. The reasons being the time factor, International Radio laws and weight. Bear in mind, one of the worst factors was lack of electric power on the aircraft at that time. Another factor was the requirement of the antenna and a good electrical ground.

A further factor was the aircraft power plant ignition noise. Navigation was also of importance, and as a result of early work in this areas, with RCA and the Marine Service, new factors were required, both on the ground and on board the aircraft.

To meet all these requirements required an organization; the result was Pamsco, a group specialized for PAA [Pan Am] and Panagra requirements. Panagra planes were originally equipped in the early 1930's with operators transferred from the Panair [Pan Am] group. As early as 1932 Pamsco units were capable of both voice and C.W., however the pilots were not licensed to operate the radio, hence the operator.

The demand for radio was critical, beginning around 1935 due to the rapid growth of airline operations in the States and abroad. This resulted in new types of equipment considerably improved over the older types. The story of the long range direction finder is interesting and it was started in 1933 because of the need for ocean flights. Flight radio operators were not on Panagra planes in the early years but after a short time, by the year 1932, planes were equipped with continuous radio telegraph operated by the pilots," not always to the pilot's liking.

In any event, after it was decided to carry flight radio operators who could handle code work, it was found very useful to have such communications aboard the aircraft even though it meant we had to lose, in passenger or cargo capacity, the weight of the radio operator and his equipment.

Harris remembered: "Carroll S. Busby, after three years as a radio operator on U.S. Cargo Steamers, decided to go to airplanes and got a job with Panagra. After employment with Panagra, he and his wife traveled by steamer from New Orleans to Panama, Atlantic side. He wrote me as follows:"

> Out of France Field on Panagra, I think P-37, DC-3. One night in Guayaquil and Lima second day. Checked in with Bob Garrison, Supt Coms and Val LaPierre, Assist. Took a couple of weeks or more to get a uniform made and the information concerning equipment, kinds of messages to expect, and the names of the checkpoints. Towns and cities on route were "You'll find out, don't worry about it.

> The first couple of months were one big change from the normally smooth and quiet ship tankers to the DC-3's with the old Wright engines. At this time there were two flights a week north and south of Lima. All communications were radio-telegraph, air-ground, as well as point-to-point, ground-ground.

> Transmitter was PAMSCO, 10F3, two tubes, plug in coils— one for communications and one for direction finder, with a 1 tube "ARA" loop amplifier, manual loop antenna. We averaged a contact every seven minutes! 30 words per minute. Our PAG ground stations were mostly of this type.

> Transmitter operated from 12-volt storage battery (gasoline engine generator "Blue Diamond" for charging, and receiver from this battery plus 45-volt B batteries. A simple flat top antenna served for 24, 36, 52 (main air) 96 mtrs for communications and 1630 KC (183 mtrs) for Radio-beacon—DF use . . .

Harris noted that Panagra ultimately developed an airline network of 9,000 miles in eight countries "through which Pan American operated in South America" although "most of the installations on the ground were bought and paid for by Panagra."[152]

> These stations were not only available and useful for communications but also for navigational purposes which until Panagra's installations were non-existent in almost all of the areas involved.
>
> By 1935 Panagra planes had been equipped with manually operated direction-finding loops for navigational purposes and antenna systems for transmitting on direction finding frequencies which were installed at ground stations.
>
> By 1940 automatic direction-finding equipment, super-sensitive aircraft communication receivers, and transmitters capable of delivering better than 100 watts to the antenna provided radio telephone facilities on 16 different crystal controlled frequencies which were installed on Panagra planes. At the same time the ground radio stations had an increase in power so that by 1943 the modernization in ground radio facilities had been completed.
>
> Special equipment to withstand variations of climate and atmosphere had to be designed for use in many different places. Some located in jungles, some in desolate arid places and in the cold barren waste of the Andes.

---

[152] *Aero Digest,* (October, 1948). History of the development of Panagra's Communications Systems.

Chapter 26: Amphibians and Float Planes

Sikorsky S38 float plane

Because the French and German airlines had preempted most of the landing fields and because technicians considered that at that stage of development, water operation was safer, Pan Am initially used aircraft—both amphibians and float planes—that could make water landings in the east and north of South America.[153]

Bill Krusen noted that "Float planes which alight on pontoons hung from struts below the normal aircraft fuselage and/or wings, are now found only in such remote places as Alaska and the Canadian Northwest. But in the 1920's float planes were common. Today a float plane is an unusual sight and a true flying boat or amphibian is a rarity in the extreme.

"Amphibians or flying boats are so called because they can take off and land either on land or water. A flying boat's fuselage is boat-shaped on the bottom, and it takes off from (or alights directly onto) the water. If flying boats or amphibians can land

---

153   Burden, 33.

on water, they can move, either under their own power or with the aid of shore personnel, up a seaplane ramp onto dry land. Pan American used flying boats exclusively in its early years and pioneered the use of the giant Clippers across the Atlantic and Pacific Oceans."

He continued, "There was a practical reason to use amphibians for carrying passengers. If his engine failed, a mail carrier could usually put his Jenny down on the nearest dirt road, or in a cornfield if necessary. New passenger-carrying aircraft were larger and heavier and needed longer and smoother landing sites. From the earliest days of aviation, the sea, a lake, or a river could offer a reliably smooth landing site—on a good day."

"On March 2, 1929," recalled Harold Harris, "the U.S. Post Office Department signed a contract with Pan American Grace Airways and we [Panagra] were in U.S. government business. At that time we had no planes that could make the flight from the Canal Zone to Guayaquil (Ecuador) since there were no landing fields available on that route. We decided that the most desirable type of aircraft would be an amphibian. The only amphibians then which could fly the required distance with a payload were the Sikorsky S-38's. Production by the factory was already 100% committed to Pan American Airways. We were able to arrange with Pan American to use one of their S-38's and crew. When we were able to take delivery of our own S-38 from the factory, this arrangement was discontinued.[154] Because some of its landing sites were on the ocean or ocean inlets, Panagra was forced to fly a combination of amphibians and land-based planes.[155]

---

[154] For the purpose of making a survey of the line, Harris' memoir notes that Panagra at one point borrowed a Grumman amphibian on a Goodwill Tour of South America from Nelson Rockefeller.

[155] Following are fragments of a conversation I had with our Dad in Sept. 1980.

AMS: . . . some of the stops were just floats in the mouth of a river.

HRH: In Tumaco [Colombia] we had a float . . . that's halfway between Guayaquil and Buenaventura . . . . when we got the flying boats,

The airline used two types of amphibians: the S-38 and the S-43, both Sikorsky productions. Harold Harris noted that the S-43 was a lot less scary than the S-38, the earlier version in which Harold Jr. and I had traveled. When the S-38 took off, "the passenger cabin with its portholes was apparently underwater. It didn't happen so badly when you were landing as when you were taking off." This is what I wrote about the experience.

> It is dying in perfect safety,
> this churning of green water
> boiling up over the windows,
> as we, in a dry womb,
> a thin metal sack, press
> madly across the ocean's breast.
> We are consigned to death. On each takeoff
> resurrection comes
> as a complete surprise.

---

that's when we opened the section between Guayaquil and Panama.

AMS: You'd have to take a land plane to Guayaquil and a seaplane from there?

HRH: ... Yes ... When we first did it, it took two days ...

A Sikorsky S43 flying boat being serviced

"Panagra started with land-based planes" Harris said," because it serviced cities that were inland, located on torrential rivers. At first it was only the Talara, Peru, to Guayaquil, Ecuador, leg that connected the Peruvian and Ecuadorean operations. Later the route would extend to Panama and by the end of its life span, Panagra was flying far longer over-water distances.

"I purchased the first Fairchild with a 220 engine. I also bought a set of pontoons. A land plane would fly up to Talara from Lima. The load would be transferred to a pontoon-equipped plane [float plane] which would be flown over the ocean from Talara to Guayaquil.

The first flight of this combination had Captain Dinty Moore as pilot (he had been a U.S. Navy participant in the first trans-Atlantic crossing by the U.S. Navy with an N.C. flying boat in 1919.) The passenger list was completely filled on our first flight. The passengers were Shorty Hebard, head of the Foundation Company in South America, and with him his assistant, a Mr. Burke. The third passenger was Ellis Briggs, then a U.S. Vice Consul in Lima, and I was the fourth. I suppose the total weight of the passengers and the Captain must have been about 1200 pounds and we had a small amount of mail. The low horsepower for such a heavy load tested the skill of the pilot but he successfully took this small plane with its burden through the ocean swells at Talara and in the air. About half way to Guayaquil, the engine stopped—out of fuel! Captain Moore had forgotten to switch the gasoline feed from one tank to the other. We were, I suppose, about 2,000 feet over the water. A perfectly calm, beautiful day, no problem for landing on the water there, but Mr. Hebard had not had too much experience with forced landings of an airplane. The program needed no careful rehearsal. As soon as the engine stopped, this assistant, Mr. Burke, reached under his seat with one motion, pulled out a bottle of whiskey, and handed it to Hebard! Of course, Captain Moore had already switched over to the full tank and the engine started again as we were gliding down towards the water. We completed the trip without further ado, landing in the Guayas River at Guayaquil . . .

The tenor of my poem about taking off in a seaplane was perhaps overly optimistic. There were several severe crashes at sea of the seaplanes during Panagra's long history. One near crash involved Grace Harris and me. How close we had actually come to disaster I only discovered when, going through the Harold Harris archives at Wright State University, I unearthed that portion of Tom Jardine's log dealing with his rescue mission.

My account represents my memory of the reactions of a nine year-old girl who has been assured that all was well and that there was little to worry about. The parallel account, from Tom Jardine's log, shows how little I was aware of what actually went on and how close we were to serious trouble.

The year was 1937; Capt. Miller piloting a Panagra seaplane (Sikorsky S-43) took off from Lima bound for Panama.[156] My mother Grace and I were among its passengers. An engine failed. We were forced to land in the ocean just off the Peruvian coast. While the other passengers became increasingly disturbed, Capt. Miller circled and circled the plane, searching for a relatively tranquil stretch of ocean to set down the fragile craft. At cruising altitude the sea had looked glassy-calm; it was only when we powered down and began a slow descent that we saw the huge waves on its surface.

Inside the cabin, the passengers were really frightened. A few uttered prayers. A Peruvian lady had hysterics. Commenting much later on the incident, Harold Harris had added: "When the engine seized, the passengers were alarmed, and one of the local passengers from the mountains started to go out the rear door while the flight was still high in the air. He had a life jacket on, and the steward stopped him. It was perfectly understandable

---

[156] I include here HRH's description of Capt. Miller's flying tricks, none of which he appeared to try the day in question: "Another of Panagra's colorful pilots was Jack Miller. Jack had operated a flying circus for years before going with Panagra. He flew the trips according to his own whim and entertainment. The rest of the crew and the passengers went along for the ride. One trick that he never failed on was either northbound or southbound crossing the Equator, he hauled the thing up into a steep power off stall. After recovery, he'd call the purser up and have him take a note back to the passengers saying that they had just passed the Equator, congratulations! Another thing he liked to do was to make an extremely steep, sideslipping approach into the airports. The last thousand feet would consist of a side slip, power off, so steep that airplane's left wingtip was actually pointed vertically straight at the end of the field. At the last second he would recover in a huge, swooping slide out and usually plunk the airplane pretty close to the end of the field on three points and then rap the co-pilot on the leg and ask him how he liked that. tremendous updraft. He had the airplane almost standing on its nose . . . "

later, since the word for life jacket in Spanish is SALVAVIDA and the word for parachute is PARACUAIDA. The SALVAVIDA caught the man's eye and he put it on thinking he was going to make a parachute jump . . . probably 2000 feet in the air."

The author with her mother about to board a Panagra flight

(I continued) The plane had appeared so sturdy, yet suddenly its thin skin made it seem pitifully vulnerable. What would happen once we hit the water? Would we bounce off, and then begin a series of ricocheting leaps until the bottom tore out?

Seated next to Grace, my mother, I apparently broke the tension. With relish, Harold Harris repeated my words: "Momma, I'm hungry!' (I don't remember that part.) People relaxed into laughter; the plane glided smoothly down and settled swanlike on the waves. Like any well-managed vessel, it had landed into the wind. As soon as we landed, Capt. Miller gunned the engine and we began bumping our way through the waves dashing up over the portholes towards a nearby beach.

I think I can remember the purser getting out the landing craft that had lain, folded, in a rear compartment. As things turned out, this action proved to be unnecessary. With enormous patience and skill, Capt Miller taxied slowly through the high waves and, thanks to the wheels with which the craft was equipped, up onto the periphery of the beach. Once there he radioed back to Lima to send a land plane to rescue us.

This plane, that actually arrived on the scene before we got to the beach, was piloted by Tom Jardine, excerpts from whose original log regarding this rescue follow.

> April 5, 1937, p-20. 'San Antonio' Lima/Mongoncillo (2:15). Jack Miller in Sikorsky on northbound trip was forced down off the coast in the area South of Mt. Mongon about 50 miles south of Chimbote. As soon as I heard of this, we loaded up a Ford with life equipment, mechanics, etc. and headed for the area. Jack was drifting on one engine off the rocky coast but was having a hard time staying off the coast due to current and wind. His radio was out and we could not communicate with him. There was only one small cove, which looked as though he could use one engine and drift into this sheltered cove if he could only be aware of it. [Lacking any means of communicating with the downed craft,] we flew over his plane and directly back to the entrance to this cove.
>
> After several flights he became aware that I wanted him to try drifting into this cove. We continued the direction flights and he carefully handled his plane into the small entrance to the cove and beached the plane. We landed immediately along the pampas area and with mechanics secured the plane. The problem was an old one: high tension coil. The mechanics replaced the coil. We took passengers (Mrs. Harris and two [?] children) to Chimbote. The Sikorsky flew to Chimbote, picked up the passengers and continued north.

The log continued, "Jack certainly did a great job of bringing this plane through the small entrance to the cove. (My secretary Benetis gave this location cove the name of Mongoncillo, as it was SW of Mongon.) We returned Lima 2:19."

For Panagra pilots it was just another routine day.

Chapter 27: Mining Assists

In *The Congressional Record for* September 18, 1963, Florida Senator Smathers paid tribute to Panagra's 35th anniversary by listing some of the vital supplies that through the previous 35 years, Panagra had transported throughout South America and north to the United States. Panagra's *normal* cargo manifests, he noted included "high-trade beef from packing plants in Argentina, fresh fruit and sea food from Chile and Peru. Panama hats from Ecuador, crude rubber from Bolivia, textiles from Colombia and such diverse items as newspapers and magazines, [as well as] oil drilling equipment, machinery, television sets, and a host of other products from the United States . . ."

The Senator neglected to mention that it was thanks to Harold Harris' enterprise that Panagra early initiated a unique service: the transport of mining machinery from the west coast to the mountains.

As well as being an expert pilot, Harold Harris was a stubborn engineer who wouldn't necessarily accept on face value the opinion of other engineers concerning the capability limits of aircraft. This quality is best illustrated by his solution to the problem of transporting heavy equipment in Panagra's frail aircraft up to mining operations high in the Andes.

Harris wrote: "In 1932 the Compania Explotadora Cotabambas, S.A. owned a gold mine called Cochasayhuas, which had been producing gold from the time of the Incas. During the most recent period, the exploitation of the mine had not proved profitable with the existing machinery there. This came to the attention of Panagra [Harris probably brought it to John MacGregor's attention in the New York office] and it seemed a very real possibility for a very unusual freight hauling, inasmuch as the mine was located deep in the Andes about 300 miles southeast of Lima. The only way to get to the mine from the ground was by a very narrow winding mountain trail, difficult and dangerous and impractical to have a widening of the road for transportation of machinery, especially the large heavy type now required. Some preliminary operations were carried out by Panagra for the gold mining company from the airport at Cuzco, 10,900 feet above sea level. In 1932 fifty-five tons of machinery were carried in by air in a satisfactory fashion and it was determined that if truly heavy additional machinery could be carried in, complete rehabilitation of the gold extraction would be accomplished."

Representing Panagra, Harris drew up a contract with the Sindicato Minero Parcoy to carry heavy mining equipment in northern Peru. "This operation required 76 hours of flying between August 30th and September 13th of 1936 from Huamochuco to Piaz, where the flight was unloaded and return flight made to Humachuco to load for further trips. The heavy cargo had been hauled by truck from Trujillo to Humachuco. The landing field there was an ancient lakebed, at about 10,000 feet altitude. Here, the cargo was loaded on a specially arranged Ford trimotor.

The reconstructed "San Fernando" with the opening in the top of the fuselage

Panagra contracted to fly in 740 tons of heavy equipment,
the largest pieces being at most two tons each with
appropriate height and length measurements. One of
the Ford trimotors of the passenger type was rebuilt as
a freighter to give an opening at the top above where the
passengers would normally sit. This opening was nine
and half feet long and four feet wide. It required very real
engineering skill in redesigning the torsional strength of
the fuselage because of the unusual length of the open area
and the very important problem of balance in flight with
the concentrated loads that were planned... This work
was accomplished under the direction of Brad Young, a
very accomplished Aeronautical Engineer.

This reconstruction was satisfactorily accomplished, even
though it was necessary to take into account the very unusual
stresses in flight, due to the high swirling winds at the
minimum of 15,000 feet altitude necessary to carry the load
from Cuzco over the mountains to the mine landing area.

Harris went on to say that "the work"—meaning the actual
flying of the modified plane—was assigned to Captain Tom
Jardine, his radio operator, C.H. Pursley, and his mechanics.
His senior mechanic was Richard Ewing and he had two junior
mechanics, M. Fargus and J. Sose. Captain Jardine had been in
charge of the 1932 transportation over the same route, so he
was thoroughly familiar with the terrain and its requirements.

Nowhere did he say that the incision into the top of the
plane and—the freight once loaded—the replacement of the
rectangular patch on top, were his idea or that he had to buck
the opinions of aircraft engineers who said it wouldn't work. So
I will say it for him.

A sophisticated method of ground to air communication was
developed for the flights to the mines that involved creating
a temporary ground radio station at both landing fields. This
allowed continuous contact with the pilot. August 4, 1934, Tom

Jardine flew the first mining equipment flight—probably the first time that radio operation was used in such a flight.

Harris noted that this radio was the type used in Pan Am planes as well as in all scheduled Panagra flights. "Through the use of this radio, it was possible not only to keep in continual contact with the weather conditions of the territory flown over, thus ensuring the success of each flight, but also to keep in continual contact with the Lima headquarters... and with other airplanes flying on scheduled airways in South America."

> The work was so successful that an additional Ford airplane, not equipped for heavy loads but carrying various miscellaneous items which could be passed through the passenger door, was flown by Byron Rickards. The transportation involved delivering the complete milling, amalgamating and a cyaniding gold plant to treat 150 tons of ore every 24 hours. An addition to the hydroelectric plant to develop 750 additional horsepower, plus a large quantity of miscellaneous machinery, equipment and construction materials were brought to the mine.[157]

> The Indians in the territory around Cuzco at Huanacopamap were so delighted with what had occurred, that a fiesta was set up by them for the flight crews with presentation of various gifts including coca, slingshots, ponchos, and pottery.

> A large black ram was brought back to Lima by plane!

"A letter to me," wrote Harris, "from Captain Jardine, with reference to the Cuzco freighter work" [follows].

> I organized the operations and did the entire pilot job in 1933 and Fritz Sterling ran the job in 1934 with Rickards as the second pilot.

157

Fritz flew the airplane with the hatch. The time for a round trip appears to average about one hour. The weights per contract were 56,000 kilos in 1933 and 760,000 kilos in 1934 (ref. *The New West Coast Leaders*, vol. XXI—No. 1119).

Sterling, starting August 17, 1934, with trip #334, flew a total of 280 trips and a total of 240 hours to October 31, 1934.

Rickards, starting September 25, 1934, flew 121 trips and 122:50 hours to October 31, 1934.

Jardine stands alongside a falling stamp mortar, one of the many pieces of heavy mining equipment he helped transport

Wrote Harris,

> On the 16th of November, 1934, the heavy cargo Ford plane, (Panagra re-constructed), carried five and a half tons of machinery from Cajamarca to Chachapoyas, a distance of 85 miles. This tonnage was transported without difficulty in three trips even though the plane had to go to 14,000 feet to get over the tops of the two mountain ranges that encircled the Valley of the Maranon River. Three freight trips were made to the Aramayo Mining Co. on Nov. 16, 1934. In 1937, p-27 made a trip from La Paz to Tipuani.

"Tom Jardine started his flights on August 4, 1934. Equipment flights were carried on by Captain Fred Sterling, who started his piloting operation on August 22nd and continued the operation, as weather permitted, until the entire shipment had been completed."

On September 30, 1934, at 3:30 P.M., Captain Sterling sent the following radio message, "Last trip, cargo finished."

Chapter 28: Adios, Panagra

A Panagra DC-2 flies the Diagonal

A June 1952 *Fortune* article titled "The Long Cold War of Panagra" focused on the core of the long running dispute between Pan Am and Grace: what Pan Am called the "constitution" of Panagra, based on a letter of August 31, 1928, from Grace's Assistant Secretary, Mr. Cogswell, to Juan Trippe. "In the key paragraph," noted the article's author," Mr. Cogswell said to Mr. Trippe: 'You will have charge of the operation from the Canal to Valparaiso, and our houses on the West Coast of South America will be the agents of the company on a reasonable compensation basis, such agency to continue during the life of the transportation projects undertaken by the company."

The article observed that the implications of the letter were at the root of the problem. In short, Pan Am saw Panagra as simply a branch of its line. Grace, on the other hand, "believes that it went into the Panagra deal as an equal partner in an individual airline, set up to go and grow in competition with other lines, including any controlled by partner Juan Trippe." The dispute was resolved only with the much later sale of Panagra to Braniff.

Trippe would not be shackled, certainly not by a small airline whose guiding light, Harold Harris, had little of the clout with the U.S. government or the financial backing that Juan Terry Trippe enjoyed.

In his historical sketch of Panagra, the author of "Pan American Grace Airways: Silver Ships of the Andes" commented on the "truly innovative enterprise in part created by a truly pioneering military test pilot, a very successful businessman and an extraordinary aviation visionary. It cannot be denied that General Harris took a small airline without a world wide route network while confronting incredible hardships in the airspaces above South America and made it a successful enterprise . . . Panagra showed other commercial carriers how an airline should be run."[158]

Harold Harris invented the airline and labored for ten years in every conceivable capacity to ensure its success. Despite Trippe's antagonism, he agreed with Grace that Panagra was independent and able to chart its own future. Consequently, he ordered planes and tested them. He flew the most dangerous routes in advance of the other Panagra pilots. In order to further the line's reach, he dealt diplomatically with the leaders of warring nations and their henchmen. He wined and dined the famous people who saw an airplane tour of South America as a new great adventure. He even became a temporary baggage handler for the Prince of Wales. Along with the pilots he had hired, he searched for lost aircraft. He dealt with the egos and eccentricities of Panagra's personnel, most of whom in the early years of Panagra he had personally

---

[158] "Pan American Grace Airways: Silver Ships of the Andes," *American Aviation Historical Society Journal*, LIV (Spring 2009).

hired. He argued for the expansion of the line, which he traveled ceaselessly, often himself at the controls, sending in to the home office a lengthy series of reports. Perhaps most important, he inspired devotion both to him and to the airline he thus ran for its first few years virtually single-handed. Without Harold Harris' guiding hand, boundless energy and foresight, Panagra might conceivably have become only what Trippe wanted: an extension of Pan Am on the west coast of South America.

To all those who were hired by him or followed him, the "little airline that could", did, with no thanks to Pan Am that refused to allow it to fly into the U.S., and refused to advertise Panagra's schedules.

Sept. 18, 1958, on its 30th anniversary, Panagra was honored by the following New York Times editorial.

> A blend of American ingenuity and pioneering spirit made possible the first United States-flag air service in South America thirty years ago this month. On that occasion Pan American Grace Airways, commonly known as Panagra, flew a single-engine four—passenger aircraft on a 600 mile flight between Lima and Talara, Peru. The flight originated from a racetrack and landed on a soccer field. These were the airport conditions in those days.

> From that humble beginning Panagra has grown into a major international airline. It operates 9,000 miles of routes linking the United States with Panama, Colombia, Ecuador, Peru, Bolivia, Chile, and Argentina. It has flown over 2 million passengers and over 100 million pounds of cargo and mail.

> Panagra developed an air transportation system where none previously existed. It had to construct its own airports, install its own radio and meteorological facilities, secure operating concessions and contracts from South

American governments and perfect its own techniques and procedures. The line has even provided guesthouses in areas where adequate hotel accommodations were lacking.

Traversing vast deserts and seas, over impenetrable jungles, and across the cordillera of the Andes, Panagra pioneered commercial aviation in South America. As transportation shifted from muleback to the airplane, a close interchange of trade and culture was brought about between the Americas. Panagra's progress during the last three decades is a tribute to American aviation.

The emotional impact of the loss of Panagra is seen in excerpts from *La Prensa*, the Lima newspaper. It commented sadly on the ultimate demise of Panagra, sold in 1966 to Braniff. ". . . we will never see again what we had always been accustomed to seeing, from childhood: the Panagra airplanes. The gringos made such propaganda with Panagra that we had identified it with Latin American friendships . . . Above all it was Peruvian. Although it was so big, it was born small, in Peru. It made its first flights—one might say it took its first steps—forty years ago, there at the old Santa Beatriz racetrack and arrived at a football field in Talara with two or three passengers and the first airmail envelope. And during 40 years it made itself so Peruvian that the people baptized the balconies of the movie theatres with the name 'Panagra' and there is a criollo dish— very criollo—which is called 'tacu-tacu a la Panagra." By that time, however, Harold Harris was long gone.

Between 1929 and 1939 John MacGregor, as Vice President and General Manager and Harold Harris, as Vice President and Operations Manager were Panagra's only officers. Following MacGregor's resignation in 1939, Harold J. Roig, a Vice President of the Grace Company, was made President of Panagra.

Krusen points out that "Harold Harris might have been expected to bristle somewhat at this. After all, Panagra wasn't

Roig's idea. But in fact, Harris was quick to credit Roig with the upcoming rapid expansion of the airline, and specifically mentions Roig's management success. The only thing Harris objected to was that the new arrangement required that he transfer to Panagra's New York office, which he did on March 1, 1939."

The family moved to Scarsdale, N.Y. Harold Harris commuted to Panagra's New York City headquarters. Harris continued as overall operations manager of Panagra and continued traveling the line. He was sent to Bolivia to take over the local German airline, LAB, for the U.S.

A fragment of Panagra's submission to the Civil Aeronautics Board Docket No's 623 and 716, originally submitted to CAB, October 15, 1941, lauds his contribution.

> From the time Captain Harris took charge of Peruvian Airways Corporation and later Pan American-Grace Airways as Vice President and Operations Manager, he was in personal charge of the pioneering and development of the Panagra operations from Cristobal to Buenos Aires. Until 1939 he resided permanently in South America and spent his entire time on the line. His ten years devoted to the development and one may even say the creation of the line, has, of course given him the most intimate knowledge of every detail of the operation and every phase of the business. In 1939 his headquarters were transferred to New York where he has continued in administration of the company's affairs.

In the interim, however, Douglas Campbell, (who became yet another Vice President,) was sent down in both 1937 and 1938 to make arrangements with the government of Colombia. Also in 1939, upon Harris's move to New York City, Tom Kirkland became Panagra Operations Manager, and in 1942, Vice President.

Administrative upgrades in 1941 included the promotion of Charles Disher to Operations Manager, and the promotion of Floyd Nelson to Chief Pilot . . . Two weeks earlier, in New York John T. Shannon had been promoted to Vice President.

In September 1942 Harold Harris resigned to join the Air Transport Command as a Colonel.

Chapter 29: World War II, the Air Transport Command; Harris' Involvement in the Formation of the International Air Transport Association (IATA)

As Harold Harris soon discovered first-hand, World War II ushered in a whole new global challenge to American aviation. In 1942 he volunteered to join the Air Transport Command where he began as Assistant Chief of Planning and was awarded the rank of Colonel. Major General Harold L. George, a career Army officer, became its head, with Cyrus R. Smith, CEO of American Airlines, his deputy. In the ATC Harris served in numerous positions including Assistant Chief of Staff, Operations; Commanding Officer of the Domestic Transportation Division; later attaining the rank of Brigadier General while Chief of Staff.

The origins of the ATC have been described in radically different ways, depending on the focus or lack of it on the contribution to the story of Juan Trippe's Pan Am. Bender and Altschul's version begins with the following statement : "In the depths of the military conflict of WW II a battle had been going on among the Allied airlines regarding the wartime activities of Pan Am ... by using its U.S. government-endorsed prerogative of providing transport for the Allies' personnel and supplies, Trippe's Pan Am had created new routes or had taken over existing airlines in Africa and the Middle East."

There was national and international resentment of Pan Am's pre-emptive role. "Unless we come to agreement, there will be a race between the Americans and ourselves to control the airlines of the world", noted a British member of Parliament.[159]

Observed General George Marshall,

> The recurring resentment of the British to Pan American's expansion in the Middle East and the fact that Pan American tends to regard a military effort as a commercial operation were among the serious disadvantages... in having a civilian airline operating so close to a combat area.[160]

Commercial airline operators agreed on the need to break Pan Am's exclusive wartime dominance based on its U.S. government-approved role. In June 1942, as a means of resolving some of these problems, the War Department established the U.S. Air Transport Command (ATC) "as the major instrument of logistical support for the far-flung combat operations on the ground and in the air. The A.T.C. contracted with major carriers for specific services, and also set priorities for their regular commercial operations."[161]

---

[159] Bender and Altschul, 371,
[160] Ibid.
[161] Bender and Altschul, 363.

An Air Transport Command Douglas C-47

Commented Bender and Altschul, much to Trippe's dismay the ATC "purchased the four-engine transports coming off the production lines and leased them to *eleven* carriers with contracts for overseas service. Trippe saw the fruits of his diplomatic labors—the international air routes—distributed among the domestic airlines for sampling. TWA and American Airlines augmented Pan American on the North Atlantic to London, United on the Pacific to Australia and India; Eastern and Braniff were assigned to Central and South America, Northwest to Alaska."

They continued, "In July, 1943 General ("Hap") Arnold, Secretary of the Air Force, called a meeting in Washington of the nineteen airlines that had contracts with the ATC; of these more than half had been operating overseas. He told his audience that the Air Force was getting out of the commercial airline business.

Freed of governmental restrictions, the involved airlines, determined to combat Pan Am's pervasive spread, created the

Airline Committee on International Routes otherwise known as the Seventeen Committee. The Committee asserted that "There can be no rational basis for permitting air transport outside the United States to be left to the withering influence of monopoly."[162] Trippe and William Patterson, President of United Airlines, refused to join.

Bielauskas' website version mentions none of this, providing instead a simpler explanation: "Just a few months prior to the beginning of the Second World War, Pan American Airways had contracted with both the U.S. and British governments to deliver U.S.-built aircraft to Khartoum in Sudan. Soon after Pearl Harbor, this route was extended and Eastern Airlines began assisting Pan American Airways with its delivery's [sic] ... During this time new delivery routes were being developed both at home and abroad and more airlines were contracted for these new routes. Eventually there were so many contracts to so many different airlines, that a proposal was made that would allow all airline contract operations be conducted under a single command reporting directly to the President of the United States and operating independently of both the Army and the Navy. Thus was born the Air Transport Command; the ATC was to be made responsible for all ferrying and transportation tasks of the U.S. A. A. C. except those tasks necessary for combat operations."

The ATC, he noted, "was an outgrowth of the Ferrying Command which had been established to deliver US-built aircraft destined for Britain under Lend-Lease from the factories on the West Coast to embarkation points on the East Coast." It was "essentially ... an airline in military uniform" ... that by the end of WW II, was "an organization larger than the United States commercial fleet" and "composed almost entirely of cargo planes . . ."[163].

---

[162] Ibid, 380.
[163] Bill Bielauskas' *Inphal, The Hump and Beyond*. The ATC was administered by former airline executives.

"As the war progressed," wrote Bielauskas,

> the Air Transport Command developed routes from the
> United States to every theater of the war. These routes
> went from the East Coast to England, by way of Canada,
> from the West Coast to Australia by way of Hawaii and the
> South Pacific Islands, from Miami and other East Coast
> bases to North Africa, across Canada to Alaska and into the
> Aleutians and south into Central and South America. The
> longest of the ATC routes, was the route to China and the
> CBI theater. The route to China went south out of Miami
> to Natal, Brazil, then across the Atlantic to Africa and on
> across the Middle East to finally arrive in India, which was
> the rear area for the CBI (China, Burma, India route).

The most famous—or perhaps infamous—of these routes
was the so-called "Hump", the flight across the Himalayas. The
U.S. was convinced that the maintenance of China, currently
under siege by Japanese troops, as an ally was essential to
the Allies' continuing deterrence of enemy forces. Its primary
military focus was to keep open an essential supply route to
vital areas of China. Yet with the fall of Burma, China had lost
its last supply line to the outside world. The only way left to
get supplies to China was by air and, since the Japanese Air
Force and Army were in Burma, the route would have to be
circuitous and very dangerous, certainly "an unlikely route
for regular flight operations due to high terrain and extremely
severe weather. It crossed a north-south extension of the main
Himalayan Mountains that ran south through northern Burma
and western China. On the very north end of the extension
terrain exceeded 20,000 MSL in height. Average elevations
lowered to the south but did not fall below 12,000 MSL for
approximately 140 miles. The routes flown fell between these
two extremes."[164]

---

[164] Bill Maher, CNAC Hump Pilots "First to Fly the Hump" website.

Reasoning that if China were to fall, the whole course of the war would be severely undermined, C.R. Smith, then an ATC Colonel—soon to rise to become a Major General—urged the creation of a regular transport service on this route 24 hours a day, 7 days a week. As a result, from April 1942 to 1945 when the Burma road was reopened, pilots flew vital military supplies over the Hump regardless of the weather. On his Hump website, Bill Maher quotes "a veteran [Hump] pilot: 'If you can see the end of the runway through the rain and mist, then a takeoff is expected.'"

The results were often disastrous. "The dangerous 530-mile long passage over the Himalayan Mountains took its toll. Nearly 1,000 men and 600 Air Transport Command (ATC) planes were lost over the Hump by the end of the China-Burma-India theater (CBI) operations". Final offensives against the Japanese, notes Maher, "resulted in one ATC transport taking off every three minutes."

Since he never discussed his ATC involvement, except to mention that he had helped provide cigars for the wife of the Prime Minister of Iceland when Nazi subs had endangered ship passage by sea, I have no way of knowing Harris' exact involvement in ATC operations. It seems clear, however, that his experience deploying pilots over the Andes certainly helped. Photos that show him dressed in Middle Eastern garb or against exotic backgrounds reveal something of the extent of his secret wartime travels.

Airlines' Self Regulation: CAA, CAB, IATA

We have seen how since shortly after WW I, the U.S. government was involved in commercial air transportation, at first through subsidizing the provision of airmail services initially domestically and later abroad. Under the Department of Commerce, legislation such as the Air Commerce Act of 1926, focusing on safety issues, had dealt with the licensing of pilots, certification of airworthiness of aircraft, etc., thus enabling the orderly development of commercial airlines nationally.

No such regulations existed for global air transport, however, and would not until intense competition for routes and services by numerous national airlines forced the establishment of both national and international aviation authorities. These regulatory agencies, arising from sheer necessity, attempted to constrain the excessive development of any one airline.

Domestically the Civil Aeronautics Act of 1958 establishing the Civil Aeronautics Administration (CAA) and the Civil Aeronautics Board (CAB), both part of the Civil Aeronautics Authority, authorized specific regulations as to air fares and routes for all carriers based in the U.S.

European nations recognized earlier than the U.S. the need to regulate air travel in foreign lands. IATA (International Air Transport Association) was founded in 1939. A modernized version that began in 1944 with the aim of establishing procedures and safety regulations common to all its member nations grew from numerous discussions by representatives from various nations with Harold Harris one of the representatives from the U.S. A Harris anecdote described one of major problems hindering the work of this international committee responsible for organizing IATA.

> When it became evident in the latter part of 1944 that the Allies would finally win WWII, the U.S. Assistant Secretary of State, Adolf Berle, decided that it was important that the world's civil aviation problems be worked out by an international conference prior to the end of the war, so that there would be no vacuum existing in control of international civil flying when the war was over.

> In order to make a really satisfactory, worthwhile and acceptable determination of proper activities to color and outline methods of obtaining desired results, preliminary discussions were called by the U.S. State Department with

separate meetings with the representatives of Russia, Great Britain, China, and possibly France.

These meetings were held in the Blair House, across the street from the White House, in Washington. The meeting was chaired by the Assistant Secretary of State, Mr. Berle. Mr. Chip Bohlen of the State Department, who later was an Ambassador to Russia, (after the war) who spoke Russian, was the interpreter for the United States delegation. The Commerce Department was represented by the Undersecretary of Commerce, Mr. William A.M. Burden. Lieut. Commander Barney Baruch, Jr. represented the U.S. Naval Air service and I was assigned as the U.S. Army Air Service representative to the Russian meeting.

Seeking 'One World' in Aviation

Leading figures in conference at the Stevens Hotel seeking world accord on flight problems include Robert A. Lovett (reading letter), U.S. assistant secretary of war for air, seated with (left to right) Fiorella H. La Guardia, chairman of U.S. Section; Col. H. R. Harris, Air Transport Command; Joaquin Cunanan of Philippine Commonwealth, and Maj. Jesus O. Villamor, U.S. Army Air Force and Bataan hero. (Daily News photo.)

Harris seated next to New York mayor Fiorello LaGuardia at the IATA Conference in 1944.

The Russian delegation was headed by Ambassador Gromyko, who was then Ambassador from Russia to the United States, assisted by two Lieut. Generals and two Major Generals sent from Moscow. The Russian group did not need a translator since Gromyko was competent in both languages. As the discussion continued, he gradually was accepted by the U.S. side as a reasonable translator without having to go through our own man. None of the Russian delegation except Ambassador Gromyko understood English. It often became a little troublesome to exchange ideas and assure a meeting of the minds of the various people there because of the completely different educational background and our assumption that the background of the West's would be understood, even though it might not be agreeable to the Russians.

One meeting that resulted in the complete breakdown of talks came about because Mr. Burden in making a point stated, "That this was desirable for civil aviation because of the profit motive." While it hadn't occurred to any of us from the West that this would fail to be understood, it turned out that the four General officers from Moscow could not understand what a "profit motive" might be. Their entire education had been without accepting any profit as a goal.

The net result in the lack of understanding of the situation finally came to light when the Chicago Conference was later arranged. The delegation from Russia started to travel to the United States by way of Siberia, got as far as Vladivostok and received orders from Moscow not to attend. So Russia was not represented at the Chicago Conference! And the groundwork for ICAO and IATA was laid without any Russian help.

Once the United Nations was established, IATA's major effort was to work with the UN's ICAO (International Civil Aviation Organization) to supervise worldwide airline prices and routes.

Chapter 30: American Overseas Airlines

In the ATC Harris served in numerous positions beginning as a Colonel as Assistant Chief of Staff, Operations and ending as a Brigadier General and Chief of Staff. He enjoyed the working companionship of several officers recruited from commercial life, notably Cyrus R. (C.R.) Smith (CEO of American Airlines) and Leon Mandel, Chicago department store owner, both of whom, following the conclusion of hostilities, offered him a job.

Harris knew nothing about the department store business, but a great deal about commercial aviation. He was more than happy to accept Smith's offer in 1945 to help lead Smith's new venture into overseas operations, American Overseas Airlines (AOA). In reality it was probably both Harris, designated Vice President and Operations Manager, and Ralph Damon, whom Smith appointed President, who convinced Smith, always obsessed with creating a superior *domestic* service, to extend American Airline's reach.

Damon, American Airlines Vice President and General Manager, had operated as its President while Smith was in the War. It was Damon who engineered the acquisition by American Airlines of American Export Airlines, subsequently renamed American Overseas Airlines.[165]

Smith rationalized his decision to go international by commenting" I want to make American what it used to be—a good and profitable airline. And I don't want to divert attention from those goals. We'll have one set of people for the domestic, and one for overseas."[166]

---

[165] Ibid, 438.
[166] *Pan American Grace Airways: Silver Ships of the Andes.*

Trippe saw both AOA and its predecessor American Export Airlines (AEA), as direct challengers to Pan Am's goal of total (Pan) American hegemony in the international skies.

American Export or AmEx had been founded in April 1937 as a wholly owned subsidiary of the shipping company, American Export Lines.[167] Transatlantic surveys were done with a Consolidated PBY-4 flying boat and in 1939 AEA placed an order for three Vought Sikorsky VS-44 flying boats, dubbed 'Flying Aces'. That same year AEA made an application to the US Civil Aeronautics Board (CAB) for routes across the Atlantic from the United States to the United Kingdom, France, and Portugal.

On July 15, 1940, in spite of strong protests by Juan Trippe, President Franklin D. Roosevelt gave his approval to AEA for a seven-year temporary certificate to serve Lisbon (Portugal) from New York City-La Guardia Flying Boat base. Later on services were also flown to Foynes, (Ireland). AEA could not begin its New York City-Foynes flying boat service before June 1942, however, due in part to vigorous objections from Pan Am.

These services ended in 1944 when AEA started operations on behalf of the ATC using Douglas C-54 Skymasters mainly between the USA and military bases in North Africa.

Harold Harris wrote: "On July 5, 1945, American Export Airlines was awarded by the Civil Aeronautics Board a certificate of convenience and necessity, authorizing it to engage as an air carrier in service between the United State and Newfoundland, Labrador, Greenland, Iceland, Eire, United Kingdom, Netherlands, Denmark, Norway, Sweden, Finland, Estonia, Latvia, Lithuania, Germany, Poland and Russia for a period of seven years. United States terminals under the

---

[167] This and the following information on AEA provided by *Airlines Established in 1937*... Hephaestus Books, n.d.

certificate were New York, Washington, Chicago, Detroit, Philadelphia, Boston, and Baltimore."

AEA launched its international presence on October 24, 1945, with Flagship New England (N90904) on the route New York City to London via Boston, Gander (Newfoundland) and Shannon (Ireland) By June 1945 both Pan Am and AEA were offering trans-Atlantic service followed by TWA in 1946.

American Airlines was interested in acquiring AEA in order to break into an overseas market still dominated by Pan Am. The US CAB (Civil Aeronautics Board) approved the acquisition of AEA by American Airlines on July 5, 1945, thus permitting the establishment of American Overseas Airlines. Although AEA's La Guardia-Botwood-Shannon route had been operated by Vought-Sikorsky flying boats using the Marine Air Terminal at LaGuardia Airport, with the CAB's blessing, AOA began operations internationally on October 24th with the first scheduled landplane (Douglas DC-4) flight to London from New York via Boston, Gander, Newfoundland and Shannon, Ireland, a flight lasting fourteen hours in the aircraft designated *Flagship New England, N90904.*

Under Harris as Operations Manager, AOA succeeded in developing a reliable, safe, service-oriented airline that was able to take over and improve on AEA's routes.

Aviation safety had always been his main concern. As early as 1925 in his Morrow Board testimony, Harris had insisted on airline safety as a priority for crew and passengers, pointing out that "unless a commercial aviation venture is economically sound and *properly engineered*, it cannot be made to pay its way". Therefore "Some form of United States Government inspection and licensing of commercial aircraft and operators" was essential.

Harris' concern for aviation safety persisted, leading him eventually to become the Chairman of the Board of Governors of the Flight Safety Foundation and an intimate friend of its founder, Jerome Lederer.

In summing up AOA's achievements for the year 1948, he wrote, "Civil Air Regulations became effective requiring Navigators, Flight Engineers, and Flight Radio Operators to possess licenses. All personnel required to hold such certificates were given refresher courses in order to assist them in passing the necessary examinations required by the CAA. We always required our Captains to be qualified navigators and in order to continue this policy, eligibility requirements for promotion to Captain were revised to include possession of a Navigator's certificate.

A caricature of Harris painted in 1948

"Complete advanced navigation examinations were given to a larger number of captains resulting in approximately 35 captains securing their Navigator's licenses. AOA Operations Training assisted in setting up the Flight Engineering training programs for AA [American Airlines] domestic operation. In addition, AA consolidated their link trainer activities at New York with AOA in our Operations Training Section in Flushing. A complete actual scale model of the Boeing cockpit mockup with workable and controllable instruments was complete at a cost of less than $2,000 . . ."

"We were highly complimented", noted Harris, "although necessarily unofficially by the CAA with the statement that they considered our flight training second to none. AOA was recognized for its contribution to safe air transportation," having operated 3 years and as of December

31, 1949, 588,551,000 passenger miles without a passenger or crew fatality in scheduled passenger carrying flight operations."

AOA launched international land plane flights on October 24, 1945, with DC-4 Flagship New England (N90904), on the route New York City to London via Boston, Gander (Newfoundland) and Shannon (Ireland). The reliable but unpressurized DC-4s were replaced on the Atlantic routes by the glamour queens of the air routes, the Lockheed Constellations (providing sleeping accommodations) from 23 June 1946.[168] From summer 1949 the Constellations were supplemented and then largely replaced by the double-decker Boeing Stratocruisers, the first AOA service by the type being on 17 August that year to London Heathrow. Pre-Jet era, the Stratocruisers provided the ultimate luxury in flight with beds for weary travelers and a bar on a top deck accessible from below by a staircase. I was fortunate to fly in one from New York to London.

Photo taken at Berlin's Templehof airport, October 1948

---

[168] A decisive factor may have been the structural problems associated with the excessive tail movement in the Constellations.

AOA played a vital role in the famous Berlin airlift of 1948 when the Soviets blockaded the entry by land into Berlin, thus cutting off the citizens' food supply.[169]

wrote Libby:

> One of the AOA pilots and head of the Carrier's European office, Captain Jack Bennett (1914-2001), was requested by the United States Air Force Commander in Europe, headquartered at Wiesbaden, Germany, Major General Curtis Le May (1906-1990) to assist in flying supplies into West Berlin during the airlift of 1948-9. Thus Bennett became the first of many civilian pilots to defy the restrictive policies of the Soviet Union in what must be considered one of the first serious confrontations of the Cold War ...

> The airlift, which managed to supply West Berliners with all of the coal and food they would need for 11 months, ultimately transported more than two million tons of goods with nearly 280,000 flights. Bennett himself flew more than 1,000 missions and, although cited as a hero for his part in the airlift, he never made any secret of his disdain for the operation, which he considered misconceived. He wrote, 'We should have simply sent tanks rolling in along the motorway. The Russians were not prepared for that. It would have worked. The airlift was an expensive mistake.'[170]

With AOA, through his constant monitoring of the line and his continuing involvement with the personnel, Harold Harris accomplished what he had achieved in his hands-on guidance of Panagra and the ATC: the welding together of a cohesive and devoted personnel while at the same time pursuing an

---

[169] Both Harold Harris and his wife Grace were aboard one of the first AOA planes to bypass the blockade.

[170] Libby, Harris biographic article.

expansionist agenda involving larger and better planes that flew faster and serviced more areas.[171]

Trippe had never abandoned his dream of his airline, Pan Am, becoming the U.S. "Chosen Instrument" around the world. This dream was not shared by the CAB or by either President Roosevelt or President Truman, all of whom saw the need for a variety of U.S. airlines to serve in world venues. In 1945 Truman went so far as to veto an "All American Flag" bill in Congress.

Sensing that C. R. Smith may have become weary of dealing with two airlines, Trippe arranged a secret meeting at which the two agreed to the purchase by Pan Am of AOA. Note Bender and Altschul, "American Overseas had an excellent reputation for service—superior to Pan American's many thought— but it operated at a deficit that cooled C.R.'s enthusiasm, particularly after American Airlines incurred substantial losses during 1947 and 1948. Undoubtedly the additional capital requirements for American Overseas' fleet of Stratocruisers fed Smith's pessimism about the transatlantic market. All of a sudden, he was singing Trippe's tune."[172]

The merger proposal went to the CAB for approval. There was a hearing that Bender and Altschul described as "aviation's Scopes trial"—on a par with the 1925 airing of Darwinism and the teaching of evolution in the public schools of Tennessee." The issue being tried was clearly Juan Trippe's "chosen instrument" argument. Regardless of the eloquence of the Pan Am lawyers, the CAB turned down the merger.[173]

Trippe knew that Truman's idol was General Marshall, and that Marshall favored Pan Am. Although the CAB had turned

---

[171] For a Summary of important dates for AOA, see Appendix A.
[172] Bender and Altshcul, 438.
[173] Ibid, 439.

down the merger, Pan Am lobbied the White House. Truman ultimately yielded and approved the merger of the two airlines.

Thus for $17.45 million cash, Trippe acquired "a valuable franchise, a fleet of the most advanced aircraft—eight Boeing Stratocruisers, seven Constellations and 5 DC-4s, almost $5 million in retroactive mail pay still due AOA. This was NYRBA in spades."[174]

In a letter to Harris dated 22 September 1950, the soon to be former Vice President of Operations for AOA, James G. Flynn summed up his pain and remorse at what he considered the sell-out of a splendid airline:

> Today is the last regular business day of American Overseas Airlines and the organization for which we all worked so hard will finally be scuttled. A set of circumstances and adversities designed to wreck the outfit could hardly have been arrived at by deliberate planning than those experienced by AOA since the day of the first landplane flight on October 23, 1945, one hour after a mechanics' strike. As a matter of fact the days of American Export Airlines were no better, although you and I were not present to bear up under them.
>
> After September 25th the best policy will probably be to bury AOA and refer to it and its experiences as little as possible. That will be a hard policy for some of us to follow; we have had so much pride in the accomplishments of the organization in spite of obstacles strewn in its path, and the unequaled esprit de corps that has been one of its most outstanding characteristics. American and Pan American will be fortunate if some of AOA's company spirit rubs off on them.

---

[174] Ibid, 441.

I have greatly enjoyed the association with you and feel that I have greatly profited from the experience. I believe we had a good working arrangement and I hope that we will have an opportunity to use it again at some later date. "You can certainly look back on the brief life of AOA with pride in your accomplishments and leadership and with the knowledge that you had as fine and loyal a group of employees as I ever expect to see in this lifetime . . .

I am reminded of the relationship between the trainer of a racehorse and the animal's actual owner. The trainer can affect the destiny of the horse on the track. But it is up to the owner to assure the animal's actual future. Harold Harris was the trainer who created a winner only to see it sold out from under him.

September 24, 1950, in a letter to the AOA Board of Directors, Harold R. Harris submitted his resignation.

Chapter 31: Pan Am and Northwest

Shortly following the end of WW II, Trippe re-organized Pan Am. Henceforth, there would be three divisions—Latin America, Atlantic, and Pacific-Alaska, each headed by a vice-president. Following his resignation from AOA, Harold Harris came on board as vice president of the Atlantic Division.

Harold Harris never wrote anything in any way derogatory of Juan Trippe or his methods. Certainly he had early recognized and was forced to accept Trippe's ferocious impulse to dominate the global airline industry. That this did not deter him, despite many bruising encounters with Pan Am, from taking on and working to help fulfill Trippe's dream is a puzzle. Perhaps as a seasoned airlines executive, he simply accepted the harsh realities attending the conduct of commercial airlines, always fighting to remain competitive in a low-profit market. Perhaps his fidelity to a dream of creating a smoothly functioning airline, its growth, and the superiority of its services overcame his distaste for Trippe's business methods. Or perhaps, simply, he needed a job.

The merger with AOA had given Pan Am valuable new routes including stations in Iceland, Scotland, Holland, Germany (Hamburg, Dusseldorf, Berlin), Oslo, Stockholm, Helsinki, as well as 1138 AOA employees including 137 pilots, 75 flight engineers, and 967 flight service, all in the Atlantic Division. A truly generous bonus!

As Operations specialist, Harris continued to pursue regular inspections along the Atlantic routes. I was fortunate to be able to tag along as a passenger on one of his inspection tours. In a brief period of time we covered Germany, Austria, Sweden, Norway, Finland, and Ireland. Everywhere he went, Harold Harris was greeted as a friend by Pan Am employees. Everywhere he asked penetrating questions and made suggestions. It was either in Frankfurt or Vienna that we met

General Kreipe, former head of Hitler's air force on the Russian front. Since Pan Am was then flying to Newfoundland, Iceland, and Scandinavia, Harold Harris was very interested in what the General had to say regarding the maintenance of the German airplanes in the subzero temperature of the Russian winter.

Since all Pan Am records were lost in a disastrous fire to its New York headquarters, further information regarding Harris' performance as head of Pan Am's Atlantic Division comes mainly from his summary memorandum to Trippe November 20, 1952, as part of his official resignation as well as Trippe's brief acknowledgement of his contributions.

The summary of Harris' achievements covering the two years between 1950-2 included substantial increases in the amount of U.S. mail and parcel post carried, total operating revenues exclusive of U.S. mail (from $35 million in 1950 to almost $45 million as of September, 1952.) In the two years between October 1949 and October 1951, Pan Am's Atlantic Division operated at a net loss of well over $3 million. Between October 1951 and September 30, 1952, however, it saw *a profit* of over $4 million.

Important was Harris' emphasis on decentralization within the Atlantic Division, even to the decentralization of purchasing. Decentralization gave him the opportunity to deal personally with a multitude of airline employees within each unit of operation. Thus Harris notes "The spirit of cooperation and teamwork which developed in our cities was something new and important. Employees of all departments and their families became interested in spreading the enthusiasm of Pan American World Airways." This cooperative spirit was enhanced by the establishment of "small monetary rewards" to all ground personnel in the area."

"The more this feeling of responsibility is decentralized," he continued, "the more people try to take the responsibility for increasing effectiveness and reducing costs of specific items, large and small."

He noted, however, "a personal inadequacy that I was never able to obtain full agreement in the System offices for this program of bringing the employees of all departments together into a more dynamic group . . ."

Among achievements during those two years the improvement of safety factors and personnel morale ranked high. Maintaining close cooperation with the CAA meant including specifications for crew training, the hiring of radiotelephone operators and professional navigators.

High powered radio beacon systems and high-powered radiotelephone stations were installed at various locations.

Intensive pilot training became a major priority and, as he noted, "The specific accomplishments in maintenance are too numerous to mention."

In accepting Harris' resignation in November 1952, Juan Trippe's report card was laudatory. "You have made a significant contribution in integrating the new fleet of DC6-Bs into the Atlantic Division under your direction. The Division's operations and earning have been considerably improved. Equally important, the company's responsibility in providing adequate airlift from West Berlin—so important to the national interest—has been effectively discharged under difficult and trying conditions."[175]

Taking into consideration Harris' sterling record at both AOA and Pan Am, it is not surprising that Northwest Airlines' Board of Directors saw him as something of a savior.

---

[175] The Berlin airlift (between 1948-9) was claimed by Pan Am on the strength of their having swallowed AOA in 1950.

In 1952, while other airlines were showing small profit balances, Northwest, under Croil Hunter, its president since 1937, encountered difficult times. It was said that the airline's problems lay in its maintenance systems, difficulties with the pilots, and inability to stay competitive against rapidly growing competition.[176]

Northwest logo circa 1947

Under Hunter, Northwest's routes had expanded from 1,000 to 20,000 miles, stretching as far as the Orient. Since 1950, however, Northwest lost a suit against Boeing for repayment of the $6 million that Northwest said was required to rid its ten newly purchased Stratocruisers of all their bugs. Then Northwest pilots refused to fly its Martin 20's after five of the planes had crashed. Ultimately sold, these planes were replaced by rentals, and, with the help of government contracts, the line appeared to show a profit in 1951. The first six months of 1952 were a different story, however, with the line losing $2 million.[177]

The Board of Directors acted swiftly. Croil was bounced up to Chairman of the Board and a search was instituted for a new president with fresh ideas. Harold Harris, with his rich background in plane maintenance, operations, and employee relations, seemed ideal. On his part, Harris saw an unprecedented opportunity to supervise the growth of an airline that was able to compete on equal terms with Pan Am and Juan Trippe. He accepted Northwest's bid and shortly after resigned from Pan Am.

"This week," noted *Time* (October 20, 1952) "Airman Harris, a cautious man with airplanes, was just as cautious about his new

[176] Time, October 20, 1952.
[177] Ibid.

job. Said he: 'First I have to find out what the airline's all about. I'm going to break my neck trying to make it resume the position it used to have in this country. Something's wrong with the airline. I don't know what yet—except that they need new equipment.'"

To help answer to what he found wrong with the airline, Harris proceeded to investigate the puzzling differences between the seeming profits of 1951 with the line's appalling losses in 1952. In an April, 1954, memorandum to each member of the Board of Directors, he noted that "different treatment has been given the allocation of certain system costs between the two years and that had the same allocation been given the 1951 figures as the 1952 figures, a very substantial reduction should have been shown for the profit for the earlier year ... The 1951 allocation problem is part of the general review to be made by the Civil Aeronautics Board in connection with our 1951 mail rate, which is the only mail rate now open. It is evident from these figures that until we can increase our domestic income and decrease domestic expenses, *we will be largely dependent upon our showing in the international field for profits.*" [Italics mine.] In other words, someone may have fudged the figures for 1951 to cover up the loss to the airline from its domestic operation and only revenue from its overseas operation rescued the line from bankruptcy.

A photo of Harris as the new President of Northwest Airlines, from Business Week, June 20, 1953

This revelation of the vital importance to Northwest of the Asian routes may have been all to Harris' liking. Regarding Trippe's takeover of AOA, Roger Lewis of Pan Am's Executive Board, had noted that Trippe "should have made a deal with American or Northwest instead of buying AOA. *Pan Am did not receive one important route after AOA* [Italics mine] and its remaining monopoly in the Central and South Pacific was jeopardized by a pack of domestic carriers clamoring to provide aggressive competition".[178] If there was a real competition between Harris and Trippe in the Far East, the two seemed finally to be on a more level playing field.

At the outset of his presidency, expansion of the Orient route was not Harris' primary focus, however. Company reorganization and moving the administrative headquarters from St. Paul to New York City were. In a May 1953 memo to the Board of Directors, he noted that the morale of both employees and stockholders was low, due to a series of accidents and the Boeing problem.[179]

Harris acknowledged that the previous year some had advocated for a merger with a smaller airline. Fortunately, stockholders had denied this move. "But the basic problem," observed Harris, was the "lack of a suitable organization, and the failure to recognize and act upon the fact that the once small local operator, Northwest Airways, was now one of the great international operators of the world . . ."

As he had done at Pan Am, Harris determined to decentralize Northwest's operations: "This great trunk line operation falls into two general geographical areas. First, the transcontinental operation, including Alaska and Hawaii and our operations in

---

[178] Bender and Altschul, 490.
[179] Some problems continued. September, 1953, saw the crash—no injuries—of a Super Constellation leased from Eastern Airlines, as well as a walkout by transportation and ticket agents.

Canada; and second, international operations between the American continent and the Orient."

The Continental Division would be headquartered in St. Paul, the Orient Division, in Tokyo. A central administrative area with a small general staff would be located in New York City.

The reorganization, he maintained, was essential to eliminate confusion in St. Paul between the administrative and operational functions.[180]

Harris insisted that the move to New York would enhance the airline's prestige: "New York is the center of the financial and business communities, not only of the United States but also largely of the world and we are not only a large transcontinental airline but also the second largest in route miles among U.S. flag carriers, much of this mileage being international." Further, "our ownership is largely held in the area centered around New York, and our capital requirements are negotiated and administered there." He even had negotiated to rent 537 Fifth Avenue where the building would be renamed "Northwest Orient Airlines Building."

Harris was dedicated to expanding the line and improving flight times. This required equipment updating. Several new Boeing Stratocruisers were ordered. Entering into a credit agreement with 14 banks for the purchase, Harris ordered six of the new aristocrats of the air, the Lockheed Super Constellations, guaranteed to fly faster and further than the present fleet. Repayment by 1959 for the planes as well as their operating costs seemed no problem, since, with the purchase, the airline would be able to carry well over a million

---

[180] Also in the works was a plan to create a new heavy-maintenance base at Minneapolis. To develop this plan he convened a Main Base Committee. It recommended that the base be moved from St. Paul to Minneapolis.

passengers in 1953 alone. *Time* noted "His policy was, as he put it last week, 'spending money to make money.'"[181]

Harris was aware it was urgent that these bold moves be accepted and endorsed by company personnel. Feedback from the media seemed to endorse the proposed changes. Employee acceptance of the financial burden he had undertaken on behalf of the airline was absolutely essential. Toward this end in June and July 1953 Harris issued a series of Employee Newsletters explaining details of the purchase, the need for expanded income to offset it, and the responsibility of each employee to promote the line among friends and family.

He included the fact that Northwest had not paid a stockholder dividend since July 1946, and noted that unlike the line's employees, the line's shareholders barely made a profit.

As though those plans were not radical enough, in the Orient, which he visited frequently, Harris launched Northwest on a fare war with Pan Am. *Time* magazine (December 1, 1953) called it a "battle of the Pacific". It began when Harris "inaugurated tourist trips from the U.S. to Okinawa, Hong Kong and Korea last month 'to stimulate travel across the Pacific'" and, as Harris explained, to "fatten a route that has been too thin to be self-supporting. Fares will average about 70% below first class tariffs. To see that Harris' diet does not get too rich, big rival Pan American World Airways was in the air with tourist flights to Honolulu 12 days later."

Already, in November Harris had recommended to the Board of Directors that the line be extended from Hong Kong to Calcutta.

December 30, 1953, Harris proposed that, due to many factors—including the CAB's reduction of domestic mail rates—making it impossible to predict revenue income for 1954, the Board of Directors not authorize the payment of the

---

[181] *Time,* March 15, 1954.

quarterly installment of the Preferred dividend, a not unusual postponement and one that was normally acceptable to the old hands on the Board. He stated that at the next meeting on January 11th, he would have estimated revenue figures as well as figures regarding the costs of the shift to New York City offices.

January 6, 1954, Harold Harris summarized for the Board of Directors his accomplishments during the past year. When he took office, he noted, the situation in the company was as follows:

(1) very low net operating income; (2) low employee morale; (3) an increasingly non-competitive fleet; (4) high operating costs; (5) an infirm route structure; (6) no future equipment program; (7) no credit beyond that already extended; (8) no long-range financial and economic planning; (9) little identification with its major market and no enough identity elsewhere; (10) an inefficient and therefore costly overhaul base; and (11) a management structure so organized and administered that it could not properly attend to the Company's affairs.

By contrast, during his administration, "Net operating income increased fourfold. Employee morale has been restored. Arrangements were completed to acquire competitive equipment needed now for critical route segments. The ratio of operating costs to operating revenues was reduced. Applications were actively pressed before the Civil Aeronautics Board to correct the infirmities in the route structure. Additional credit was obtained. An equipment-acquisition program to protect the company's needs after January, 1955, was put into effect. Long-range financial and economic planning was begun. A program was undertaken to increase the Company's identification. The necessary steps were to collect and analyze the facts—and to arouse community interest—so that the problem of the overhaul base may be resolved. And the management was drastically reorganized in many respects, but most importantly so that top management can attend to policy formulation and functional direction, with the daily details of the Company's business being administered by a newly created high-level second echelon of management . . .

"At year's end", he wrote, "it is obvious that the Company will survive and, as attested by greatly increased net operating income, can sustain itself. The groundwork has been laid for the task of increasing the future value of this Company in spite of many obstacles still to be overcome."

Harris had argued successfully that besides the usual group of lawyers and financial representatives, several of whom were new to the Board, the Board of Directors should include at least one hands-on engineer. This was not enough, however, as *Time* (March 15, 1954) observed, to outweigh the voting power of a couple of New York firms interested primarily in short-term stock holders' dividends rather than in the airline's positive profit status or its long term picture. "About 25% of Northwest's common stock, noted *Time*, "is owned by Wertheim Co. or held for customers of two New York brokerage firms, Merrill, Lynch, Pierce, Fenner Beane and Carl M. Loeb, Rhoades Co." These groups that had little or no experience with major airlines except to travel on them, were relatively new arrivals on the Board, Harris noted.

"To the Board's distress", *Time* continued, "the stock sank lower under Harris, from 14 1/2 in 1953 to 9 a year later, though the operating income rose 81% during 1953, from $603,000 to $1,277,000." When Malcolm Mackay, the vice president who took over the reins when Harris was in the hospital, announced the dividend deferral, the stock fell another 1½ points to 7 ½.

January 10th Harris collapsed in Minneapolis and was taken to the Abbott Hospital. He had undergone a severe heart attack. The very next day, January 11th, the Board met and voted to grant him an indefinite leave of absence. They also voted to defer indefinitely most of Harris' well-laid plans: to postpone Harris' order for six Constellation aircraft, to cancel the proposed sale of the Company's old DC-4's along with the purchase of additional DC-6B aircraft as replacements. In the same crushing manner Harris' plan for the location of the main base for repairs and parts in Minneapolis was sent back for further study.

From his hospital bed January 15th in a letter to the Board of Directors Harris penned a letter of self-vindication. He began "On the evening of January 10, 1954, I was informally told by three of the directors that 'lack of confidence' among non-management Board members had led them to the determination to find a new President and Chief Executive Officer of Northwest Airlines. I have since learned that this opinion is not shared by all of you . . ."

The day after the stock fell to a new low, "without a word to President Harris, an executive of the company notified a St. Paul newspaper that Harris was out." (*Time*, March 15, 1954) As Wayne Parrish noted in an editorial for that same issue, the Board's move "serves as a symbol of what happens when financial groups who know virtually nothing about running a public carrier obtain dominant control and seek to be management themselves."

Harris cited "irreconcilable differences" with members of the Board, "who presently constitute a majority of the company's Board of Directors. These disagreements involving the reversal of policies previously approved by the Board, relate to basic policy underlying the planning for the company's future so that the company may properly discharge its obligations to the public, provide security and expanded opportunity for its employees, and offer a fair return to its owners."

March 4th Harris, along with two of his closest aides, quit. His contract with Northwest still had almost four years to run. Wayne Parrish observed that "In his one year as chief executive officer, Harris had made a highly creditable record. Given the time which any management needs to prove itself, he could have restored Northwest to the position it deserves to have, but the financial junta has decreed otherwise."

Chapter 32: Creator of Aviation Financial Services and State Department Consultant During the Cold War

Harold Harris was never satisfied with the prospect of retirement. Relying on the fund of knowledge and enormous network of friends and acquaintances he had developed in the previous almost half a century dealing with all aspects of aviation, he determined to place his connections and expertise at the service of newly created airlines looking for funding. Thus in 1955 Aviation Financial Services was born.

The moment was opportune. Immediately following WW II, the challenge to American aviation had lain in developing a US-based global airlines system utilizing American equipment. In the 1950's the challenge to the American aviation industry lay in the new European turboprop designs and the possibility of European-based jet fleets. It was time for American manufacturers to come up with newly designed aircraft and for airlines to unload their propeller airplanes and acquire jet aircraft. The result was that the conventional aircraft market became glutted with an unprecedented flood of used propeller aircraft.

A letter Harris received dated July 23, 1958, from Edward Lund, President of Lund Aviation, dealers in transport aircraft, outlined the problem thus indirectly giving blessing to the new service. "I have never seen," Lund wrote, "so many airplanes available and so many airlines that could use them with so little cash to pay for them. If this situation is not checked by some concerted, cooperative action between government, banking circles and the aviation industry, it may well deteriorate into a national catastrophe."

Lund enclosed a staff report titled "An Appraisal of the Needs of the Surplus Transport Aircraft Market". It noted that the inability of American airlines to absorb the available used planes for sale was particularly critical. "There would be 600 large [used] transport aircraft" on the market "within the next 3 to 36 months" while at the same time "some 50 major airlines are committed to take delivery of over 600 large, brand new turboprop and turbojet airliners." The new jets, coveted because they were twice as large and incredibly fast, were also incredibly expensive.

Since the American market for used planes was saturated, Lund suggested that young airlines should look abroad for funding where used or "remanufactured" American—created piston airplanes might be welcome. The advantage would be that once accustomed to American products, the foreign purchasers would in the future continue buying American aircraft. Either the U.S. government or commercial banks would finance the necessary loans for the new equipment.

Seeing a perfect opportunity to promote Aviation Financial Services, Harris quickly circulated Lund's report among a large number of his contacts including various arms of the federal government. The result was that Harris was invited to Washington to meet members of the Aviation Division of the State Department. His memo to Mr. W. B. Harding on the events of this day, March 17, 1958, follows.

> They [State Department members] are very much concerned about the possible infiltration of Soviets in the free world's commercial aviation activity. They are also concerned with the growing attempt by the British to improve the British position in the free world commercial aviation field. Their principal concern at the moment is the Middle East and they feel that they would like to have some U.S. entity—not a U.S. flag carrier— establish a maintenance base at Beirut, Lebanon. Their first idea is that such a set-up would also serve as a sales office for secondhand U.S. piston engined aircraft as they become available from the U.S. carrier fleets.

State is concerned that the Soviets may dump Soviet transports, perhaps even turbine powered, in the various local airlines through the Arabian world as a move toward placing technicians and other personnel in a sensitive transport industry in nations whose political positions could be modified in favor of the Soviets by means of the intimate contacts assured.

State wants a set-up whereby the local carriers can secure U.S. equipment on long term lease or time payment purchase, in order to keep the U.S. in the forefront of the local carriers activities and make listening posts available to the U.S. rather than to Russia.

We had a detailed discussion about the most suitable location, the types of aircraft and power plants presently operated, and the types which would be readily available and useful in connection with the specific problems of the local carriers involved. As a result of this detailed discussion, it became evident that more up-to-date specific information would be required and the State will query their representative, Putt Turner, who has recently been transferred to Beirut from Montreal, and whom I have seen in action in Germany and Austria (I think well of him), as well as the CAA people stationed throughout the whole territory, the air attaches, etc.

I told them that until a much more definitive program than was presently possible could be set up, that no one could readily properly evaluate the financial way to go, but indicated that I felt sure that a reasonable program was possible when the information was available.

Lockheed has suggested an investment of $8.5 million by the Government in such a set-up at Beirut, which would be a Lockheed named maintenance center and would act as a sales representative of Lockheed primarily, plus any other manufacturer's products that the State desires to add. A part of this $8.5 million, the State would pay for two Lockheed Electras to be used as demonstrators in the area. State does not think too much of this since it gives one manufacturer an advantage and the program is more costly than they believe necessary.

After further discussion, I believe I convinced State that the proper way to approach the overall problem is in two parts—(1) with the establishment of a maintenance base and, (2) the establishment of a disposal agency for secondhand U.S. aircraft. While these two could and probably should, work closely together, the problems of one should not necessarily involve the other.

Additional discussion was had on the desirability of similar general arrangements in the Indonesian area, with a discussion of Singapore, Bangkok, Manila, Formosa, etc., considered as bases. Also, mention was made of a similar Latin American problem, where discussion was had about a possible base in Lima, Panama, Sao Paulo and/or Buenos Aires. It was agreed that the Far East and Latin America were not as important at the present moment as the Middle East.

My impression is that State would like to have Trans Ocean[182] do the job in Beirut but they are not sure that Trans Ocean has the capital or the competent manpower to swing it. Apparently Trans Ocean has the made a good impression on the State in connection with their activities with the Iranian Airlines with whom Trans Ocean has a management contract. My impression is that PAA [Pan Am] has not made nearly so favorable an impression in the areas where they are operating management contracts, i.e. Turkey, Afghanistan, Thailand, and I believe, Pakistan. State seemed to think well of TWA's work with Ethiopia.

---

[182] I have no information about this operation.

State has tried to come to an agreement with the British
with respect to joint effort in Beirut where the British have
taken over PAA's position in the Middle East Airlines and
have set up a maintenance base for Vickers products. The
British are intensively pushing the Viscount for all Middle
Eastern air carriers and are offering very favorable terms
as an inducement to switching to British aviation products.
Consequently, the British have not reacted favorably to the
State's approach.[183]

My impression is that the suggestion that I made
that George Kraiger who has recently retired from
management of Aramco Airlines may be employed as a
consultant to make a survey trip throughout the Middle
East for the Department of State, in order to make up a
definitive program for the U.S. in that area. In any event,
I suspect we will not hear further from State for another
couple of months."

Harris's proposals seem to have been taken very seriously
by relevant sections of the U.S. Government. On June 19th a
report from the Operations Coordinating Board of the National
Security Council asserted that the Government "should offer
reasonable assistance to U.S. private industry in establishing
in the Middle East a regional aircraft main overhaul base and
a regional aircraft leasing firm to provide normal commercial
services to Middle East users of American manufactured
products..."

The report emphasized the necessity for adequate financing,
the promotion of private loans to the aircraft industry
interested in the Middle East project and the relaxation of
Government credit restrictions. The aim was to "place suitable
aircraft with airlines of the Middle East," something that

---

[183] A later meeting revealed that the British and Trans Ocean had
agreed on "some sort of joint maintenance theory."

heretofore had been accomplished more efficiently by the British than the Americans."

July 3, 1958, Harold Harris became a Foreign Affairs Officer (Consultant) for the State Department, authorized to deal with classified documents. State Department documents show that he was authorized between that date and August 4, 1958, to be reimbursed for travel to New York to talk to bankers.

July 7, 1958, Harris met again with State representatives who notified him that by the middle of August the State Department was responsible for presenting to an interdepartmental group "a proposed program." This program would be based on a joint proposal created by Generals Harold Harris and Robert Walsh—the latter another State appointee—"to make American aircraft available as replacements or as additions to the fleets of the air carriers based in the Middle Eastern area." The proposal would not be limited to the Near East, but could extend to all corners of the globe and would include both used and new airplanes.

The Harris/Walsh proposal provided in short a bailout for U.S. airlines holding unwanted unsold airplanes while also providing insurance that Middle Eastern governments and others around the globe would receive American planes instead of those donated by the Russians. As well it would put the British on notice that their hegemony in the Middle East was terminating.

Subsequent Washington meetings dealt with the need to establish a Trading Company that would negotiate the deals, depending on the Export-Import Bank and private commercial interests for the start up loans necessary to the interested nations. These loans would be guaranteed by the U.S. Government. They should be seen as necessary "pump priming" in an area of the world where free enterprise in the form of venture capital is rarely successful.

July 9th Harris and Walsh met with Government officials to discuss a paper issued by the CAB (Civil Aeronautics Board) itemizing the potential aircraft needs through 1962 of various Middle Eastern air carriers. Sixteen Middle Easter nations had submitted bids to the U.S. for aircraft as follows:

- Aden, 4 F-27s
- Afghanistan, 3DC-6s
- Egypt, 8 F-27s
- Ethiopia, 2 240's
- Greece, 1 DC-6B
- Iran, 1 DC-4, 4 F27s, 1 Viscount
- Israel, 27072, or 2 DC-8s
- Jordan, 5 F-27s
- Kuwait,2 Viscounts
- Lebanon, 4 440s, 1 DC-4, 1 DC-6, 9 DC-6a
- Libya, 3 240s
- Saudi Arabia, 8 340s, 1 DC-3
- Sudan, 2 F-27s
- Syria, 2 F-27s, 3 Viscounts
- Turkey, 1 Viscount
- Yemen, 1 Viscount

Regarding Israel and other unnamed nations, the Harris/Walsh memo noted that further discussions would be necessary since these nations either could arrange their own financing "or would be assisted by the British in connection with the purchase of equipment from Britain."

July 11th Harris and Walsh submitted a memo to the State Department titled "Aircraft Financing Needs for the Middle East" as follows.

> On the basis of rough estimates concerning aircraft needs in the Middle East over the next five years, we can assume that there will be a need to finance the acquisition by local airlines of $70-80 million worth of new or used aircraft beyond those now on order and perhaps $15

million turbo-props. Some $25-35 million might be new aircraft and perhaps $15 million turbo-props. Of the total anticipated financing needed in the area, we estimate that close to $18 million might be financed from non-United States sources in the normal course of events, leaving $50-60 million during the next few years which might be largely through American sources.

It seems clear that there might be some difficulty in arranging dollar financing of aircraft in this area to the extent of $50-60 million during the next few years if entirely normal methods of financing are used as in the past. Accordingly, it is proposed that an Aircraft Trading Company be established to engage primarily in lease and lease-purchase arrangements, hopefully in terms which would be more advantageous and more flexible while still being commercially sound for a profit-making enterprise. Better terms might include lease-purchases with a moderate down payment, with payments related realistically to the life and utilization of the aircraft and to the operating income of the airline, and with the possibility in some cases of repayment partly in local currencies. The Trading Company might operate separately but in conjunction with (but probably separate from) a maintenance /overhaul facility in the area, which could presumably absorb a certain amount of local currency.

We have estimated that, of the total $50-60 million, about two-thirds might be provided through 'normal financing', which is understood to mean that the local airlines might be expected to arrange financing through normal channels already now existing, especially if we assume that a somewhat more liberal attitude is adopted by the Export-Import Bank with respect to used aircraft. In the case of one-third, or some $17 million, there might be a greater need for the more advantageous terms which could be offered by the proposed trading company, or without such terms it might be difficult to assure that aircraft needs were met in keeping with United States objectives. (In some cases the terms needed might be non-commercial, but in such instances the additional risk and financial involvement would be borne by the United States Government.)

It is not intended that the Trading Company would limit its operations to the cases just described (related to the estimate $17 million). It would undertake such of the 'normal' financing as it deemed commercially desirable. If it were to participate eventually in, say, one-half of the 'normal' financing, this would mean an involvement of perhaps another $17 million and bring the total to some $35 million. The figure might be somewhat lower if current receipts from company operations were used to sustain a line of credit, in the nature of a revolving fund.

The target areas of special interest to the trading company, it appears, would be in the United Arab Republic (Egypt-Syria), Lebanon, Jordan, and perhaps Libya. Perhaps two-thirds of such financing would involve used aircraft. It seems likely that a good part of the 'normal' financing arrangements in which the trading company might participate would be in the same countries or in Saudi Arabia, Turkey, Sudan, Greece or Ethiopia.

It is not clear at this stage what the initial involvement in aircraft would be in order to put the trading company into business; for this purpose an on-the-spot survey would be needed. It seems likely, however, that the trading company would want to start off with a small fleet of aircraft suitable to meet the immediate leasing or lease-purchase needs, and for talking purposes, we might assume an initial fleet composed largely of or entirely of used aircraft and valued at not more than $5 million.

What we need to know at this stage is the extent to which private equity capital will be willing to participate in the proposed trading company operation, and the extent to which commercial banks, insurance companies or other private sources will participate in the financing of the aircraft which would be placed in the area. It may be assumed that the United States Government would arrange acceptable guarantees to assure dollar transferability and protection against risks of expropriation or war; and that Government-financial institutions, such as the Export—Import Bank, would be prepared to participate in the financing along with private capital.[184]

July 17th Harris and Walsh submitted a memo to the State Department refining the details concerning funding of purchases by Middle Eastern nations of American aircraft. To emphasize the need for haste in the implementation of this program, the two included with their report a July 10th New York Times clipping detailing the Soviet offer to sell "an unspecified number" of the latest jet airliners to the United Arab Republic.

The establishment of a Trading Company "to handle both new and second-hand aircraft" and the involvement of both private banks and the U.S. Government-sponsored Export-Import Bank to advance loans seemed essential. Essential also, however, was the need to keep direct Government involvement at a minimum.

Attached to this document was a series of tables outlining characteristics of M.E. [Middle East] commercial airlines. The first table detailed the differences between the airline operation of the various interested M.E. nations and U.S. commercial airlines. Next came a review of the overall traffic

---

[184] Attached to this document were several tables detailing methods of possible financing by various Middle East nations.

volume, number of points [destinations] scheduled, and route miles scheduled of each M.E. airline, the revenue ton-miles per airport, the length of hop, route-mile turnover, passenger trip length, and percent of non-scheduled to total capacity.

Overall revenue load and capacity per aircraft; overall revenue load factor; revenue passenger loan and available seats per aircraft; the passenger load factor; the revenue per ton-miles—percent distribution by class of traffic; revenue ton-miles percentage change 1951-6 ; aircraft on hand and on order; list of foreign airlines operating in ME countries; international traffic flow—passenger, mail, and freight; airlines of foreign registry operating in Middle East countries as well as summary of types of aircraft on hand and on order; summary of international traffic flow—all were dealt with in this report.

Also included were route maps, miles from airport to airport, and frequency of operation of the following airlines: Bahrain, Cyprus, Afghanistan, Iran, Greece, Ethiopia, Egypt, Turkey, Syria, Sudan, Saudi Arabia, Lebanon, Iraq, Israel, Jordan, Kuwait.

The final map indicates scheduled services of air carriers of Middle East Countries for February 1958.

Harris and Walsh handed in this, their final report. Their job was done.

Chapter 33: Aviation Financial Services, the Wings Club

Harold Harris returned to Wall Street and Aviation Financial Services. A thin booklet, "Aviation Equipment Financing, A Presentation of the Services Offered" (April, 1959) demonstrated how, backed financially by Smith, Barney Co., Harris was able to offer financing services tailor-made for the needs of a company or an airline requesting help.

The brochure noted that 43 companies and 11 airlines were able to profit from his experience, his contacts, and the brokerage houses' fiscal aid.

"These transactions," it asserted, "involved flight simulators, modern transport aircraft, automotive equipment and commercial appurtenances" as well as "spare parts, aircraft engines, ground equipment, and mechanical appliances."

The company was also deeply involved in the development of two pieces of legislation: (1) the Government Guarantee Act, Public Law 85-307; and (2) the Equipment Trust Amendment to the Bankruptcy Act, Public Law 85-295.

The brochure listed 13 cases in which AFS was successful in aiding a company's development.

I. Carriers desiring the use of flight simulators for crew training in advance of delivery dates of their jet equipment are able to lease this equipment for long terms from wholly owned subsidiaries set up for the purpose by AFS.

II. A manufacturer of airline equipment collaborates with AFS in the design of a program for the financing of its product which permits an airline to make use of this equipment on a pay-a-you-go basis without capital investment. The manufacturer uses this plan as a sales tool.

III. A United States airline needs to add newly developed equipment to its fleet. It owns some modern transport aircraft, which it has leased on a long-term basis to another carrier. Arrangement is made for a private investor to purchase the aircraft subject to the long lease. Thus the airline owner is able to recapture his investment and order new equipment.

IV. An international carrier operating long range piston engined aircraft, long range jets, and medium range propjets, is confronted with the problem of maintaining and overhauling three different types of engines.

V. The traffic and operations department of a United States carrier determine that their anticipated route and traffic requirements necessitate the use of 4 ½ large jet aircraft for optimum performance. AFS designs a program which gives this carrier part-time use of a jet aircraft identical to the 4 which it has on order to provide the additional services needed for economic operation.

At the same time the requirement of another carrier for part-time utilization of this aircraft is also satisfied.

VI. An international airline is confronted with the necessity of obtaining funds for the purchase of new equipment. AFS arranges for the purchase of some large piston engined transports from this carrier and for their lease to a major United States trunk airline which requires additional equipment to serve newly awarded routes.

VII. A government owned foreign carrier is reluctant to appeal to a dollar-short treasury to buy needed new jet powered equipment. Its present fleet of modern piston engined aircraft is sold to AFS. New jets are leased to the carrier for its long-term use.

VIII. A major airline carries three times as many passengers during its peak seasons it does during the winter months of the year. Another airline carries 30% more traffic during the winter months than during the balance of the year. AFS arranges for the purchase of the desired aircraft and its lease on a long term basis to the first carrier during its peak season and to the second carrier during its heavy traffic months.

IX. An air carrier having recently purchased modern equipment which was financed by a medium term loan, is faced with the competitive requirement of ordering pure jets which are now available. A large part of the present loan is still outstanding so it becomes necessary to refinance this loan and obtain additional funds for the purchase of the required jets.

X. A local service carrier requires modern flight equipment. AFS arranges with insurance companies and banks to make use of the government guarantee for the supply of funds necessary for the purchase of modern flight equipment.

XI. A revolutionary development in the air transport industry has been the return or sale of used equipment to airframe manufacturers as part payment for new aircraft. In response to the need of major aircraft manufacturers of the United States, AFS prepared to submit programs for the disposition of secondhand equipment, as required, by the manufacturers of airframes.

XII. An international carrier is in search of additional capital to meet commitments already entered into for the purchase of new jet aircraft. The carrier owns a substantial number of modern piston engined planes. A percentage of this fleet is purchased by AFS and leased back to the airline until it takes delivery of the jet equipment. Cash generated by the sale of the present fleet is applied to the purchase of the jet aircraft.

XIII. A substantial amount of highly specialized ground equipment is necessary for the operation of each of the long range jet types. AFS buys the ground equipment and leases it to the carrier for its use on a long-term basis."

Amazingly, although it was a tremendously risky as well as creative business, AFS survived until Harris retired in 1965.

It was concerning this period that—much later—I was inspired to write the following.

When John Glenn circumnavigated the earth at an altitude higher than any man had ever gone, our Dad was working at the business of promoting financing for small airplane companies that were, literally and metaphorically, simply trying to get off the ground. I remember watching Glenn's thrilling ride on TV and phoning Daddy in New York to tell him that I was thinking of what he represented as a living embodiment of almost the entire American experience with flight. I had no sooner launched into my story than Daddy stopped me. "Thank you, dear, for calling" he said abruptly, "but I'm really busy right now.

So when it came time to ask my son Alex to draw a suitable illustration for the cover of my father's 85th birthday celebration invitation, I wrote this:

I said to my son, give me
some illustrations something
to epitomize the career
Of a business man who, when notified of John Glenn's
bold leap outwards, said simply
Thank you, but I'm busy right now,

meaning that he had been caught
in midflight, mindflight
between vectors and passenger
capacity, not that his soul was ever anywhere but in
the pure empyrean
where the towering cumulus
dazzle and torment, walking
like silent giants noiselessly
beside the silver craft—
needle in a blue haystack.

I talked of parachutes and biplanes
cartoon-style. My son who bathed
early in the jet stream,
knew better, drew instead
the bright eyeblink in the clouds
signifying heaven.

Retirement from active participation did not mean that Harold Harris abandoned the field of aviation. In 1954 he and associates had created the Wings Club high in a Manhattan office building, dedicated to" the advancement and development of aeronautics". Besides providing a convenient meeting place for like-minded executives to make valuable contacts, as of 1963 the Club featured an annual Sight Lecture, so-named by Harold Harris because each lecturer was asked to produce "insights, hindsights and foresights" of aviation.

Harris was elected President of the Club in 1958/9. Following a string of lectures by aviation notables, it was Harris's turn to deliver the Sight lecture, thereafter called the General Harold R. Harris Sight Lecture in his honor. His 1984 talk, aptly titled "The First 80 Years" was a summation of his lifetime involvement in and passion for aviation.

TWENTY-FIRST WINGS CLUB
GENERAL HAROLD R. HARRIS
'SIGHT' LECTURE

Chapter 34: The Summing Up

To accommodate the demands of his work, the Harold Harris' family moved several times. Upon arrival from Lima in 1938, the family moved briefly to Scarsdale, N.Y. With the onset of War, the house was sold in 1942 and Grace joined her husband in Alexandria, a Virginia suburb of Washington, D.C. The War's end saw the family in New York City, ultimately retreating in 1948 to Westport, CT. and then, finally, to New Canaan, CT. where for some years Harold Harris commuted to New York City, maintaining his involvement in both the Wings Club and Aviation Financial Services. He began compiling material for an autobiography.

Lovingly tended by husband, son, and daughter, Grace died in 1978 on Cape Cod, where father, mother, and son had been accustomed to retreat in the summertime. In 1979 Harold Harris sold the New Canaan house—our mother's antique joy—and the three of us and my four children joined forces in Falmouth, MA., where Harold Harris lost no time in joining the Congregational Church and generally attaching himself to the community.

The community was delighted. The Falmouth Enterprise published a series of articles accompanied by photographs of his early exploits that helped Harold Jr. and me and my four children bathe in the luster! Harold Harris quickly made

285

numerous friends, continuing a habit of giving talks about his experiences.

Dorothy Turkington, wife of the co-editor of the Falmouth Enterprise and a longtime much-loved high school English teacher, after meeting him, wrote the following:

To Harold R. Harris

You must have been at home
in planes and sky, with winds—those errant ones—
but you have been at home, too
with books and foreign places.
And now you join us,
        to a more circumscribed place,
        this apostrophe of land
        between the continent and the sea,

between the country and the air.
Sea birds are common here:
wood ducks, mergansers, teals, scoters,
And swans more at home than on the Thames.
We are accustomed to the weather:

Fog, spray, and winds—those errant ones.
        Winters in monotones:
No bazaars here, no souks, camels,
        Bullfights, mosques, gilt, glory.
So now you join us,

        The Pilgrims moored here briefly.
        Paul Revere's bell is here, and Thoreau was.
In a small Cape theatre group someone said,
        "Mr. O'Neill has got a whole truck of plays,"
        and that was his beginning.

And now you join us.
We are honored and enriched,
Not for your past adventures, feats, even fame,
        but for you now:

your humor and quick riposte,
your charm and cheerfulness, you interest in our favorite institution—
        town meeting—

your quick intelligence,
your being comfortable wherever you are.
For being and still becoming
we are honored and enriched
        now that you belong here.
        Dot Turkington

It was in his favorite chair on July 28, 1988, that Harold Harris peacefully died. With his passing, friends from many parts of the world grieved, the writer of his obituary in the London Times, a close friend, referring to him as "Hal".

Many associates and employees had loved and respected him. Retired USAF Major Dana Seiler, who became Harold Harris' traveling companion during his last years, noted in his speech at Harris' memorial service that Harris' "selflessness, devotion to duty, honor and unrelenting perseverance in his contribution to the progress of aviation, both in the military and civilian areas were his watchwords".

Shortly after the publication in the New York Times of Harold Harris' death, our local Falmouth Enterprise received and printed a reminiscence that illustrates the nature of the man. David C. Frailey, author of the article, a former American Airlines employee, provided this account.

> When General Harris' Thumb Got in the Way of the Champagne Bottle

The report in the New York Times of the death of Falmouth resident Harold R. Harris listed many of his achievement during a long and illustrious career in the Air Force and in the airline industry. He was one of aviation's greats.

What the obituary did not mention was that General Harris could be a mighty good sport. I know that from my only personal experience with him when I was starting my own airline career in the 1940's as a young public relations representative for American Airlines and its trans-Atlantic division American Overseas Airlines, which he headed as vice president and general manager.

We christened a lot of airplanes in those days—some of them more than once. Put a new airplane on an old route, or an old airplane of a new route, and we'd ask a civic official or a congressman or a diplomat or their wives to christen the plane. All the planes had names, and we could change those names with a bit of paint or with a silver masking tape bearing the new name.

Airlines all had what we called 'christening plates', a sharp-edged metal piece that could be attached to the fuselage to protect the plane's skin from the impact of the champagne bottle. Experience had taught us to 'score' the champagne bottles with a file for easier breaking and also to wrap the bottles securely with tape to prevent shattering.

Service to Reykjavik.

So came a day when General Harris' American Overseas Airlines was to inaugurate service from Washington's National Airport to Keflavil Airport service Reykjavik, Iceland. The plane on the first flight, an old DC-4, if I remember correctly, was to be christened, naturally, the Flagship Reykjavik. The wife of the Icelandic ambassador, Mrs. Thor Thors, was to swing the champagne. As the

Washington public relations person I was to arrange press coverage, have the champagne handy and—for further insurance—a hammer, gaily decorated with a ribbon, in case the bottle refused to break.

But there was a problem. Although I had scored a champagne bottle, taped it and tied a nice ribbon around it—in Iceland's colors, no doubt—the American Overseas Airlines headquarters public relations staff, holdovers from the time when the airline had been a subsidiary of a shipping company, sent me a bottle of champagne prepared for a ship christening. No score, and covered with a heavy, ropelike material. (After all the ship christener stands way back, gives the bottle a boost and lets it fly and pick up momentum as it heads for the heavy metal of the ship.) General Harris, loyal to his own people in New York, chose the ship-type bottle. He and Mrs. Thors ascended the steps to the plane; he said a few words about how pleased the airline was to begin serving Iceland from our nation's capital, and then he asked Mrs. Thors to christen the plane.

Time for the Hammer

She swung the bottle time and time again against the metal plate. And nothing happened. It just would not crack. General Harris asked me to get the hammer.

And then several things happened very quickly. While Mrs. Thors placed the bottle next to the christening plate, General Harris gave the bottle a hefty tap with the hammer. The bottle spurted a small mist of champagne. He obviously decided that the deed had been done, the christening accomplished. Mrs. Thors just as obviously thought the bottle had been readied for the real thing.

General Harris placed his hand on the plate—to indicate, I guess, that it had helped to do the job—at exactly the moment Mrs. Thors let fly again. This time the bottle exploded as it caught General Harris' left thumb. My thumb hurts to this day just writing about that accident. That was the only christening I can recall when the spewing champagne was mixed with a shower of blood.

And the remarkable thing was that General Harris did not so much as whimper. He did not stop smiling. He thanked Mrs. Thors for handling her inaugural role so beautifully. And then he posed for photographers while airline attendants cleaned his wound and applied an enormous bandage that probably saved his thumb.

He didn't even complain when all the inaugural publicity showed only his thumb being bandaged. There was nothing about the newly christened Flagship Reykjavik or the new service or Mrs. Thors flailing away at the plane.

General Harris was a wonderful sport about it all.

I have never forgotten the incident and I have had through the years the utmost respect for him.

Of the many photos we have of our Dad, there is one we particularly cherish. Taken at Cape Cod's Otis Air Force Base on May 22, 1987, the day of the Annual Base Air Show, it shows him flanked on either side by eight members of the Air Force Blue Angels Flying Team. Shrunken and stooped with age—he was almost 92 when the photo was taken—he stares from under his black Portuguese fisherman's cap into the camera, eyes narrowed, his whole frame alert. In every sense of the word, he is one of them.

In *Wind. Sand and Stars*, Antoine de Saint Exupery, whom Daddy met when the famous author was flying a mail route in Brazil, wrote:

The events of a life are not notches on a perpendicular bar, one above the other. They are not embedded in one spot in time. They are more like horizontal beads in a tapestry. That red thread that appears at only one point in your life, the red center of a flower—has it not been there all the time, hidden underneath on the backside of the tapestry, waiting till it should find its place in the pattern, disappeared once it had fulfilled the role, but underneath all the time, forming part of the whole firm, intricate, varied structure of the woof?

There is no doubt but that Daddy's red thread was flight. Always optimistic, always looking into the future, he followed its unerring path. I think he still does.

       This poem I titled "Flying the Time Line."

          It is chilly in the cockpit.
          The pilot, resting his eyes,
          pushes up his goggles, presses
          gloved fingers against the lids.

          Cold air needles stab his face.
          Except for the engine's regular
          shudder, he is alone.
          Checking location, he looks down.

          Below, undulating lazily,
          flows a red line. He turns
          his gaze. Behind, lost in clouds,
          their pilots pinned inside,

          lie a million twisted wrecks.
          Ahead, in the new dawn,
          a handful of bright stars.
          Towards these he sets his course.

The 102nd Fighter Interceptor Wing

The Caterpiller Club
and
Friends

PROUDLY HONOR HAROLD R. HARRIS, BRIG. GEN. USAF (RET.), ONE OF AMERICA'S FOREMOST TEST PILOTS, ON HIS 65TH ANNIVERSARY AS THE FIRST PILOT TO SUCCESSFULLY PARA-CHUTE FROM A DISABLED AIRPLANE, AND THE FIRST MEMBER OF THE CATERPILLER CLUB.

October 20, 1987
Base Activity Center
Otis Air National Guard Base

Acknowledgements and Bibliography

Deepest thanks to the following that supplied me with invaluable information and with most of whom I corresponded via email on a fairly regular basis.

The Archives Section of Wright State University Library, Dayton, Ohio, whose personnel led by Lynda Kachurek, Archivist/ Collections Manager, offered special viewing apparatus along with permission to use and copy whatever resources were available.

Justin H. Libby, author of numerous articles on early aviators, including "Harold Ross Harris", *AAHS Journal,* v.55, 4, Winter 2010, who provided me with at least one long unpublished article on Harold R. Harris that is mentioned in footnotes as simply "Libby bio". He also provided a comprehensive Harris Bibliography. Prof. Libby was kind enough to read my first draft as well as providing me with information and comments regarding the magnitude of the contribution Harold Harris made to the development of aviation.

Donald Beatty, Memoir of the Search for the San Jose. Available in Harold R. Harris's archive, Wright State University, Dayton, OH.

Bill Bielauskas, *Imphal, the Hump and Beyond*, website

Bill Maher, CNAC Hump Pilots "First to Fly the Hump"website

James Hoogerwerf, biographer of the beginnings of Delta Airlines.

Ralph Cooper, creator of a website on early aviators.

Walter Ringle, focus on helicopter pilots.

Captain Paul Willey, author of *Memories of Panagra, Pan American-Grace Airways.*

As well as the following sources:

Bibliography

Airlines Established in 1937. Hephaestus Books, n.d.

Mabry I. Anderson. *Low and Slow: An Insider's History of Agricultural Aviation.* San Francisco: California Farmer Publishing Company, 1986.

Marylin Bender and Selig Altschul. *The Chosen Instrument: Pan Am Juan Trippe, The Rise and Fall of an American Entrepreneur.* New York: Simon and Schuster, 1982.

Robert Lee Boughten, Jr.,. *From Clipper Ship to Clipper Ship: A History of W. R. Grace Company.* B.A. dissertation, Princeton University, 1942.

William A.M. Burden. *The Struggle for Airways in Latin America.* New York: Council on Foreign Relations, 1943.

Dominguez Air Meet, 1910. Published by Hatfield History of Aeronautics, Northrop University, 1976.

A.W. DuBois. "Panagra the Beginning", in Captain Paul Willey, Memories of Panagra, 2009.

Richard Hallion. *Test Pilot: The Frontiersmen of Flight.* New York, Doubleday, 1981.

Harold R. Harris. *The First 80 Years,* General Harold R. Harris "Sight" Lecture. New York: Wings Club, 1984.

Harold R. Harris. Unpublished Memoirs.

James A. Hoogerwerf. *Roots: From Crop Dusting to Airline; The Origins of Delta Airlines to World War II.* Ph.D. Dissertation, Auburn University, 2010.

Nick A. Komons, *Bonfires to Beacons: Federal Civil Aviation Policy under the Air Commerce Act 1926-1938.* Washington: Smithsonian Institution Press, 1989.

William A. Krusen, *Flying the Andes: The Story of Pan American Grace Airways.* Tampa: University of Tampa, Press, 1995

Edward Davis Lewis. *Dear Bert, An American Pilot Flying in World War I Italy.* Logisma Editore, 2002.

Fortune. *The Long Cold War of Panagra,* 1952.

Newsletter of the Florida Aviation Historical Society, May, 2009.

Ralph A. O'Neill. *A Dream of Eagles,* Boston: Houghton Mifflin, 1973.

Panagra, *Confidential Report to the Civil Aeronautics Board reference Elimination of Axis Airlines in South America during World War II.* 1943.

"Pan American Grace Airways: Silver Ships of the Andes". The American Aviation Historical Society Journal LIV, Spring, 2009.

Jim Ray. *The Story of Air Transport.* Philadelphia, John C. Winston Company.n.d.

Florence Sprenger. *Spirit of the Toilers: An Intimate Epic of the Unique Educational and Social Adventure that Became Manual Arts High School*, 1977. Dallas: Taylor Publishing Company.

Hudson Strode. *South By Thunderbird,* Random House, 1937.

Edward Pearson Warner. *The Early History of Air Transportation.* Norwich: Norwich University. 1937.

Appendix A: Correspondence, Ross Allen to Harold, June and Jessica to Harold

None reveals better the complex personality of this multi-gifted man—who still loved the ladies!—than the following letter to the whole family describing an exciting musicale Ross attended on October 28, 1932.

> I went to a small musical Sunday night, at a native Australian's, 'by invitation only'. I ran away from church after the anthems and was late, of course. But Mein Herr Philo Becker greeted me, all smiles. He has had all his teeth out and looks it. His charming lady looked lovely in blue satin. The music was furnished by a trio, piano, violin, and cello.
>
> A really beautiful young lady with the eyes of a seraph and glorious coloring (synthetic?) was at the piano. Mein Herr explained to me, "That is Paloma." Now Paloma is Spanish for Dove and she was some pigeon! She flirted with Heaven with those soulful eyes. And with me—sitting in front of her (a young man would have been flattered)—I was hypnotized. It must be confessed that she pivoted like a dying top on the piano stool. But how she could play!
>
> A great artist—I studied cello with him in a former incarnation—was the cellist, sitting up so straight he had to brace his feet on the chair rung to keep from falling backward. He, too, played as if inspired.
>
> The violinist looked like a Hebrew Nihilist"...[185] (There is only a slight chance that our grandfather could have

---

[185] Nihilism, defined as "a doctrine or belief that conditions in the social organization are so bad as to make destruction desirable," was a label applied in the media to the pre-1917 Revolution

known what a Hebrew Nihilist looked like. It seems apparent the characterization was meant to imply a fierce-looking individual unkempt, with shaggy hair.)

but he was certainly a master of the violin and viola. Some antique numbers of the 15th and 16th century were rendered—perfectly. And a glorious sonata by Brahms. I was entranced—and wondered if the divine Dove smoked. Smoking—by ladies—is my pet peeve, you know.

After the program was finished, everybody was introduced to everybody else, while men and women smoked cigarettes and talked—banalities—conversation is a lost art. I was introduced to the heavenly Paloma Schram—twice. And incidentally learned that the gangling 18 year-old girl—who resembled her mamma not at all—was her daughter. In fact she has three children. Mein Herr said "Olga Steef (his most celebrated pupil) heard Paloma play and said, 'I am going to play as well as Paloma'" and did it! After his instruction, of course.

I met a number of distinguished people; and wished I myself were as distinguished. They had but few ideas beyond the commonplace. (Nor had I! In that I was one with them.) But the truly great are ever thus!

Then we were ushered thru ornate rooms, stuffy with furniture, great paintings, and hangings, to the dining room, oriental as a Pasha's palace. Here we were served exotic refreshments and occidental liquids. Mine host asked if I would prefer wine or beer. I said (with my usual French tact and finesse) "Thank you. I don't drink anything

---

opponents of the Russian czar. Perhaps more specifically it signified Ross's reading of the media coverage of the trial and subsequent execution in 1889 in Odessa of most of a band of 28 Nihilists, 8 of whom were Jews, as reported in the NY Times for May 14, 1880.

stronger than H20.'Everybody else took one or the other beverage; as the highly spiced viands made us all thirsty.

A plainly dressed lady passed in the milling crowd. I asked, quite innocently, 'Do you know where I can get a glass of water?' 'I'm shaw I cahnt tell you'.

Horrors! I wondered if she <u>were</u> a maid. I had met there a <u>rich</u> physician (yes!); a versatile portrait painter, who had recently returned from a trip around the world; and a lot of others in the local Who's Who. Maybe this maid was a Lithuanian princess in disguise! For it was a Bohemian bunch.

A scion of the royal family of Italy, a De Medici—that was his real name—a celebrated violinist; a splendid young American—he knew a physician I was acquainted with; Spanish, Swedish, Brazilian and German highbrows. I was the only misfit or was it my inferiority complex?

Well, it was lots of fun—and one doesn't have enough real fun anyhow. And the music and Paloma were celestial— while they lasted. But Idyllwild or Balboa [California resorts] is preferable. Anything but princesses in disguise.

What can we learn from this description about the nature of its author? We are treated to the widower's powers of critical description—"Mein Herr Philo Becker greeted me, all smiles. He has had all his teeth out and looks it;" his persisting sexual interest: "A really beautiful young lady with the eyes of a seraph and glorious coloring"; his social snobbery: "I went to a small musical Sunday night, at a native Australian's, 'by invitation only', and "The violinist looked like a Hebrew Nihilist"; his proclamation of moral superiority : "I don't drink anything stronger than H20".; and, perhaps most significant, his prejudices and insecurities: "I met a number of distinguished people; and wished I myself were as distinguished . . . I was the only misfit or was it my inferiority complex?"

I wonder at this display of humility and self-abasement by a man known as the stern patriarch of his family who had already accomplished so much in his lifetime. Did it arise solely from his financial insecurities, and if so why did these arise? Were they simply a product of the times—when people cut back on physician's services? (In the family letter describing the 1932 Los Angeles-based summer Olympics, Ross writes that "Work is falling off as it is apt to in August. But I keep reasonably busy. All the doctors are weeping—no work and no collections. Be glad" he tells his son, "You've a job.") Was it due to his simple mismanagement of funds, i.e. poor investments? Or did it also stem from something in his childhood?

Finally, the way Ross Allen's narrative leading up to the discovery—and implied letdown—that a sexual idol—"A really beautiful young lady with the eyes of a seraph and glorious coloring"—actually was married and had in tow an unbeautiful teenage daughter reveals the humor—including that directed at oneself—that was and continues to be an essential element of the Harris family zeitgeist and that of its offspring.

Ross Allen had an eye for the girls, no doubt about that. It is interesting that in a family letter he was quite open about his admiration for good-looking women. In this regard, his beloved younger daughter Jessica (our Aunt Jessica) remembered a time shortly after the death of her mother, when the two on their daily stroll, Ross Allen suddenly turned to her and asked what she thought of his proposing marriage to the 17-year old daughter of the family living next door.

Jessica was shocked. Although her beloved mother had died four years earlier, the union seemed in all ways inappropriate and undesirable. Summoning her best diplomacy, she argued with him gently, noting how unfair it would be for an elderly man facing death in a few years to chain down as a widow a young person on the brink of her adult life. He apparently was persuaded since she never heard more on the subject.

In the letters Ross Allen's financial difficulties were persistent and acute, although they do not specifically mention his purchase and subsequent loss of various properties.

At the same time excerpts from a letter dated October 9, 1932 seem to indicate that he had indeed acquired several properties and was consequently—in the light of a vastly diminished income—saddled with excessive mortgage repayments as well as taxes : ". . . there is no used deceiving myself as to my financial status. My assets at a forced sale would perhaps amount to 60 or 70 thousand dollars. Yet, with taxes and assessments as they are I am constantly in the hole. I reproach myself for not forcing my way into the army ; I tried to get in and as you know was recommended for a Captaincy when your telegram came "Under no circumstances accept anything less than Major." I wrote to Washington to that effect, not mentioning you or your message. Now lesser men than I who got in are freed by a mistaken California law from paying taxes at all, which makes the taxes all the more burdensome for us who must pay.

"Now don't get panicky and think I am going to ask you to pay my November taxes. I shall pay them as far as I can. As for the rest, I shall let them become delinquent unless . . ."

"I have thought of a number of ways out," he continued. "I owe you $1000 in round numbers. I owe $5000 in mortgage on this house. No other indebtedness except for auto repairs, some $25 . . . I have work to do, some of it not very remunerative, but am glad when a $1 a-call patient comes in."

Despite feeling that he would have at most another ten years to live, with the implication that death at least would end his indebtedness, Ross Allen persevered in looking for ways out of his financial dilemma.

He discussed the possibility that through the "Immanuel Presbyterians" he should be able to publish for profit some of his writings." "A man in New York"—a Mr. Stevenson—who had passed some of Ross' manuscripts onto a manuscript reader" had praised his "superb individualistic style", and felt certain there was a market for his work.

In response Ross intended to shower him with "a short, serious poem" and perhaps a chapter or two of the novel he was working on.

He then proceeded to suggest that he take on a mortgage of $6500 "or possibly $7000" on the family home that Ross reckoned was worth at least $25,000, "since Wilshire has been opened (Orange Street)." Thus he could pay off the $5000 mortgage on the home and all his taxes, "insure the places on which the insurance has lapsed (I have to keep mortgaged property insured), and by that time I believe I will have a better income."

A letter of December 28, 1932, refers again to the mortgage idea for the family home. But by this time Ross had pointedly suggested that his son take over the mortgage and give him the requisite cash. He was quickly rebuffed. Harold Ross' reply came in the form of a registered letter enclosing a $10 check. Ross Allen's son had rejected the scheme, and the father in what was clearly a face-saving gesture, quickly agreed:

"I don't wonder you couldn't 'see the point' in transferring the mortgage from a local bank to your act. [account]. It was that, as it is now, that the bank could foreclose at any time that the terms of the mortgage were not literally fulfilled."

He explained that he maintained the home, paid the insurance and until recently also the taxes. However, the current taxes of $326.90 in default found him without funds. He argued that his son should realize that he, Ross, didn't have long to live and that Harold could probably utilize that fact to good advantage. ["I thought you would be protected by your future ownership of my effects as soon as my time has run (when death occurs) so you would be certain of the mortgage and interest finally anyhow"]. He noted that if Harold took over Ross's mortgage, he might not hold his father in default. ["In case I did default temporarily you would not foreclose, and thus make it impossible for me to carry on my work . . . For I am still strong and able to work, if I can get work, and this office is at a fairly good strategic situation."

He concluded his failed attempt: "But I can see your view point and will not urge you to do what you don't want to do."

Regardless, in January 1933, clearly desperate, Ross was back on the attack. Writing again to Harold, he noted that "Taxes are overdue and interest on the mortgage. This is the cheerful situation! Mrs. Lamb, the Avalon purchases" [I Googled "Avalon" and found a reference to a Hollywood nightclub and a Catalina Island resort. This might refer to either of these pieces of land.] . . ." has defaulted. De Morris, who sent me most of my surgical cases, was buried a week ago—cancer. Mrs. Marshall [housekeeper/secretary] is sick, possibly appendicitis. I have been unable to sell any of my brainchildren; but keep writing and have an interesting variety of rejection slips. If in spite of all these prognostications, you are willing to lend me the money, I will give you a note at 7%. Please let me know right away because otherwise I must try elsewhere. The amount is $700 for first taxes(with 10% interest) second installment taxes (now due) and mtg. interest (and 45 cts.)"

His strength despite his advancing years was reassuring to Ross. In a special message to his son, a written attachment to a typed family letter describing the July, '32 Los Angeles Olympics, he writes that "the sun baths have made me over, as much as a prehistoric machine can be made over." Observing the beautiful young men and women athletes, He laments his lost youth. "Oh for reincarnation with their opportunities," he says wistfully, "which they seem to esteem so lightly."

By October he boasted: "I thought—in a year and one-half I shall have lived out this allotted span of man's life [70]. I never felt younger—or, in a way, happier. The good old days were not when I was twenty, thirty, or forty. They are now, if ever they were. They will be better if I can make them so . . ."

Yet in the January '33 letter his claim that he was physically fit seemed designed to show that he was still eager to make money and however possible dig himself out of debt. "I am as young and capable (?) as ever". he asserted. He concluded that "Suicide wouldn't pay my debts nor cancel my mistakes. Labor and courage and cheerfulness may. I am not discouraged."

February 20th, 1933, found Ross ecstatically welcoming his son's check (for $700 to pay taxes): "I signed this morning for your incredible airmail registry. I hardly dared open it" but did so finally "with a small knife blade—oh, so carefully." He tells Mrs. Marshall "my Secretary, to take it immediately to the bank." The bank, unfortunately, sent word that they could not cash the check until receiving verification via an airmail letter from New York [the main branch of Harold's bank?)] Regardless "a great burden is rolled off my mind."

Ross complained of a throbbing headache, due probably—he said—to the fact that three days previous he lay under a hot sun and fell asleep for an hour. His head was severely burned. That was on a Thursday. By Friday he had a painful headache that hadn't yet, at the time of writing, left him.

Since he was a doctor, by Sunday, when he stayed in bed most of the day, he was running over a list of possible causes for the headache: "spinal meningitis, brain tumor, dural adhesions and other pleasant themes." Yet always a moralist, Ross noted that his foolishness should serve as a warning to others.

Harold seemed to have indicated that he was due to return to the U.S. shortly. Ross greeted the news with pleasure but added that of course he understands that his son would probably be too busy to fly cross-country to see him.

His mention that Grace seemed too frail to teach leaves me mystified. He added that if Grace wished to stay with him, she and the children could stay in the spare rooms that thus far he had had no luck in renting out.

He mentioned his daughters: June (not yet divorced) and Jessica (married with baby Dorothy). Aunt Lou will soon be 80, Ross said. He wrote a birthday Ode to her, his half-sister, who served as a substitute mother for him throughout his childhood. He harkened back to his old proposition—that Harold take over the balance of Ross' mortgage. The times are terrible, he said; no one trusts the banks and people are being advised to withdraw all their funds and convert them into gold coins. "It reminds me of a sign", he said, "in a San Francisco restaurant, 'Your check may be all right, but we don't trust the banks.'"

He told of his current joy in writing music: "Taking some celebrated melody like the Swan, Meditation from Thais . . . I have harmonized them for mixed or male voices . . .

Five days later he characterized himself as "an invalid." The headaches had worsened; the attending physician thought the cause was an enlarged pituitary; Ross has vomited "great quantities" of bile and thought it might be a bilious attack such as his half-sister Lou was prone to get. He spoke of "the torturing headache that is undermining my morale."

The transfusion of a young man's blood had been recommended. He knew the second blood donor very well:" He is a very fine Christian aviator . . . German, but in sickness one forgets all racial prejudices."

He concluded that he "bragged too much of good health and well being . . . If it be true . . . that 'Whom the Lord loveth, he chasteneth,' I must be the object of His solicitude." He assumed that, rather than the Lord's wrath, "It is largely of my own indiscretion in eating, and general cussedness, and irregularity in sleeping."

A few days later Ross, now dictating to his German blood-giver friend, who had become his nurse, wrote the Lima family to allay any fears raised by his last letter: "Dr. Oliver Wendell Holmes wrote, 'A sick man is a rascal.' I would add, 'A sick man is frequently an imbecile when it comes to opinions and prejudices."

Ross's physician is a Dr. Purcell, a woman who seems for her time competent enough. She gives him shots of pituitary extract and pills for his headache, by now accompanied by a raging fever. His German blood-giver helps Ross onto the sleeping porch where it is a bit cooler. They joke about the wet towel on his head—to ease the fever—that makes Ross look like Mahatma Gandhi.

On March 4th, again dictating, Ross blames his illness on personal indiscretions of "eating, drinking, and exercise." The original diagnosis of heat stroke was revised by Dr. Purcell to an under-active pituitary gland. Now he is told he has Indicanuria in which the urine runs blue. [See the film "The Madness of King George."] He finds humor in the fact that contemporary diseases force one to look in the dictionary for their meaning.

He describes the bath his German male nurse laid him in to reduce the fever. Coming out of it he fainted and would have drowned if Ernest was not there to haul him out. Would drowning have been so bad? he wonders. "I came to the conclusion that nothing matters, indeed, since there was no assurance of getting well and staying well . . .

"Now I can sympathize with the suffering of Mae, Grace, Harold and little Harold and Alta Mae; with June and Bert Snow and little Bert; with Jessica, Dorothy, and Arthur; and Lou, Mabel, and Pearl . . .

This is the last letter from Ross Allen.

Correspondence between Jessica, June, and Harold

June, the elder of the two, and Jessica, both considerably younger than Harold—whom they both adored—were close friends. Both were endowed with their mother's fiery red hair. Jessica was inclined to be as corpulent as her mother, whereas June was wand-slender. Divorced with one child, Bert, now living in southern California, June had a successful career as a buyer for a prominent women's clothing store. Jessica, who became a successful commercial artist, married Arthur Goodearl. Their union produced two children: Dorothy and Donald. These letters reveal the contrasts in the youthful personalities of the three: Jessica, steady with attention to detail; June, bubbly and warm; Harold, calm and logical: all three concerned and generous in response to their father's illness.

March 9, 1933. Jessica writes, "Father is very ill and I thought yesterday that he would surely die. Today he seems to have rallied a little but his condition is heart breaking. He is in such pain and is so weak that I hate to go in to him . . . His mind wanders . . . You know of course about his pituitary gland and his hemorrhoids." (The doctor was giving him digitalis for his heart and insulin for the sugar in his urine.)

"Of course there is no money to speak of, and no cash so I have been using my money (what there is of it!) Mrs. Marshall hasn't drawn her salary for weeks and Mrs. Clark is due $5.00. Father told me that in a recent letter you had sent him $700 for his taxes. Thank you, Harold, I'm grateful to you. Arthur [her husband] and I couldn't help him out there as Arthur is now supporting his folks and has had so many salary cuts that we have to go carefully. The banks being closed of course complicates matters. We'll manage some way until they open again. I am going to stay here two weeks or longer if absolutely necessary.

"Mrs. Clark is going today and I will take her place house-keeping... Will write later. Please write to Father. He asks every day about you."

March 10, 1933. Jessica again. "Just a note to let you know father is going to the hospital this afternoon—perhaps never to return. I called in Dr. Lissner and he believes from the rough tests he made this morning that it is either a tumor of the brain or spinal meningitis Perhaps other complications, If you are coming up soon and could make it a little earlier, it might be well—but not at all necessary as Father will probably be under opiates and wouldn't know you anyway."

March 14, 1933. June writes of the earthquake that shook the hospital the day Ross was brought in. The consolation, she notes, was that he probably wasn't aware of it. "The earthquake was everything the papers say it was—terrible. Ed and Haven [I don't know who they were] took some pictures in Long Beach and some of the buildings were simply flattened to the ground. Some of the houses twisted off their foundations. "[The Long Beach earthquake of 1933 with a magnitude of 6.4, caused widespread damage to buildings throughout Southern California.]

In regard to her father, there were more tests with no specific results. He suffered mostly from a terrible headache that wouldn't go away. The doctors refused to give him opiates for the pain because they might cause him to die. "J and I decided that he would be happier to go that way—he has always said so, you know—instead of suffering so. It seems very inhumane to me to let him suffer. We think he knows he hasn't long to live. He was talking to J today about his will . . ."

With help from Ross's male nurse, Ernest Frisius (at $1 per day!) who tended the patient at night, and a female nurse at $25 weekly during the day, the sisters established Ross back in his home in a rented hospital bed.

By March 17th the patient appeared to have turned a corner. He sat up in bed, demanded coffee, and read the morning paper. The terrible headache persisted.

March 19, 1933. June writes her brother that the doctor says that since Ross has survived thus far, he probably would improve. What with the cost of the nurse and Ross' medications, they are running out of money: "Well good night Harold, it's heck to be far away, where you can't get all the dope isn't it?"

March 20, 1933. A cablegram from June and Jessica to Harold Ross: "Improved normal temperature this evening occasionally rational insulin digitalis pituitary extract continued may pull through."

March 20, 1933. In response Harold writes June and Jessica that he was heartened by their cablegram. He asks for all details and expresses surprise at the rapidity with which Ross went from self-proclaimed excellent health in February to near death in March. He suggests that they amass information as to all of their father's assets and liabilities. Why not ask Mrs. Marshall and her husband to move into the Harris home, thus making her more available as a nurse as well as cutting down on the couple's cost of living and thereby possibly allowing a reduction in her salary? [It is a very sensible cogent letter, dictated, no doubt, to his secretary].

March 21, 1933. June writes Harold that their father has gotten very stubborn, won't accept medication, even from Jessica, and, eyes closed, refuses nourishment. Jessica is exhausted because her father keeps asking for her; no one else would do. "The suspense," June says, "is the hardest part of this business. We don't see how he can be so terribly ill and weak and not get a break one way or the other ... Dr. Higgins said he would never be well again. Father is so unlike himself except his stubbornness is very pitiful. I may have to holler for more money, you poor guy, a regular <u>goat</u>! Is your supply inexhaustible? Our earthquakes go on and on, but they are sort of incidental to F's illness"

March 22, 1933. Jessica writes that Ross nearly died "this A.M. but the doctor gave him a shot that brought him around. He eats nothing and drinks little. Their day nurse thinks he cannot last more than a few days. "Father asked me about you this afternoon and I told him how you had telephoned and cabled and he said 'Dear boy, how I love him!'"

March 25, 1933. June writing. Attending doctors informed June that previous diagnoses of syphilis were incorrect, (a pronouncement that must have relieved the daughters' minds immeasurably). They now decided that Ross had a brain tumor, "but admitted it was a very baffling and complicated case." The patient had become very paranoid, dismissed the latest diagnosis as "a bunch of tommy-rot" and announced he didn't like Dr. Hunter, his personal physician, since "he smelled like a cigar factory."

June laments once again that her father is being kept alive in great pain when without medical intervention he could easily have slipped away. She notes that Mrs. Clark (Grace's mother) phoned to announce the birth of a sixth child to her son Roy—"six kids in twelve years—oi, oi!" writes June.

She describes the exhaustion that both she and Jessica are feeling as a result of nursing their father with little outside help.

Harold continues to send checks—"Jessica and I fell on your three airmail letters yesterday. They were swell Harold and we think you're one good guy! The checks are highly appreciated also. Your $50 to me was a big surprise and thank you a lot but I have enuff money to get home all right."

June states that she has deposited all monies in a separate account in order to pay off bills, including the mortgage.

She says that the sisters do not believe Harold should come to Los Angeles, but at the same time she wants to know his plans, since the sisters could delay the funeral. It is the indefiniteness of the whole matter that is troublesome . . .

March 27, 1933. An unsigned cablegram to Harold: "Consultation of specialist think brain tumor possibly live month or more come if wish but unnecessary."

Appendix B: Panagra's Confidential Report to the Civil Aeronautics Board

The most important feature of Panagra's past national defense activities relates to its successful efforts in eliminating, or contributing materially to the elimination of, Nazi-controlled airlines operating in Peru, Ecuador, Bolivia and between Chile and the Argentine. At the beginning of 1940, Panagra confronted competition from Nazi-controlled airlines at four stages of its route. In Ecuador, the Sociedad Ecuadoriana de Transportes Aereos, the so-called SEDTA line, was operating. In Bolivia an important airline operated by German groups, known as LAB, was active, connecting with flights from the east coast of South America by planes operating as part of the Lufthansa group. In Peru, Deutsche Lufthansa Peru operated extending into Bolivia and connecting with LAB, and finally in the Argentine and Chile Lufthansa-controlled Condor paralleled Panagra's trans-Andean operation.

> During the latter part of 1939 and continuing throughout 1940, Panagra worked in close cooperation with the United States Department of State and other interested agencies of the United States Government on a thorough and extensive program for the elimination of German-owned or German dominated airlines in South America. The details of Panagra's activity, especially in Ecuador and Bolivia, are set forth. The arrangements made were at all times accomplished in cooperation with the interested officials of the United States Government. Numerous conferences were held in Washington, attended by Panagra's chief executives, in which the direction and character of the program were decided upon. Acting upon understandings arrived at in these conferences, Panagra undertook to work out the details locally with the South American Governments involved. A Panagra representative [probably John MacGregor] went to South

America expressly for this purpose and great use was also made of the facilities of W. R. Grace Co. in South America. Panagra's representative was in constant communication with the chief executives of the Company in New York who, in turn, kept the officials of the United States Government informed of progress being made, and made suggestions for what steps should be taken to overcome the various difficulties which arose from time to time in the negotiations. The entire project was a cooperative one with Panagra working in close contact with the United States officials.

The German operations in Peru were the first to be eliminated. Deutsche Lufthansa Peru was 100% German-controlled. It operated between Arequipa and Lima and sometimes made landings at Arica and Puno. Of more importance was its connection with Lloyd Aereo Boliviano, another German operation, at La Paz, Bolivia. Panagra had no active role in the elimination of Deutsche Lufthansa Peru. This was brought about on March 31, 1941 when the Peruvian Government seized the line's two planes and property following an attempt by the Germans to destroy certain German vessels held by Peru at Callao Harbor. Shortly after this episode Panagra, commencing on June 3, 1941, increased its Peruvian services, thus substituting in large part for the displaced German operations.

One of the new services undertaken was between Lima and Oruro and was flown by Panagra voluntarily without mail pay, from June 3,1941 to August 26, 1941. No claim is being made for payment on this mileage.

The activities of Panagra in opposing these German-controlled operations in cooperation with the State and War Departments are colorful chapters in this country's fight against fifth column activities.

In the case of Ecuador, it should be recognized that the SEDTA line was operating less than 1,000 miles from the Canal Zone, and, indeed, northern airports on SEDTA's regularly scheduled operation were as little as 800 miles flying distance from the Canal Zone. In effect, this meant that German-controlled planes could reach the Canal Zone in five or six hours' flying time. It was recognized that German planes could go to the Canal Zone, at least one way, carrying bombs, and that conditions were such as, perhaps, even to permit the return of these planes to base.

The SEDTA line had been operating actively in Ecuador since 1937. It flew German planes and used entirely German equipment. Its executive personnel were Germans and the principal funds, which permitted the continuance of the operation, came through a German subsidy. As far as the public in Ecuador was concerned, however, SEDTA posed as a local Ecuadorian company. Its principal directors were dummy directors, chosen from prominent citizens of Ecuador. The German interests also controlled important news outlets in Ecuador, and these publicity connections were used to distribute much propaganda, which consistently played up the SEDTA operation as a local Ecuadorian operation of which the citizens of Ecuador could well be proud. The news and propaganda activities, as well as the operations of SEDTA itself, were closely coordinated through the activities of the German legation in Ecuador.

Panagra first tangled with SEDTA in 1937, when it sought to establish Quito as one of the main stops on its international route. At that time a representative of Panagra [either John MacGregor or Harold Harris?] went to Ecuador to make the necessary arrangements for stopping at Quito. He met immediate resistance from the SEDTA officials, who urged that they had exclusive operating rights within Ecuador. Panagra had already established Guayaquil as an airport on its route, and the SEDTA group insisted that operations between Quito and Guayaquil, though conducted only as part of the international run, would result, in effect, in the establishment of a local Ecuadorian operation, which it was claimed, violated the SEDTA franchise. This opposition was overcome and Panagra obtained permission to land at Quito after working out arrangements with the Ecuadorian government for the improvement of airports at Quito and Guayaquil, for which Panagra was to be repaid gradually on the basis of a certain amount for each landing at these points. In working out this arrangement Panagra obtained permission to carry passengers and express between Quito and Guayaquil, but did not get permission to carry domestic mail, the franchise for domestic mail remaining in the hands of SEDTA.

Late in 1939, Panagra was approached by the State Department and asked to undertake additional operations in Ecuador with a view to eventually eliminating the SEDTA line. Several alternative methods were discussed, but the determination of the final arrangement, as well as the principal burden of conducting negotiations with the Ecuadorian government, was left in the hands of Panagra officials who consulted everyone concerned including officials of Panair [Pan Am] who were asked for advice based on that company's experience in Colombia. It was decided to establish a Panagra operation, which would parallel those being conducted by SEDTA, and Panagra's representatives commenced negotiations looking toward the necessary arrangements in the early part of 1940.

Almost three months were required to work out the final arrangements. The government of Ecuador was friendly to the United States, and because of close relations which had existed for many years between the W. R. Grace Co. and Panagra organizations and high officials in the Ecuadorian government, the government was also very friendly to Panagra. As a result and due to effective ground work by the American legation in Ecuador and aid from interested agencies of the Federal government it was possible to obtain an early decision from the Ecuadorian government permitting Panagra to conduct local operations. This was, of course, but the first step. There were many details which had to be worked out against the constant opposition of SEDTA and those interested in that Nazi-controlled operation. Panagra had to spend 800,000 sucres ($60,000 United States currency) to build a new airport at Cuenca and to improve facilities at Loja, Manta, Esmeraldas and Salinas. Several of these airports were extremely primitive prior to Panagra's operations. Some fields became so muddy in rainy seasons as to require extensive drainage before being safe for all-weather use. It was necessary to abandon and re-locate the field at Cuenca. Other fields had to be increased in size, filled to eliminate dangerous gullies and irregularities and finally leveled. In some instances grass stood waist high on the landing areas and trees or buildings constituting serious obstructions had to be removed. Except for several small sheds SEDTA had constructed no passenger facilities. Panagra has sought to make the history of its activities in Ecuador in connection with its local services beginning in the latter part of 1940 one of rapid, continuous progress on a sound operating basis.

With the cooperation of the Ecuadorian government and with Panagra financing, adequate all-weather airports were constructed at Salinas, Manta, Cuenca and Loja, the airport at Cuenca being in an entirely new location as the airport formerly used by SEDTA was impossible of satisfactory improvement. An entirely new airport was constructed at Esmeraldas, which it is expected will prove to be usable throughout the year, although the coming rainy season may prove that further improvement is necessary. Airport facilities, radio facilities and passenger stations were constructed at Esmeraldas, Manta, Salinas, Cuenca and Loja, and the existing Panagra facilities at Guayaquil and Quito were expanded and improved. Ecuadorian Airport Managers, Mechanics, Radio Operators, Dispatchers and other personnel were employed, given intensive training and assigned to the new stations. Trained men from other points on the Panagra lines were assigned to supervisory duties in Ecuador. Frequency of service between all points except Esmeraldas, where traffic density is exceptionally low, was increased by successive steps and the routing of services was changed in some cases to provide greater convenience of service to the public and to minimize the effect on local passengers of unavoidable delays in the international schedules which during seasons of unfavorable weather in the southern part of the continent and in the Caribbean area had been the cause of bitter complaint by prominent Ecuadorian local passengers.

Actual operations by Panagra were undertaken late in 1940. The company has, since that time, served all points that were served by SEDTA. Two DC-2 planes were used exclusively for the operation. In some instances the schedules flown by Panagra established greater frequencies between certain points.

Throughout the negotiations Panagra encountered vigorous opposition from the SEDTA group. The first action taken by the SEDTA line was to appoint the brother-in-law of the President of Ecuador as President of the Board of Directors of SEDTA. Elaborate briefs, challenging the legality of the Panagra proposition, were submitted to the Council of State and to other high officials by SEDTA, and a very energetic publicity campaign attacking Panagra was instituted through the Nazi-controlled news outlets.

The final contracts had to be approved by the Council of State of Ecuador, which is a group made up of high government officials and which functions for the government while the Ecuadorian Congress is not in session. The Germans brought great pressure on the Council of State in an effort to have it turn down the contracts. Such action would have required that the entire proposition be presented to the Ecuadorian Congress when it reconvened at a later date. This activity by SEDTA was effectively met by Panagra officials and the Council of State eventually approved the entire arrangements.

As a final resort, the German Minister to Ecuador filed a vigorous but unsuccessful protest with the Ecuadorian government, urging that the application of Panagra to operate local services be refused.

Panagra promoted a large amount of traffic in Ecuador, carrying as many as 700 passengers a month. On the other hand, the SEDTA line lost little of its patronage and continued to carry, during 1940 and the first part of 1941, approximately 300 passengers a month. This was made possible by the SEDTA policy of offering very low rates and free transportation, and by the further fact that persons sympathetic to the Nazis customarily flew on SEDTA'S line. SEDTA was able to continue in operation through its German subsidy. It was materially helped by a very astute move on its part through which it was given the right to carry airmail at regular mail rates. This arrangement which was worked out by the SEDTA interests, effectively blocked Panagra in the mail field, for Panagra was still authorized to carry mail only at air mail rates and any reduction of its air mail rates was not favored by the Post Office Department. The result of this arrangement was that all domestic mail, or at least the great bulk of it, continued to be carried by SEDTA.

The effect of Panagra's activities in Ecuador, then, was to establish an air service for all local stops and thus to pave the way for action by the Ecuadorian government in eliminating the SEDTA operation entirely. As long as no competitor for SEDTA existed, the Ecuadorian government could not take action, for air transportation was an essential part of the country's development. The lack of adequate ground transportation facilities made the airline very important to the country's economic development. As soon as the Panagra service was well established, however, it became possible for the government to act.

On September 1, 1941, the government of Ecuador suspended all operations of SEDTA airline. This action completed the elimination of German aircraft from this section and left Panagra with exclusive flying privileges in the territory.

Panagra encountered a more difficult situation in Bolivia. Here the Germans had established an airline, BOLIVIA Lloyd Aereo Boliviano, known as LAB, as early as 1925, with a plane that had been a gift from the German colony in Bolivia. LAB was owned by Bolivians and native Germans, with a substantial stock interest held by the German airplane manufacturers who supplied equipment. The company was, however, entirely German controlled. The planes flown were German Junker planes, the pilots were either German pilots or Bolivian pilots many of whom were sympathetic to the German cause, and the executive management was German controlled and German dominated. The company operated its main route from La Paz to Corumba and made connections between Corumba and the east coast of South America through arrangements with Condor (Lufthansa), which was very active in Brazil.

LAB was, like SEDTA, used to further German propaganda. The pilots and other officials of the line were active agitators for the Nazi cause. Propaganda leaflets, motion pictures, illustrated booklets and other material were repeatedly flown by LAB to its main base in Bolivia and from there distributed throughout the country. LAB had active connections with the German legation in Bolivia and attempted to develop good will by offering cut rates and giving free service to Bolivian officials. The company was much more firmly entrenched than SEDTA because of the great interest, which many native Bolivians or Bolivians of German extraction had in the company's activities through their ownership of its shares.

Panagra undertook to operate in Bolivia in 1935, at that time establishing an operation from Arica to La Paz. It was necessary to obtain permission from the Bolivian government to operate in and out of La Paz and a Panagra representative was sent to Bolivia to make the necessary arrangements. In 1937 Panagra extended this operation on the so-called diagonal route from La Paz through Oruro and Uyuni to the Argentine. Strong opposition from LAB was encountered, but there was little the company could do at the time to effectively check Panagra. Through the good auspices of the W. R. Grace Company officials in Bolivia, it was possible to convince the Bolivian government that it stood to make tremendous gains by having a direct air connection with the Coast and Argentina.

Bolivia has no coast line and has in the past been a very isolated region. The development of its commerce and trade depends to a large extent upon connections with the outside world through air transportation. Of course, the establishment of Panagra's diagonal service did nothing to hinder the continued development of LAB's operations throughout Bolivia. On several occasions Panagra called the attention of the State Department to the LAB operation, and early in 1940 the State Department made a request of Panagra to look into the matter and see what could be done to supplant LAB with an American flag line. In order to understand what next transpired, it is necessary to go into some detail.

Early in January, 1941, a Panagra representative [Harold Harris ?] while in Bolivia, made an extensive investigation of certain files relating to LAB. These he was able to procure with the assistance of the W. R. Grace Co. organization. An examination of these files disclosed that, during the war between Bolivia and Paraguay, the Bolivian government had, in effect, taken over LAB because of its military importance. During this period the operation of the line was financed through advances from the Bolivian government, and it was understood that at the end of the war a settlement would be made between the government of Bolivia and LAB, at which time the Bolivian government would obtain an interest in LAB which was proportionate to the amount of money it advanced.

The war ended in 1936 and the government of Bolivia appointed a commission to look into this matter and work out a settlement. The commission reported in favor of an arrangement that would give the government a 64% interest in LAB. This arrangement, of course, placed the Germans in the minority. Accordingly, they immediately took steps to counteract the government's move. They refused to accept the report and arranged that the matter should be arbitrated before the La Paz Chamber of Commerce.

The documents disclosed that the arbitration panel of the La Paz Chamber of Commerce was definitely pro-Nazi and that the entire arbitration had been engineered by the Germans in an underhanded effort to counteract the move on the part of the government of Bolivia. The award of the arbitration panel, however, gave the Bolivian government a 48% interest and the German group a 52% interest. It was further shown that the Germans had protected their position by giving the government its 48% in Class B shares, which had no voting power, and in giving the Germans their 52% interest in Class A shares, which held the sole voting rights. As a result, the German group remained thoroughly entrenched in LAB's management from 1937 to 1941. The Bolivian government did not challenge the arbitration award.

Panagra's representative [Harris ?] disclosed the above facts to high officials in the government of Bolivia and urged that the government take immediate steps to set aside the arbitration award. On May 14, 1941 he was successful. On this date Bolivia issued a decree stating that the arbitration award had been illegal and acquiring all shares that had been issued to non-government shareholders. The decree stated that the final disposition of the matter would be further studied and a new disposition of the matter made. Under the terms of the decree a three-man commission was appointed by the Bolivian government to reorganize LAB. The membership of this commission was pro-American and anti-Nazi in its makeup. The Germans, in retaliation, called a stockholders' meeting in an effort to remain in power. The government of Bolivia appeared at the stockholders' meeting and announced that it would discontinue its monthly subsidy in the event there was any effort on the part of the LAB stockholders to obstruct the execution of the decree or to have it set aside. This subsidy from the Bolivian government, which had been in operation for many years, was the lifeblood of LAB, and the Germans were forced to recognize that they must accede to the decree in order to keep the line in operation.

The decree of May 14th was followed on May 24th by a decree authorizing Panagra to operate twice a week between La Paz and Corumba. It was understood that Panagra would commence operating one trip to Corumba immediately and that an additional trip stopping at more intermediate points would be instituted as soon as improvements had been made in the additional airports. This decree was of great significance since it eliminated LAB's exclusive rights to operate between these points in Bolivia. Panagra started its first trip from La Paz to Corumba early in June, after survey flights in May that revealed grave inadequacies in existing airports and other facilities.

Meanwhile, the United States Government, through the Legation in La Paz, and a special group representing the Federal Loan Agency (later Defense Supplies Corporation) who proceeded from Washington to La Paz for this express purpose were actively working on the problems involved in the LAB reorganization. Their work was of basic importance and value and resulted among other things in an advance by the Federal Loan Agency to LAB of $660,000, made on June 20, 1941. This loan was to be made in the form of a cash payment of $300,000 and $360,000 in the form of three Lockheed aircraft and spare equipment. This loan was subject, however, to the condition that LAB would enter into a management agreement with Panagra. As a preliminary to the final execution of the management contract, all Germans in the LAB organization were paid off, their contracts canceled or allowed to expire, and all German influence thus eliminated.

On July 31,1941, six further steps were taken to complete the elimination of German influence in LAB. These arrangements had primarily been negotiated by Panagra's representative ably assisted by a Panair [Pan Am] legal expert sent especially to La Paz for the purpose, with the Bolivian government, or were made with his concurrence. The first was a contract eliminating the distinction between LAB Class A and Class B shares and providing for the issuance of additional shares which would give the Bolivian government a 56% interest in the company. LAB also arranged to buy up the German shares. The second contract was a new charter for LAB that modified many provisions of the original contract originally written under German influence. The third contract consisted of new by-laws under which the Bolivian government was assured of selecting four directors out of eight, and the other stockholders were given the right to elect three. The seven directors thus selected were given the right to elect the eighth member, who would be Chairman of the Board. Thus the Bolivian government was given assurance that it could control the chairmanship and a majority of the Board of Directors of LAB.

The fourth contract consisted of a new operating arrangement between LAB and the Bolivian government. LAB agreed to undertake all routes other than the main route served by Panagra for a subsidy of $16,000 a month. Due to the fact that Panagra had taken over the operation between La Paz and Corumba, this arrangement resulted in LAB flying about one-half its former mileage in return for the same subsidy. Thus more funds per mile were made available to it and it was assured that it could make improvements that would make its operations more efficient. The fifth contract was an arrangement between LAB and the Bolivian government that increased the postal revenues of the airline. In the past LAB has been paid an amount somewhat less than that which persons were required to pay for airmail, the difference being absorbed into the Bolivian treasury. The new arrangement, in effect, gave LAB a larger proportion of the amount paid for airmail by persons using the facilities of the line.

The sixth contract was a management contract between LAB and Panagra. Under this management contract the LAB Board of Directors delegated various important functions to Panagra and was, in effect, prevented from interfering with Panagra's discretion in the operation of the line. Panagra was given the right to prepare budgets, to hire and fire personnel, and to run all departments. Its power over schedules, routes, maintenance, radio, tariffs, accounting systems and methods, the selection of equipment and ground improvements, relations with the governmental agencies, etc. was complete. It is provided in the management agreement that Panagra shall report periodically to the Board of Directors and that certain types of agreements, such as agreements with other carriers, arc subject to the Board's approval. Panagra's responsibility, on the other hand, is only that of a manager. LAB must meet all liabilities incurred through the operation. In return for these numerous services Panagra receives $1500.00 a month, a very small contribution indeed to the administrative and technical duties undertaken by Panagra. Of this amount $700.00 is paid in cash to cover the salaries of a technical operating official and one or two other employees necessary to immediately supervise the LAB operation. The remaining $800.00 a month is paid in shares of lab's stock, and the management agreement provides that Panagra has the option to buy up to 20% of the outstanding shares of LAB at a price established on a basis of the book value of the shares on May 31, 1941.

As in the case of Ecuador, these complicated arrangements were made only in the face of very serious opposition. The active work on the part of Panagra's representative [Harold Harris], the extremely important assistance rendered by the Grace organization and the effective co-operation of the American Legation made the arrangements possible. The opposition was exerted in several principal directions. Among other things, the Germans were able to stir up much opposition in the community by appealing to their local Bolivian shareholders and to place many legal obstacles in the way of final arrangements, and finally, at the last moment, an attempt was made to bring about a revolution.

The importance of having the LAB operation under American control was demonstrated in July 1941 when German agents attempted the revolution, hoping for support of the Bolivian Army. While full details of the plot are not known, it was unsuccessful and some LAB pilots and the LAB manager were jailed the next day. It is known that Ernst Wendler, German Minister to Bolivia, had for some time worked in close cooperation with Major Ellas Belmonte, a pro-Nazi official who served as Bolivian Military Attaché in Berlin. A letter written by Belmonte from Berlin to Wendler disclosed that a revolution was planned for July. When this letter was made available to the Bolivian government, a Cabinet meeting was held and Wendler, the German Minister to Bolivia, was expelled. The letter indicated very clearly that the revolutionists had planned to make use of LAB to bring about the revolution. It was apparent from the text of the letter that revolutionary activities were to centre at Cochabamba, where the main office of the airline was located, and that the planes would be used to further the purposes of the revolution. The letter, which was later, released to the public read as follows:

Legation of Bolivia in Germany

Berlin, June 9, 1941.

His Excellency

Dr. Ernest Wendler

Minister of Germany

La Paz

Dear Friend:

I have the pleasure to acknowledge receipt of your interesting letter in which you inform me of the activities of yourself and your personnel in the Legation and our Bolivian civil and military friends, which are being carried out in my country with such success.

I am advised by friends in the "Wilhelmstrasse" that according to information received from you the moment is approaching to strike our blow to liberate my poor country from a government that is weak and with completely capitalistic inclinations. I go still further and think that the action should be fixed to take place about the middle of July as I consider that the most favorable time. And I repeat that the time is propitious as from your reports to the Ministry of Foreign Relations in Berlin I am please to note that all of the Consuls and friends of the whole Republic of Bolivia, and especially our most friendly centers such as Cochabamba, Santa Cruz and the Beni Province have prepared the way and have organized our forces with ability and energy.

There is no doubt we shall have to concentrate our forces in Cochabamba as preferred attention has always been given to this point. I have learned from friends of mine that the meetings are continuing without any interference from the authorities and that the drills by night are continuing. Furthermore I see that a good quantity of bicycles have been accumulated which will facilitate our night movements as autos and trucks arc too noisy. I therefore think that during the coming weeks the activities should be carried out with much more care than before in order to dispel all suspicion. The meetings should not be held and all instructions should be given from person to person in place of giving them at meetings. Of course, the iniquitous transfer of the L. A. B. to the Yankee imperialism is an inconvenience as I had in mind taking over control of this organization immediately upon my arrival at the Brazilian border, but this I will solve with my friends here as I will make my flight accompanied by another plane which will follow me all the way. We have received the detailed maps showing the most favorable sites for landing. These show me once again that you and your staff are making excellent preparation for the realization of our plans for the welfare of Bolivia. I have taken particular note of what you write me with reference to the younger element of the Army. I have always counted on them and they are no doubt the ones who will best cooperate with me in the great work which we will carry out to fulfillment in my country. As I have already said, it is necessary that we move rapidly as the moment is opportune. We must undo the tungsten contract with the United States and cancel or at least substantially modify the tin contracts with England and the United States. The handing over of our airlines to Wall Street interests is treason to the country. As concerns the Standard Oil, which is working actively for an "honorable" solution in order to "reestablish Bolivian credit", it is criminal. Since my brief affiliation with the Ministry of Government I have been fighting this.

What eagerness to deliver the country to the United States under the pretext of financial aid which will never come! The United States will follow its old policy of obtaining great advantages in exchange for small loans, which we would not even be allowed to have a voice in. Bolivia does not need American loans. With the victory of Germany, Bolivia will need work and discipline. We must copy, even though only modestly, the great example of Germany since National Socialism assumed power.

The "famous" treaty of Ostria with Brazil is truly a crime. Once we are in control of the situation, this will be one of the first things we will change. The government with the aid of my good friend Foyanini did whatever was possible to prevent the execution of this treaty. It is clear that the famous "give-away" Chancellor, Ostria, is completely influenced by capitalism and if it were up to him we would already be an American colony.

I await your final word in order to leave from here by plane to start the work which will first save Bolivia and later the whole South American continent from North American influence. Soon other nations will follow our example and only then, with one purpose, with one ideal, and with one supreme leader will we save the future of South America and start a new era of purification, order and work.

(signed) Elias Belmonte P.'

It was to the developments indicated by this letter that President Roosevelt referred in his historic speech of September 11, 1941, when he discussed several outstanding examples of Axis penetration in South America.

From the foregoing, it is clearly apparent that the Nazi program called for establishing a pro-Nazi government in Bolivia, and that the activities of Panagra, in cooperation with the State Department, which led to the elimination of LAB, materially weakened the Nazi influence in Bolivia and prevented an effective revolution. As a result of the negotiations which have been outlined above, plus the operating plan and controls instituted under the negotiated agreements, all Bolivian airline schedules are now operated either by Panagra in its own name or by LAB with the assistance of Panagra through its management contract. Particular pride is taken in this result because it was accomplished in spite of vigorous opposition and because it required the most skillful negotiation both with the local officials and those old LAB employees who were retained under the new management. Panagra feels that because of its experience and knowledge of South America and its important connections with W. E. Grace Co., it was able, with the assistance of the State Department, to thwart Nazi penetration in Bolivia in a manner far more effective than would have been possible if the matter had been left entirely to diplomatic channels.

LAB's Bolivian operation is important as a freight operation, though the importance of its passenger-carrying facilities should not be overlooked. It must be recalled that LAB did not itself come through to Peru, and the facilities of LAB in Bolivia were not comparable to those now provided under Panagra management. The area served, especially that north of the altiplano, is not accessible to South America's west coast by truck or railroad. Indeed, the altiplano has presented such an impassable barrier to trade and commerce that interior Bolivia's contact with the outside world was almost impossible.

The effect of the LAB operation has been in no manner better demonstrated than by the nature of the cargo carried by air into the region north of the altiplano since the operation commenced. This cargo has included such things as salt, flour, sugar, toilets, washbasins, rice, potatoes, anvils, slices, cement, carbonated water, cloth and hats.

The Panagra and LAB Bolivian operation has tremendous political significance. It serves to unite Bolivia with other South American countries in a manner that has never before been possible, and it opens for the United States channels of trade and commerce into Bolivia, which never before existed. This integration of Bolivia into the South American scene, which the Panagra operation has done so much to bring about, of course has its military as well as cultural significance.

Upon taking over the LAB management, i.e. e., both the operation of express service in Panagra's name between Oruro and Corumba and supervision of the remaining LAB local Bolivian services, Panagra found an extremely chaotic set-up, operating without any semblance of orderly control and far below American standards of safety and efficient service. No flight maps, details of airports, radio, meteorological facilities or fuel supplies were available. Panagra's supply of flight personnel and aircraft, already overtaxed by the Ecuadorean expansion, had to be further extended. Panagra was fortunately able to borrow one survey plane through the efforts of the Federal Loan Agency and charter one DC-3 from Pan American Airways. Temporary ground radio stations were constructed, local radio operators employed, local non-German agents appointed, fuel stocks ordered, and spare parts and material flown in to assure safe and satisfactory operation. Since most of the key men in LAB were Germans or German sympathizers, they had to be dismissed and replaced by trained Panagra representatives in the Maintenance, Operations, Traffic and Accounting Departments. The extraordinary accounting methods used by the German management required months of overhauling in order to determine the true financial position of the Company and to assure the extraction and compilation of the necessary information to guide the management and Directors for future operations. Prior to the arrival of the two Lockheeds, the German aircraft had to be continued in service even though all instruction booklets and marking of the aircraft controls were only in German. Promptly upon the change in management, the Germans had withdrawn one of the German planes in use by LAB under charter arrangement from Sindicato Condor. During the interim period while the line was being operated by the reorganization group set up by the Bolivian government, as previously described, two aircraft were wrecked, one of which had to undergo extensive repairs before it could be put back in service.

Upon taking over, Panagra discovered that LAB had only four radio stations operating on LAB's main line, most of the stops having no facilities of any sort except a marginal airport which were unusable in rainy weather. An airport rehabilitation program was immediately instituted to furnish suitable landing fields, radio stations, passenger and refueling and servicing facilities. The tariff structure of LAB was found to be unsound and work is going forward in an attempt to secure revision. Agency and solicitation facilities were of the sketchiest variety, which required both time and effort to improve and correct. Only three radio navigation beacons existed on the entire LAB operation. Panagra is putting in radio beacons at each point touched by its services as well as those served by LAB. Operations had to be carried out with one Bolivian pilot and two Bolivian co-pilots who were rapidly advanced to Captain's position. Not until late in October could one American pilot be secured, and a second American pilot was not secured until January, 1942. Upon the arrival of the first Lockheed on August 13, 1941 and the second Lockheed on September 8th, 1941, schooling on this radically different type of aircraft had to be carried out with the able assistance of a representative of the Defense Supplies Corporation. Instructions for the use of these aircraft and their equipment were not available in the Spanish language. Strict operational flight control was instituted both as regards flight technique and as regards overloading, both of which procedures were new to the Bolivians. To add to the difficulties, over 100 hours of search flying was required by the LAB planes in connection with the disappearance of two Bolivian civil aircraft in the months of September and October.

Other obstacles which had to be overcome in connection with both the local and express services in Bolivia, may be indicated by reference to the great difficulties encountered in getting adequate machinery and to the lack of water, bad sanitation, mosquitoes and other unfortunate health conditions which prevail in some areas. These problems were met at considerable expense, but the maintenance of the operation on a sound basis continues to require substantial expenditures, in fact expenditures in excess of those that are required for comparable activities on other portions of the Panagra route.

With the elimination of German-dominated airlines in Ecuador, Bolivia and Peru, there remained but one portion of Panagra's route where Nazi competition was encountered. Between Buenos Aires and Santiago, the German-controlled Condor Airlines had been operating for some time once or twice a week. It was desirable to eliminate this important Nazi link between the Argentine and Chile. The State Department sought Panagra's help in this connection to further negotiations, which were in progress through the American Embassy in the Argentine. At the suggestion of the State Department, Panagra undertook to establish a daily service between Buenos Aires and Santiago. This involved the addition of a fifth weekly trip on October 8, 1941 and two additional services commencing November 29, 1941. With the establishment of daily services between these points, services that were more efficient than those provided by the Condor line, it was possible for the State Department to bring about the eventual elimination of Condor, which was accomplished in December, 1941. Panagra undertook the three additional weekly flights between Buenos Aires and Santiago under arrangements with the Postmaster General whereby it received the contract rate of mail pay on somewhat less than half the miles flown and no pay on the balance.

The statement continues, "Panagra has not received any mail pay compensation for the Bolivian operations or for a substantial portion of the local operations in Ecuador. The Ecuador and Bolivia operations are off Foreign Air Mail Route No. 9, and the Postmaster General felt it was not within his power to negotiate the amount of compensation to be paid pursuant to the provisions of its Foreign Air Mail Contract. In each case, therefore, the operations were undertaken on the understanding that Panagra would receive mail pay at a rate to be fixed by the Civil Aeronautics Board, and Panagra has made appropriate application to the Board requesting it to fix such rate.

These national defense services were undertaken to meet an emergency, and Panagra was glad to be of assistance to the Government in this regard. Naturally Panagra was required to incur substantial expense in this connection. Many of these expenses are difficult to ascertain or to evaluate. Exhibits elsewhere present certain ascertainable actual out-of-pocket costs incurred for the services in Ecuador and Bolivia, and present other related information which the Board should have in mind in fixing a rate to pay Panagra for its services during the period since the services were commenced . . .

One further condition deserves brief mention. The elimination of foreign competition in Ecuador, Bolivia, Peru and across the Andes between the Argentine and Chile has been for the moment accomplished by the strenuous and effective cooperation of Panagra and numerous agencies of the Federal government. It has been accomplished, however, on the assumption that Panagra can and will provide sufficient efficient service to meet the needs of the countries concerned.

Appendix C: Harris' Summary of Important Dates for AOA, 1945-1950

Oct. 23, 1945: Inauguration of Flagship (DC-4 landplanes) to London—three flights a week.

Nov. 19,1945: Inauguration of Chicago-London service by one-a-week schedule.

Nov. 23, 1945: Inauguration of Washington and Philadelphia to London service by one-a-week schedule.

Dec. 26, 1945: Start of daily transatlantic service, consisting of five flights weekly out of New York (one stopping at Boston and another starting from Washington), one flight out of Chicago.

Feb. 1, 1946: First International Carrier to provide service to Scandinavia—weekly trips to Copenhagen and Stockholm.

Feb. 19, 1946: Start of Netherlands service—weekly trips to Amsterdam.

April 5, 1946: Extension of Scandinavian service to include Oslo.

April 8, 1946: Delivery of first Lockheed Constellation L-49.

May 18, 1946: First international flag carrier service to Germany—Frankfurt and Berlin via Amsterdam.

May 31, 1946: Operations in England transferred from Burn to London Airport coincident with AOA's first Constellation flight.

July 28, 1946: Commercial schedule frequency increased to 14 flights weekly, averaging 2 per day.

Nov. 2, 1946: Carried 30,000th passenger since start of landplane operation, Oct. 23, 1945.

Dec. 7, 1946: Start of "Operation Reunion"—contract with Army to fly wives and children of G.I.s in occupied Europe to Frankfurt.

Dec. 16, 1946: Increased schedule to 16 transatlantic round trips weekly.

March 7, 1947: Three AOA flagships flew U.S. State Department representatives to Moscow, Russia, for "Big Four" foreign ministers' meeting.

March 17, 1947: First U.S. commercial carrier service to Iceland—thrice-weekly service to Keflavik.

April 1, 1947: Increased schedule to 24 transatlantic round-trips weekly.

May 21, 1947: Beginning of "Project Reunion"—contract with Army to fly G.I. brides and fiancées from England to the U.S.

June 1, 1947: Increased schedule to 24 transatlantic round trips weekly.

June 2, 1947: First U.S. carrier to serve Scotland—twice-weekly service to Prestwick.

June 9, 1947: AOA granted first license by Federal Communications Commission to transmit public correspondence via radiotelegraph from in-flight aircraft; first airline in history of U.S. civil aviation to provide this service.

June 24, 1947: Inauguration of service to Finland by first U.S. scheduled airline thrice-weekly service to Helsinki.

July 17, 1947: Announcement of the doubling, in the first six months of 1947, of passenger and cargo volume for the corresponding 1946 period, giving AOA the lead over all transatlantic air carriers in the numbers of flights and passengers transported between the U.S. and Europe.

Feb. 5, 1948: Introduction of the "Irish mercury" to AOA's daily non-stop service to Ireland.

March 8, 1948: CAB authorized AOA to serve four German cities of Hamburg, Bremen, Dusseldorf and Cologne.

June 8, 1948: National Safety council award for AOA's perfect safety record during 1947 presented.

June 26, 1948: Russian blockade of Berlin becomes effective— AOA provides the only U.S. commercial air service between Berlin and Western Germany.

Nov. 29, 1948: Introduction of Scottish "Mercury" on AOA service to Scotland.

Dec. 13, 1948: AOA announces that an agreement has been concluded for a consolidation of AOA routes with the transatlantic service of PAA, subject to CAB approval.

Jan. 23, 1949: AOA Constellation sets new speed mark between New York and Shannon—8 hours, 47 minutes.

May 12, 1949 Russia lifts Berlin blockade. AOA transported 28,546 passengers, flew 7,850 150 passenger miles, 12,800,000 pounds of cargo on 2,000 flights between Frankfurt and Berlin.

May 17, 1949: 1948 National Safety Council Award presented to AOA.

May 19, 1949: Introduction of "private channel" radio teletype facilities to all AOA communications between U.S. and Europe.

June 2, 1949: "Beachhead Revisited"—D-Day tour through European battle areas for 44 ex-war correspondents activated; White House audience with the President; christening of AOA flagship "Normandy" by General Eisenhower and Gen. Bedell Smith.

June 21, 1949: First double decked Stratocruiser delivered to AOA at Seattle, Washington.

Aug. 17, 1949: Commencement of AOA Stratocruiser service from New York International Airport (Idlewild).

Sept. 5, 1949: "The American Discovery Flight": fifty publishers, editors and writers representing 14 European countries, begin air tour of U.S. aboard AOA Stratocruiser.

Sept. 13, 1949: AOA and PAA announce extension of merger contract to March 13, 1950.

Oct. 31, 1949: Stratocruiser service extended to Frankfurt.

Nov. 15, 1949: Introduction of Constellation Sleeper-Lounge service to Scandinavia marked by "Wings to Vikingland': 20 outstanding women journalists and broadcasters fly to Iceland, Sweden, Finland, Denmark, Norway and Ireland.

Nov. 18, 1949: Speed record between Seattle and New York set by AOA Stratocruiser: 6 hours 26 minutes.

Nov. 21, 1949: Fastest time between Boston and Shannon by AOA Stratocruiser lowered to 7 hours, 13 minutes.

Dec. 31, 1949: 97, revenue passengers transported by AOA during 1949.

Jan. 10, 1950: Passenger and cargo service departments move from LaGuardia to New York International Airport (Idlewild). Inauguration of Stratocruiser service to Glasgow and Amsterdam. Introduction of combined Stratocruiser-Constellation service to Scandinavia.

Jan. 23, 1950: AOA announces 1949 record year for passenger traffic and cargo volume.

May 22, 1950: New non-stop record, 11 hours, 37 minutes, Shannon—New York, established by AOA Captain Edward A. Stewart.

June 8, 1950: 20,000[th] transatlantic crossing—American Airlines system.

June 14, 1950: National Safety Council announces award to AOA for completing over three years of scheduled operations and 588,551,000 passenger miles without a passenger or crew fatality.

June 23, 1950: AOA inaugurates new internal Germany service, Hamburg-Berlin.

July 1950: The President and the CAB approve the sale of American Overseas Airlines to Pan American World Airways.

Sept. 1, 1950: Completed more than 738,000,000 scheduled passenger miles without a passenger or crew fatality.

Sept. 2, 1950: AOA inaugurates the first through air service between New York and Cologne-Dusseldorf, 4th and 5th German cities to be linked with direct air service by AOA.

Alta Mae Harris Stevens was born in 1928 in Lima, Peru, along with her father's first commercial airline, the world's first regularly scheduled airline south of the equator. A graduate of Bryn Mawr College with an M.A. in English from Dalhousie University and a B.Ed. from Mt. St. Vincent University, she was for a decade a high school teacher in Halifax County, Nova Scotia. While there, she represented the province in a national creation of feminist curricula at the high school level sponsored by the Canada Studies Foundation. She earned a Ph.D. in Anthropology from Brown University when she was 70.

Publications include The Fountain Image in English Poetry from 1550 to 1667, her Dalhousie M.A. thesis (1971); a review of women's roles in early Manitoba, co-authored with Linda McDowell(1975); Hallelujah and Amen! Immigrant Haitian Mothers, their Teenage Children, and a Protestant Fundamentalist Church, M.A. thesis (1990); "Manje in Haitian Culture", Journal of Caribbean Studies, (Spring 1996); and Haitian Women's Food Networks, United States of America (1998), her Brown dissertation. She has four children and five grandchildren. She lives with her brother, Harold R. Harris Jr., on Cape Cod.

Alex Stevens, a professional artist and photographer and long time admirer of his grandfather's career, designed the cover and interior text. His most recent publication is a book of photographs, *Silver and Gold, Cape Cod in the Quiet Season* (2013).